Praise for
THE FRAMEMAKING SALE

"Finally! *The Framemaking Sale* equips you to transform a sales process into a cheat code to create confident buyers. It could not come at a better time." —Tim Hardin, president, Decisiv

"Everyone claims to be focused on the customer, but this book is cutting edge in shifting the mindset of sellers to help customers make better decisions. This is a must-read book for the selling profession." —Mike Etzel, VP commercial excellence, Cargill Inc.

"*The Framemaking Sale* will leave you wide-eyed, questioning everything you thought you knew: Should we really stop trying to gain customer trust in our solutions? Should we no longer highlight our product's superiority? Is thought leadership actually a bad thing? A must-read for anyone looking to truly understand the evolving landscape of B2B sales." —Jeff Lowe, chief commercial officer, SMART Technologies

"The uncertainty of a rapidly changing environment, an abundance of data, and the complexity of integrated solution selling has led many customers to feel safer taking no action on buying decisions. *The Framemaking Sale* provides a powerful, clear path forward to inspiring confidence in customers to make the high-leverage decisions needed to propel their own businesses forward." —Zak Lowe, VP sales, Land O'Lakes

"Next level! *The Framemaking Sale* is a way to continue our team's growth and development focused on being better and being different by finding ways to help customers be confident in not only your solution but confident in themselves, especially when it requires significant change to how they have always done things." —TJ Stoffer, SVP sales N.A., Electrolux Group

"As more buyers choose to go it alone, sellers face a pivotal moment—evolve or be left behind. *The Framemaking Sale* is the answer to this new reality: a bold, evolutionary framework that redefines how sellers create value and drive growth. This book is the blueprint for those ready to lead in the new era of selling."

—Randy Kobat, president, Repair onDemand

"With compelling data, relatable metaphors, and humor that is uniquely Adamson, this book presents an opportunity for sellers to make their numbers with practical application of how to build a customer's confidence in their own decision making. Rather than mourning the death of human-to-human selling, read this book to celebrate the rise of the modern seller." —Hang Black, author of *Embrace Your Edge*

"If you want to become the one seller or sales team a customer actually wants to talk to, then this book is a must-read; an instant best seller and lightning in a bottle. In *The Framemaking Sale*, Adamson and Schmidt have futureproofed the concept of seller relevance. It will, I'm sure, become the blueprint for modern B2B sales success."

—Alex Ayers, sales director, Gamma

"*The Framemaking Sale* isn't just another book about sales and marketing, it's a go-to-market blueprint for thriving in a world where customers increasingly prefer to buy without sellers. Adamson and Schmidt arm you with the tools to become the seller buyers actually want to talk to. This is a must-read for any commercial leader serious about making sales matter again."

—Ray Wizbowski, chief marketing officer, ECI Software Solutions

"Selling—and importantly, *buying*—has become complicated and messy, leaving buyers uncertain, unconfident, and resistant to the very sellers who are able to help. Adamson and Schmidt don't just diagnose the problem, they give sales leaders a powerful framework for enabling better buying decisions and building customer confidence at scale. This book is both timely and actionable."

—Patrick Armstrong, chief revenue officer, ReSource Pro

"For over two decades, I've wrestled with questions about how to truly enhance buyer decision confidence. Adamson and Schmidt have not only addressed these questions—they've delivered a masterclass. *The Framemaking Sale* is an essential read for anyone serious about building a resilient, high-performing sales organization."

—Matthew Smith, head of strategy and
implementation, Veritex Bank

"This might be a more important book than *The Challenger Sale*. I'm serious. Expect 'Framemaking' to become common language amongst B2B sellers and marketers for years to come."

—Matt Heinz, founder & president, Heinz Marketing

"In the relentless arms race of better and more content, our customers are caught in the crossfire. My differentiation has become just one more problem for my customer to resolve. *The Framemaking Sale* resets the relationship between buyers and sellers. If you're not helping your customer find the signal, you're just more noise!"

—Barry Parsons, chief commercial officer, Acteon

"*The Framemaking Sale* focuses customers on developing their own internal self-confidence and the required courage to make informed, complex decisions. Disciplined research and compelling data to prepare commercial teams to excel in next-generation market capture."

—Michael Kleppinger, president commercial operations,
clinical research group, Thermo Fisher Scientific PPD

"I've been a fan of Adamson and Schmidt for years—and they have done it again! *The Framemaking Sale* exposes the issues of today's 'selling'—or I should say 'buying' environment. Understanding how buyers need to consume information to make a purchase decision is our responsibility as members of the sales discipline, to add value in every interaction."

—Bill Sisson, executive general manager, LexisNexis

"*The Framemaking Sale* details how our current, long-trusted way of selling through logic is fraught with 'no decisions.' The opportunity for B2B sales today is to find ways to directly, positively, and productively impact customers' *self-perception*, helping them feel more confident in their ability to navigate decisions and achieve positive outcomes. *The Framemaking Sale* shows us exactly how that's done!"

—Sheevaun Thatcher, VP revenue enablement, Demandbase

THE
FRAMEMAKING
SALE

THE FRAMEMAKING SALE

SELL MORE BY BOOSTING CUSTOMER CONFIDENCE

BRENT ADAMSON
and KARL SCHMIDT

BASIC
VENTURE

NEW YORK

Basic Venture
Hachette Book Group
1290 Avenue of the Americas, New York, NY 10104
www.basic-venture.com

Printed in the United States of America

First Edition: September 2025

Published by Basic Venture, an imprint of Hachette Book Group, Inc. The Basic
Venture name and logo is a registered trademark of the Hachette Book Group.

The Hachette Speakers Bureau provides a wide range of authors for speaking
events. To find out more, go to hachettespeakersbureau.com
or email HachetteSpeakers@hbgusa.com.

Basic Venture books may be purchased in bulk for business, educational, or
promotional use. For more information, please contact your local bookseller or
the Hachette Book Group Special Markets Department
at special.markets@hbgusa.com.

The publisher is not responsible for websites (or their content) that are not
owned by the publisher.

Library of Congress Control Number: 2025000912
ISBNs: 9781541705821 (hardcover), 9781541705838 (ebook)

LSC-C

Printing 1, 2025

To our kids
and finding their way in the world with
empathy and human connection

CONTENTS

THE
FRAMEMAKING
SALE

INTRODUCTION

I n early 1993, the team at Mosaic introduced the world's first widely adopted Internet browser, and everything changed.

For the first time, the general public had direct, individual access to massive amounts of online information previously available only through professional experts. Virtually overnight, we could find things, learn things, even buy things in ways completely unimaginable only a few years earlier. It was an incredibly exciting time.

Unless, of course, you were a travel agent. Within just a few short years, the travel agent industry had virtually imploded.

It's kind of crazy to think that not that long ago, we'd have to take a number, wait in line, and then speak with an actual human being just to access simple travel information or complete basic transactions. There was simply no other option.

Then suddenly, we had options. Faster, cheaper, better options. Why go to all the trouble of talking to a travel agent when you could hop online and book everything on your own—even late at night, in your pajamas, snacking on a huge bag of Cool Ranch Doritos? Travelers no longer needed travel agents to get information. Supported by sites like Expedia and Travelocity, they could now find a hotel, book a flight, compare prices, even view photos of possible destinations.

And travel agents weren't alone. To one degree or another, virtually every retail sales sector has since faced similar structural decline, leaving the broader consumer sales profession virtually unrecognizable relative to the not-so-distant past.

But that's consumer sales. Surely, the world of business-to-business sales is completely different, right? Maybe not.

B2B BUYERS' PREFERENCE FOR A "REP-FREE" EXPERIENCE

Of all the data published in our time with the Gartner sales practice, the finding that generated the greatest attention was a pair of statistics first discovered in 2020. In a survey of nearly one thousand buyers of complex business-to-business (B2B) solutions, a concerning 43 percent reported they would prefer to make that purchase without ever speaking to a sales professional *at all*.[1] Within just one year, that number had climbed to 75 percent.[2] That's three-quarters of B2B customers expressing a clear preference for a completely "rep-free experience" when buying even the largest, most complex, expensive solutions.

Yikes.

Clearly, customers have had it. They're tired of putting up with the many impersonal, unhelpful sales reps who seem more interested in making their own number than helping customers make a better decision.

And yet, in an ironic twist, the research found that among those B2B buyers who *do* successfully complete an actual purchase decision, the buyers who prefer no rep involvement at all experience a 23 percent *higher* level of regret for whatever it is they ultimately choose to buy compared to those who value seller support.[3]

So, clearly, today's customers are not better off going it alone. They could really use some help. Yet remember, 75 percent of customers see today's sellers as completely unhelpful.

So, now what?

For many, these data served as a wakeup call not only for individual sellers but also for the entire sales profession. Could this be the death of sales as we know it?

Dire as the data might seem, the immediate reaction from sales leaders was strangely mixed. As we presented the findings around the world, some considered the data deeply disturbing and argued for drastic change. Others were far more ambivalent.

Although sales leaders agreed in principle to the existence of the overall trend—some even calling it self-evident—relatively few considered it relevant for their specific organization. "This might be true in general," they'd say, "but it doesn't really apply to us. We're different."

In their view, their solution was uniquely complex, requiring custom configuration or collaborative design, so it was impossible for customers to buy their solution without interacting with at least *someone* on their sales team. As a result, they struggled to apply the implications of the trend to their own context. After all, it didn't reflect their everyday experience. For them, the primary takeaway was closer to "not my problem" than "this changes everything."

And whether you're a senior executive, a sales manager, or a frontline seller, this might be your reaction too if these numbers fail to correspond to your day-to-day lived experience.

But here's something to consider.

To be precise, these data don't tell us that 75 percent of B2B customers are currently buying without speaking to a sales rep. Rather, they indicate that 75 percent *would if they could*. In other words, the data don't represent customer *behavior*, but customer *preference*. And that's a distinction bearing meaningful difference. Essentially, the vast majority of B2B buyers find so little value in most sales interactions that *given the chance* they would prefer to eliminate those interactions altogether.

That's a finding worthy of reflection for anyone in sales, at any level.

More than anything, this widening gap between customer reality and customer preference represents *risk*. Specifically, risk that the overall sales profession—or, at the very least, you/your sales team—becomes fully disintermediated as customers develop ways to interact more in line with their actual preference, ultimately shifting even relatively complex sales to digital-first channels.

Sound crazy? Honestly, we don't have to look far to see this shift already underway. Consider, for example, the massive departure from human-led sales across virtually every consumer category over the last several decades—including travel agents. There was a time not that long ago when buying clothing, electronics, home appliances, cars and trucks, and even shoes (!) all required direct interaction with a professional salesperson. There was simply no other way. But, today, the vast majority of consumer purchases are now digital-first, if not digital-exclusive. Heck, you can even buy a car from a vending machine. A vending machine!

Why do consumers buy this way? Simple. Because they *can*.

If one trend has clearly emerged from years of research into sales and marketing, it is this: As goes consumer behavior, so goes business behavior. Typically, with a lag of at least five years. That leads one to naturally wonder, Which seller-led business purchases today might offer a completely rep-free alternative sometime in the near future? The answer is probably just as unimaginable for us today as online shoe shopping was twenty-five years ago. And ten years from now, it will be just as normal.

Especially with the rise of generative AI, a future of rep-free B2B buying may be far closer than most of us imagine. And as that future unfolds, the data clearly indicate that for roughly 75 percent of customers, the sooner, the better.

That is the risk.

But this book isn't about risk. This book is about opportunity.

REINVENTING SELLING FOR TODAY'S BUYING REALITY

Counterintuitive as it may seem, today's widening gulf between customers' buying reality and their purchasing preference represents the single biggest opportunity for today's sales professionals to stand out and offer far greater value in the eyes of customers.

How, exactly?

If we return to the story of the travel agents, the surprising twist isn't the industry's ultimate demise but its dramatic comeback. In fact, today many travel agencies are absolutely thriving. Reinvented, to be sure, but flourishing nonetheless.

And the reason why is deeply instructive.

How have some travel agents turned existential crisis into commercial opportunity? In many ways, the answer has just as much to do with buying as it does with selling.

Have you tried to plan a complex trip lately? Not just buy a flight, rent a car, or book a hotel room—but plan an entire complex trip? Maybe a multiweek group excursion, or a family trip to a destination theme park? There are hotel sites, booking sites, recommendation sites, comparison sites. There are untold experts, reviews, videos, top lists, social posts, and an endless array of online influencers. And everyone's got an opinion! There are even "aggregator" sites, compiling all the information from all those other sites. It's pretty overwhelming!

Many would-be travelers, exhausted from the research alone, need help. Not so much with making the purchase, but with making the decision. Where to go? Where to stay? How to get there? What to do? What to pay? It's exhausting.

In fact, you know what would be so much easier? If you could just talk to a real human being. Some kind of expert who could guide you, step-by-step, and help you figure out exactly what to do.

That's why travel agents have made a comeback. The good ones just make things so much easier, providing guidance and creating confidence for overwhelmed customers otherwise unable to make a decision on their own. Essentially, a good travel agent acts like a "decision coach," walking clients through an overwhelmingly complex decision in a way that makes everything feel so much more doable.

And that's exactly the opportunity in front of today's B2B sellers, because today's business-to-business buying looks a lot like a would-be traveler struggling to plan a complex vacation.

Let's face it. Modern B2B buying is broken. Across every major industry, geography, and go-to-market model, customer buying teams are struggling with too many people, too many options, too much information, and too little collective consensus, meaning 40 to 60 percent of deals lost today are actually lost to "no decision" at all.[4] That's roughly *half* of all lost deals derailed by customers' inability to achieve any better outcome than "never mind" or "not right now."

Over time, this gravitational pull toward the status quo inevitably infuses each subsequent purchase decision with an increasingly toxic mix of skepticism and resignation. Simply put, buyers are losing their mojo. It's not so much that sellers are struggling to sell effectively as that B2B buyers are struggling to buy effectively—or sometimes even buy *at all*.

Is this, in fact, the death of sales as we know it? Or more provocative: *Should* this be the death of sales as we know it?

Maybe.

But we emphatically believe it doesn't have to mean the death of sales *altogether*.

Instead, what if sales professionals could engage customers in a way that customers actually found profoundly valuable? A way specifically designed to help buyers navigate their own internal decision complexity, make sense of overwhelming amounts of information, align more easily on competing internal objectives, and feel more certain about complex outcomes? What if, in other words, every sales interaction was specifically designed to make customers feel more confident in their own decisions? That's a future worthy of any profession—and arguably the most viable, profitable path forward for sales professionals looking to thrive.

It's time for reinvention.

INTRODUCING FRAMEMAKING

At the heart and soul of this book lies a simple, powerful question: How can you become the one sales professional—the one sales team—that customers actually *do* want to talk to?

If the single biggest headline of B2B commerce today isn't that sellers struggle to sell but that buyers struggle to buy—or more to the point, they struggle to *decide*—then the single biggest opportunity for today's sales professionals is to provide them *help*. To become B2B buyers' travel agent, as it were.

We call this approach Framemaking.* Framemaking is all about selling more by helping your customers buy better.

Framemaking is the act of making a complex task or decision feel more manageable, both by establishing clear, credible boundaries around its scope and by prompting key considerations and prioritizing best next steps that customers might otherwise easily overlook on their own.

By using Framemaking to take something hard or overwhelming and make it easier, sellers are able to boost customers' productive

---

* Framemaking is a trademark of A to B insight, LLC.

progress through a purchase process, thereby dramatically increasing the likelihood of closing a deal.

Leading countless research initiatives at CEB, now Gartner, and beyond, we have spent the last two decades studying the ins and outs of B2B sales in data-driven detail. Much of the early output from that research is captured in the two bestselling books *The Challenger Sale* and *The Challenger Customer*.[5] Since their publication over a decade ago, however, the world of B2B commerce has fundamentally changed. While we still stand by the core premise of *Challenger*—engaging customers with insights that challenge the way they think about their business—the B2B buying reality that that research was designed to address has evolved dramatically, rendering much of the *Challenger* work still necessary but now insufficient to overcome the challenges today's B2B buyers face. Today's commercial context is simply *different*. Indeed, given modern B2B buyers' struggle to buy, a sales approach largely based on *frame-breaking insight* creates an even bigger opportunity for *frame-making help* at the same time. Otherwise, customers already struggling on their own are simply left with one more thing to struggle with. Based on years of primary research into B2B selling and buying, including extensive qualitative analysis along with thousands of interviews and conversations with commercial leaders, senior executives, and sales professionals, all supported by cutting-edge behavioral psychology, *The Framemaking Sale* provides a practical blueprint for creating sales interactions designed to help today's buyers buy. Interactions customers will run *to* rather than run *from*.

Framemaking is a data-backed, customer-based, practical answer for engaging today's B2B buyers in a highly differentiated, profoundly valuable way. Through a combination of powerful research, real-world stories, and practical tactics from some of the world's best leaders and sales professionals, we'll lay out the compelling case for creating customer confidence, examine the forces undermining that confidence today, and then detail step-by-step a completely new approach to selling, specifically designed to reestablish the value of sales interactions in today's radically different context of buying.

As we dive into this powerful new approach to selling, we'll start with today's world of B2B buying, seeking to understand what it takes for customers to successfully complete larger, more complex B2B purchases in the first place. We will introduce the critical role of customers' decision confidence, foundational not just to Framemaking selling, but, more importantly, to customers' likelihood to complete what we call a "high-quality, low-regret purchase." That insight provides a compelling backdrop for an introduction to the Framemaking approach, which we'll unpack in an incredibly practical tour through the world of Framemaking selling, with a review of the four primary challenges currently undermining consumer confidence today: decision complexity, information overload, objective misalignment, and outcome uncertainty. Along the way, we'll examine ways to *establish* a frame for guiding customers through each challenge, *engage* customers in a Framemaking conversation to boost confident action, and then help customers *execute* that decision far more predictably. Then, we'll round out our tour of Framemaking with a review of some of its broader, organization-wide capabilities, spanning key design principles of Framemaking interactions as well as content strategies to guide customers to those interactions in the first place. Finally, we'll place Framemaking into its historical context as an emerging means to maintain differentiation in an otherwise rapidly commoditizing world.

At the end of the day, the primary purpose of Framemaking is to enable more purchase decisions, not to push more solutions sales. But for all of us on the sales side, more business is the benefit. After all, both the data and practical experience tell us that if we solve for buying, we simultaneously solve for selling. Creating customer confidence is our North Star for better qualification, shorter sales cycles, and higher quality deals with less customer regret.

We started this project with a simple question: Given the dramatically different world we live in today, what would "the sales book for our time" look like?

The Framemaking Sale is that book. If you're looking to secure your future in sales, then this is your story.

CHAPTER 1

Solving for Customer Confidence

Have you ever tried to buy something relatively simple online, maybe a gadget for your home, or a gift for a friend? More than anything else, the promise of online shopping is its convenience. You get in, you get out, and you move on with your life. Except all too often, it doesn't actually happen that way. Welcome to the dark side of shopping online.

It starts out easy enough—you head over to Amazon, enter a couple search terms, and boom! Results in an instant! Gratification is only minutes away! Except . . . no. Your search turns up 1,500 items, all with four stars or more.

OK, no problem. Maybe you start with "Amazon's Choice" and dive in. You read over the description, check the delivery date, and you're ready to buy. Just one last thing—might be a good idea to check out these one-star reviews. Then things start spiraling. "It arrived broken!" "It stopped working in a day!" "Doesn't work!" "This thing's horrible!" "Don't buy!" Phew, looks like you dodged a bullet there. Better look for a different one.

TWO HOURS LATER, you're still shopping! And now you're getting frustrated. But you're not mad at Amazon. After all, they're just doing what they're designed to do—serve up lots of options. You're actually mad at your own inability to make a decision on something so simple.

But it's OK. Amazon's got your back. In fact, there's a button on Amazon that reads "Save for later." And if you click that button, all the pain stops. Granted, you don't get whatever you came to Amazon to buy. But you do get your life back. And you can move on, hoping to never have to go through that again.

Sound familiar? This is the world of online buying, and it happens all the time.

In fact, last time we checked, our combined families have over 590 items "saved for later" on Amazon. That's 590 purchase journeys stalled in frustration, confusion, exhaustion, and, ultimately, resignation.

And if consumers are struggling this much to buy relatively simple products online, imagine the difficulty of B2B buyers buying much more complex solutions as part of large, diverse buying groups. In a typical B2B purchase, it's not a single person making day-to-day decisions but a group of them, spanning a wide range of opinions, priorities, budgets, and functions. And many of us don't have to imagine just how hard it is for that kind of buying group to make long-term, large-scale decisions on behalf of an entire company, especially these days, when some of those people have quite possibly never met in person, or even met at all.

For example, we recently spoke to the president of an enterprise software company whose team had just lost a multimillion-dollar deal because the twenty (!) members of the buying group have never made a collective decision before—and simply couldn't figure out how.

Add to the mix a flood of information, all offering expertise, research, business cases, and "raving fan" testimonials, and it's like making a "simple" online purchase all over again. Except now it's complex five-, six-, and seven-figure solutions, possibly running on multiyear contracts, with all sorts of implications for both business operations and personal credibility.

It's no wonder B2B has its own "save for later" button. It's called "no decision."

In fact, it's actually kind of a wonder that B2B commerce still happens at all. After all, if we struggle to buy a pair of socks as an individual, how are we expected to buy complex solutions as an organization?

As sales professionals selling into this complex commercial context, if we want to understand how to sustain our business—let alone *grow* it—in the face of unrelenting uncertainty and overwhelming complexity, then it's absolutely critical that we understand the "physics" of modern B2B buying. Specifically, we have to understand what needs to happen for today's customers to do the nearly unimaginable—to take decisive action and make bigger, better buying decisions on purpose.

So how the heck is *that* supposed to happen? We can find an answer in the research.

THE HIGH-QUALITY, LOW-REGRET DEAL

Research initiatives across the sales and marketing practices at CEB and then Gartner spanned the better part of six years focused on the drivers of a high-quality, low-regret deal. A high-quality, low-regret deal is simply a complex B2B purchase where buyers report they didn't settle for status quo or "good enough," but bought the bigger solution, with the broader scope, usually at a higher price, often across a longer contract.

Admittedly, the term "high-quality" is supplier centric, representing the specific deals most suppliers prioritize to escape price-based commoditization in search of organic growth. Effectively, it's the classic "solutions sale" central to much of today's B2B business strategy, where the total value of an integrated "solution" is meant to deliver greater value than the sum of its component parts (i.e., 1 + 1 + 1 = 4). That can only happen, of course, when customers buy the broader solution in the first place.

That said, despite their potentially greater value, broader "solutions" can often trigger increased buyer regret due to purchase complexity, implementation difficulty, and increased financial commitment. So, what we really want to understand are the cases where customers buy the higher quality deal but simultaneously experience significantly lower regret—a commercial unicorn.

Identifying B2B buyers who successfully completed a high-quality, low-regret (HQLR) purchase of a complex solution revealed various deal attributes that mattered most in driving that outcome. Across years of research, this included virtually every supplier attribute imaginable: sales behaviors, marketing strategies, organizational characteristics, product performance, service delivery, content characteristics. You name it.

Over time, that effort proved incredibly revealing.

For example, a supplier's brand typically has no direct impact on customers' likelihood to buy an HQLR deal. Counterintuitive as it may seem, this result proved relatively stable across many different research efforts.[1] This doesn't mean a supplier's brand doesn't matter for commercial success, but in the world of five-to-eight-figure deals, it's, at best, table stakes. To be sure, if a supplier has a completely unknown brand, or worse, a poorly perceived brand, it likely won't make it into customers' consideration set to begin with. But once on the short list of the top two or three candidates, those suppliers are all considered good enough on brand. At that point, they're far more likely competing on some combination of price and capability to deliver on customer requirements. Brand gets you in the door, but it rarely gets you a bigger, better deal.

Alternatively, certain sales behaviors demonstrated meaningful impact on increasing the likelihood of an HQLR deal. For example, as expected, a number of dimensions associated with previous Challenger research indicated a marked increase in the probability of a HQLR deal. Of those, the seller behaviors most closely associated with teaching customers new ways to make money, save money, or mitigate risk that they themselves had yet to discover on their own—providing "frame-breaking" insight—had the greatest impact.

But across multiple surveys of thousands of B2B buyers, the single biggest driver of an HQLR deal, *by far*, turns out *not* to be any set of supplier attributes at all, but rather a very specific collection of *customer* attributes.

To understand our most meaningful opportunity to drive bigger, better deals, in other words, we need to shift our perspective from selling to *buying*.

Because the data clearly indicate, that's where good deals go to die.

THE CRITICAL ROLE OF CUSTOMER CONFIDENCE

Practically speaking, the actual outcome we're all seeking to achieve isn't so much a high-quality, low-regret *sale* as a high-quality, low-regret *purchase*. After all, suppliers sell something only when customers actually buy something.

Self-evident as that shift may seem, it matters greatly as it dramatically expands the variables possibly impacting a successful sale well beyond supplier-centric considerations like seller skills and content strategies. In fact, when we apply that broader lens across thousands of B2B buyers spanning a wide range of industries and geographies, all engaged in some kind of complex purchase, we find something remarkable:

B2B buyers reporting a high degree of decision confidence were over ten times (!) more likely to make a high-quality, low-regret purchase than customers exhibiting average confidence.[2]

Nothing else in the research was even close. That's not a 100 percent increase, but a nearly 1,000 percent increase. The impact is a full order of magnitude greater than anything else we've ever studied. Bottom line: Customer confidence matters. A lot. It is the single biggest driver of an HQLR deal we've ever seen, *by far*. As such, it represents the single best bet for driving organic growth—through both new-customer acquisition and existing-customer expansion.

Arguably, this one, simple finding dramatically changes the way sales professionals, sales leaders, and B2B executives need to think about sales. Simply put, absolutely *everything* we do as suppliers—sales tactics, content strategies, digital engagement, expert advice, you name it—and every dimension of the customer experience should be purposefully designed to help customers feel more confident in the decisions they're making on behalf of their company.

Now, that conclusion may seem somewhat self-evident on the face of it. But how many of us could claim an organization-wide sharp focus on customer confidence right now? To be sure, we might agree with the importance of customer confidence conceptually, but how many of us are systematically solving for confidence across every customer interaction along the *entire* end-to-end customer experience (from demand gen to customer acquisition, to retention, through success, and on to customer expansion)?

To be fair, it's hard to know without a more practical understanding of customer confidence, so let's go there next.

THE MANY RELATED FLAVORS OF CUSTOMER CONFIDENCE

If customers' confidence matters above all else in driving growth, the natural question becomes, confidence in what, exactly?

Customers' decision confidence captures the aggregate impact of attributes, such as:

As a customer buying group, how confident are we that we:

1. Asked the right questions?
2. Conducted sufficient research?
3. Thoroughly explored alternatives?
4. Reached consensus on the most pressing problem?
5. Reached consensus on the best possible solution?
6. Can effectively implement the chosen solution?
7. Will receive adequate value for our investment?
8. Will have made the best choice on behalf of our company?

This is a list you'll want to flag. Think of this list as a customer confidence checklist.

As such, these eight attributes represent a powerful, tactical framework for opportunity qualification and deal reviews. In fact, we often suggest sellers use this list in pipeline meetings or line-by-lines as a means not only of reinforcing a customer-centric perspective but also of ensuring that this customer-first perspective centers on the attributes most important for deal success, statistically speaking.

Practically speaking, one might, of course, remove or add similar sentiments, but these eight capture not only the diverse flavors of customer confidence but also the manifold dimensions across which customer confidence may fall short more generally. After all, B2B buying is fraught with potential for doubt across every step of the buying journey.

In fact, if you consider your own experience as a buyer, either personally or professionally, some version of this very list will likely feel quite familiar. Take the first attribute on the list—for example, "In pursuing this purchase (or solution, or course of action), how confident are we that we've actually asked the right questions to begin with?" After all, a complex B2B purchase spans multiple parts of the customer organization, and it's both understandable and absolutely necessary that the team making that decision identify and address questions pertinent to all parties. But which questions, exactly? How many? And across which categories? There are business needs, current capabilities, target performance, potential value, user experience, ease of integration, switching costs, emerging technologies, generative AI, data security, environmental impact, financial impact, brand impact, productivity impact, employee engagement, operational efficiency, and on, and on. Really, there's no end to the questions that matter. And in the face of both high decision complexity and rapidly evolving technology, that list of important questions easily expands faster than it contracts, especially if one is making that decision for the first time, or the first time in a long time.

Likewise, consider the second dimension of that checklist of customer confidence. It's equally hard for customers to feel confident that they "have conducted sufficient research" when the world is awash in massive amounts of content—white papers, infographics, videos, websites, slide decks, review sites, customer communities, even TikToks. Information is endless. And for many, the inclination to keep "researching" is harder to overcome for a B2B buyer than it is for a consumer buying something simple from Amazon. Not because we're "B2B buyers," but because we're human beings. And in today's digital world, there's nothing more human than consuming ever more content.

In fact, as you work your way down that list you'll find this same, familiar potential for a high degree of doubt embedded within every dimension of customer confidence. Naturally some customers, in some contexts, won't struggle at all across some dimensions (e.g., repeat purchases, transactional purchases). But the potential is always there.

So, if we step back and take it all in at once, this composite characterization of customer confidence—along with its massive impact on commercial outcomes—reveals something critically important about B2B business today. No question, there's the headline conclusion: customer confidence *really* matters for deal success.

But this deeper dive into the specific attributes composing customer confidence actually upends decades of conventional wisdom regarding B2B customer engagement and overall go-to-market strategy in two critically important ways.

B2B Buying Is Based on Feeling, Not Knowing

There's an old saying in retail sales that consumers "buy emotionally and justify rationally."

In business-to-business, however, we have long relied on the exact opposite notion, building large, complex, data-driven business cases to demonstrate an objectively higher "return on investment," "lifetime value," "rate of return," or lower "total cost of ownership." After all, while it may be true that *humans* act on equal parts emotion and reason, *companies*, on the other hand, function in an objective, rational fashion designed very specifically to maximize shareholder value. In business, it's all about the numbers.

Except it isn't. At the end of the day, the people making those business decisions aren't *machines* (at least, not yet), they're *human beings*, acting on behalf of the business. And as individual human beings held personally accountable for collective business performance, our research reveals that individuals' emotions play an outsized role in B2B buying. In fact, CEB partnering with Google and Motista found that the emotional connections B2B buyers establish to certain suppliers are actually *stronger* than those consumers develop with even the most iconic of brands.[3] After all, the stakes in B2B are far higher as bad business decisions prove costly not only to the companies pursuing them but to the employees making them (not to mention their colleagues as well).

Bottom line: B2B buying is fraught with emotion.

But which emotions, exactly?

There's the old FUD factor—fear, uncertainty, and doubt. But causing more fear, less certainty, and increased doubt among potential buyers can cut both ways. If I'm afraid, uncertain, and doubtful of the status quo, I'm undoubtedly more likely to pursue change. But if I'm afraid, uncertain, and doubtful of *change*, I'm far more likely to embrace the status quo. In *neither* case, however, am I necessarily likely to opt for anything bigger or broader than the most minimally viable course of action. After all, if I'm motivated to change by FUD, I'm typically changing because I *have* to, not because I *want* to. And as a result, my main objective is to minimize downside risk rather than maximize upside potential. It's all about playing it safe.

Instead, for customers to embrace a bigger, broader purchase, their orientation needs to be closer to "what's possible?" than "what's preventable?" And that kind of mindset comes from customers' confidence, for example, that they asked the right questions.

But that naturally raises a practical question: Exactly which questions are the right questions? What exactly does "right" even mean? And what happens if I think *these* are the right questions, but you think *those* are the right questions? After all, the right questions for the chief marketing officer (CMO) will almost certainly be different from the right questions for the plant manager, or the head of finance or IT. So, how in the world can we be confident that we've asked the right questions, when it's not even clear what "right" actually means?

The simple answer is, we can't. Ultimately, there is no *objective truth* on which questions are the right ones. In the context of a B2B purchase, at least, "right" has only relative meaning, not absolute. So it's critically important that the buying group feel pretty sure that the questions they've asked will prove to be "sufficiently right" to meet their current need.

Similarly, exactly how much research is sufficient? Is "sufficient" measured in time? Maybe weeks or months? Or maybe it's measured in terms of volume of content consumed? Maybe fifteen websites?

Fifty? How many white papers, videos, demos, or sales conversations constitute "sufficient"? In a reference to the timeless classic mock-umentary *Spinal Tap*, one senior executive reported their research "goes to eleven." But even so, if whatever decision we make based on that research ultimately goes south, then it won't matter whether our perceived efforts were deemed sufficient or not. The natural conclusion will be that we missed something important. Clearly, our research needed to be sufficient-er.

Interestingly, we find this same phenomenon across every dimension of confidence. Did we "thoroughly" explore alternatives? Agree on the "most pressing" problem? Identify the "best possible" solution? Assess our ability to "effectively" implement the solution? Ultimately realize "adequate" value? And make the "best" choice? Not a single one of the words in quotes offers an objective finish line.

Think about that for a moment. In aggregate, these various dimensions of confidence represent the biggest statistical driver of sales success *by far*, and yet none of them can be "known" to be true because none of them is objectively knowable.

When it comes down to it, high-quality, low-regret B2B buying decisions aren't based on what customers *know* but what they *feel*. Specifically, they feel *confident* that they've done "enough." They asked the "right" questions, conducted "sufficient" research, and so on down the list.

So how does this conclusion upend decades of conventional sales wisdom? Because right now, most of us are trying to win deals with an appeal to logic rather than emotion—typically, through an alphabet soup of math: ROI, TCO, LVA, IRR, NPV . . . And only when that math comes up short do we resort to emotion. But when we appeal to emotion, we're generally trained to stoke fear and deepen doubt.

But decision confidence, the single biggest driver of an HQLR deal, stems from *neither* logic nor fear. To be sure, the math really matters. But it matters in *context*—specifically, within the context of customers' confidence around what they're trying to do—or more accurately, what they're trying to decide. After all, if all that math simply raises more questions than it answers, or makes customers feel the need for ever *more* research, then it's actually reduced customer confidence, not increased it.

Customer confidence is the indisputable engine driving B2B commerce. Everything suppliers do to sell into today's commercial environment should be purpose-built to fuel that engine at scale.

Customer Confidence Is Supplier Agnostic

The second way decision confidence upends traditional views on customer engagement centers on the key question, "Customer confidence in what?"

It's no secret that suppliers invest mountains of money into boosting customers' confidence in their product, their brand, their service, and their people, all in an effort to become a "leading brand," a "thought leader," and a "trusted advisor." That's what all that math is for as well: "Look at the incredible value of our solution!"

Indeed, supplier claims designed to earn customers' confidence and trust are so common they've become cliché. What company *doesn't* describe themselves like this:

- "Where companies turn for a partner they trust"
- "Trusted by 85 percent of the Fortune 500"
- "The number one choice of leading companies like [place logos here]"
- "Delivering cutting-edge solutions for customers' most mission-critical priorities"
- "The industry leader"
- "The top provider"

Every one of these statements—and literally hundreds more just like them—is built to bolster customers' confidence in a supplier's ability to deliver value. So it would be natural to conclude that customer confidence is well-trodden territory for most B2B suppliers.

But it actually isn't. At least, not the kind of customer confidence that matters. If we return to the dimensions of customer confidence that matter most, notice *none* of them has anything to do with a supplier at all.

- How confident are we that *we* asked the right questions?
- How confident are we that *we* conducted sufficient research?
- How confident are we that *we* thoroughly explored alternatives?
- How confident are we that *we* reached consensus on the most pressing problem?
- How confident are we that *we* reached consensus on the best possible solution?
- How confident are we that *we* can effectively implement the chosen solution?
- How confident are we that *we* will receive adequate value for our investment?
- How confident are we that *we* will have made the best choice on behalf of our company?

See the pattern? It's actually hidden in plain sight. Every expression of customer confidence captures customers' perceptions not of suppliers but of *themselves*. Decision confidence, in other words, isn't just customer centric, it's *supplier agnostic*.

Ironically, while we spend the vast majority of our time in sales focused on customers' *supplier* perceptions, our customers are far more concerned with their *self*-perception. They're less worried that a supplier will fall short and more worried that *their decision* will fall short. After all, they're the ones on the hook for that decision.

Yet, the entire infrastructure of B2B sales—all the content, process, training, coaching, annual "initiatives," you name it—is designed to encourage customers to think a specific way about *the supplier*: who we are, what we do, how we help, and how we're different.

Meanwhile, the single biggest obstacle standing in the way of customers' completion of a large-scale, high-quality, low-regret purchase isn't customers' confidence in supplier performance, but self-confidence in their ability to make a decision.

That's the challenge, and the *opportunity*, of B2B sales today—to find ways to directly, positively, and productively impact customers' *self-perception*. To help them feel more confident in *their* ability to navigate decisions and achieve positive outcomes along a purchase journey.

And now that we've identified the opportunity, the core purpose of *The Framemaking Sale* is to show you exactly how that's done. Today's B2B buyers face a deepening crisis of customer confidence, so let's first identify why that's happening. After all, we can't build customer confidence unless we understand what's reducing it in the first place.

THE CRISIS OF CUSTOMER CONFIDENCE

In the words of Canadian Prime Minister Justin Trudeau at the 2018 World Economic Forum, "The pace of change has never been this fast, yet it will never be this slow again."[4] No question, asking customers to find common ground and take decisive action on a five-, six-, or seven-plus-figure purchase in today's relentlessly evolving environment is asking a lot. Yet, as disruptive as this endless arc of change may be, the primary challenge facing today's B2B buyers is, in reality, both considerably more prosaic and far more enduring.

Quite simply, it's about customer stakeholders struggling to reach collective consensus. Indeed, we've been tracking these changes since long before the onset of the global pandemic or the rise of AI. In fact, in many ways, today's buying complexity traces back to supplier efforts starting in the early 2000s to sell larger, more complex, integrated "solutions." As those solutions connected more parts of the customer organization through technology and data, it's only natural that more stakeholders from increasingly diverse parts of the customer organization became involved, all conducting independent due diligence to determine how exactly that broader solution might fit within their corner of the organization.

So, fast-forward to today, if one considers a typical B2B buying journey as a kind of project to be managed based on logical steps following a relatively linear process, then it's completely fair to ask, "Just how hard could this possibly be?" After all, B2B purchase decisions feel pretty straightforward:

Step 1: Identify a need. > Step 2: Explore solutions. >
Step 3: Identify requirements. > Step 4: Select a supplier.

But when we actually map a typical B2B purchase process, we find it follows *anything but* a predictable path. What feels like it should be a straightforward, linear process turns out to be a big, tangled mess (Figure 1).

THE SPAGHETTI BOWL OF B2B BUYING

We call this the "spaghetti bowl" of B2B buying.[5] Although meant to be illustrative, the diagram inevitably triggers a strong, visceral reaction as it feels so familiar. At some point, virtually all of us have starred in this movie in one way or another as we've engaged in our company's own purchase journeys. And it can only be described as painful.

To orient you to the image, across the middle you see four key B2B buying "jobs": problem identification, solution exploration,

The Spaghetti Bowl of B2B Buying Today

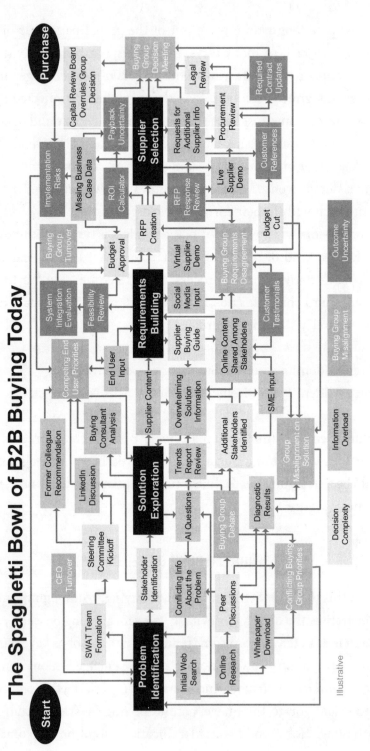

Illustrative

Figure 1

requirements building, and supplier selection. As a typical B2B buying decision flows across those buying jobs from start to finish (with an actual purchase by no means guaranteed, of course), that presumably linear journey proves to be anything but. Often, it's two steps forward and one step back. Sometimes, it's actually *one* step forward and *two* steps back.

So, perhaps we've identified a problem worthy of organizational time and attention, but in the process of exploring solutions, we realize we've underestimated its scope or failed to understand contingent issues requiring simultaneous attention. That discovery leads back to a reassessment of the problem.

Or, perhaps, we've made it all the way to supplier selection only to discover through the late-stage involvement of procurement that our preferred partner isn't on the company's short list of preapproved providers. As a result, we're forced to reassess our preferred solution, or possibly even deprioritize the original problem.

Really, customers find themselves facing all manner of setbacks, questions, and additional considerations along their journey, forcing them to retrace steps repeatedly. In fact, the vast majority of B2B buyers return to earlier steps across the four buying jobs at least once, repeating sometimes several buying jobs along their journey, even for relatively low-complexity purchases.[6] We call this phenomenon "looping" as it's a perfect description of how B2B buyers actually move along a purchase path—they don't really progress through a purchase nearly so much as *wander* through it.

And all that looping takes a massive toll, not just financially but psychologically. It's *exhausting*.

Across the last eight years, we've asked well over five thousand senior B2B sales and marketing executives about their own professional experience with a large-scale purchase that they've participated in *on the buying side*. Then we asked them to choose just one adjective to describe that process.

We've asked this question all over the world on stages big and small, with both live and virtual audiences. And across all those thousands of people, we have yet to hear a single positive word. It's always negative—things like long, hard, awful, frustrating, painful, time-consuming, inefficient, exasperating...

At an executive meeting in Washington, DC, one head of sales said, "Landmine!" To which we responded, "But that's not an adjective." In a flash, he exclaimed, "Landminish!" And that became our word of the year describing B2B buying. B2B buying is landminish. It's perhaps the very best, most evocative way to describe the spaghetti bowl of B2B buying. It's an unmapped minefield. And just like any minefield, you're always on edge, as you never quite know when one false move might blow up months of hard work (metaphorically, thank goodness).

Even more memorably, at a Chicago meeting, a chief marketing officer who'd just completed the purchase of a CRM system blurted out, "Ineverwanttodothatagain!" All one word. I. Never. Want. To. Do. That. Again. And you could tell by the look in her eyes, she wasn't kidding. The pain on her face was palpable as she relived her entire experience right before our eyes. She truly never wanted to do that again.

But let that sink in for a moment. This isn't just a fun—or funny—thought exercise. This is our current B2B reality. B2B buying is broken. And these thousands of examples of an incredibly common sentiment prompt a powerful, if not painful, question for all of us trying to sell into this environment: What do you do when the number one word your customer thinks about in making a large B2B purchase is "I never want to do that again"? That's a problem. And that's what we're up against trying to sell complex solutions to exhausted buyers every single day.

It's no wonder many CEOs invest in engineering a better "customer experience," seeking to "ease customers' buying journey," by making their own organization "easier to do business with." In many ways, their instincts are right—we must find ways to make B2B buying *easier.* That said, well intended as they may be, the focus of their efforts is largely misplaced because those same customers tell us repeatedly, the vast majority of their frustration has little to do with the supplier selling to them and everything to do with their *own company.* It's all the meetings, the requirements, the second-guessing, the bureaucratic setbacks, legal considerations, shifts in strategy, budget constraints, and on and on. At the end of the day, we're all so frustrated because we're all convinced we work at the world's most dysfunctional company. And we've become convinced that we're all correct. Because we're all human, and regardless of organization, we're all struggling with some version of the same four buying challenges.

THE FOUR CHALLENGES UNDERMINING CUSTOMER CONFIDENCE

We once designed a keynote reviewing obstacles impeding B2B buying, which a colleague dramatically dubbed "the four horsemen of the commercial apocalypse." Over the top? Undoubtedly. Nonetheless, the turn of phrase is evocative of the high stakes at play across each of these four B2B buying trends materially undermining customer confidence.

Decision Complexity

If we think of a large-scale B2B purchase as a kind of organizational project, the first dimension along which buyers struggle is simply project management. Who should be involved? Which steps should we take? Which steps are we overlooking? Which people are we inadvertently omitting? Without a clear, consistent project plan, buying decisions quickly become "landminish" as unanticipated obstacles, questions, and concerns repeatedly disrupt efficient progress toward a completed purchase.

From a supplier perspective, B2B marketers, in particular, have prioritized "mapping the customer buying journey" in order to drive deals forward by "meeting customers where they are." Commonly, step one in most journey-mapping exercises is to document customers' buying process based on their direct input (usually via surveys and interviews). But what happens when customers themselves no longer have an answer? What happens when you seek to meet customers where they are only to find out that "where customers are" is . . . lost?

Information Overload

Across the last decade, the story of B2B buying—and more specifically, the story of B2B learning—has largely been a story of customer empowerment. With the rise of online content, customers no longer rely on sellers to educate them on speeds and feeds or features and benefits. Instead, customers learn on their own, conducting independent research and due diligence such that by the time they proactively reach out to a supplier sales rep to get their input into whatever they're seeking to do, there's often little left to discuss but price.

But what if today's B2B buyers aren't "empowered" by information nearly so much as they are overwhelmed? Today's customers struggle mightily to simply make sense of the massive amounts of high-quality information available through countless channels, online and off. In this world, showing up with yet another perspective—differentiated and disruptive as it may be—may actually *exacerbate* customers' struggle to act decisively. So how do you engage customers with a helpful perspective when they're struggling to sort through too many competing perspectives already?

Objective Misalignment

B2B buying is a team sport, which naturally raises all sorts of questions: Who's involved? In what way? What are their priorities? According to which criteria? Who breaks ties? It's not unlike a group of friends trying to pick a restaurant—one's a vegetarian, two are gluten-free, one loves meat, another wants sushi, and one isn't even hungry and would prefer to see a movie. Good luck! Now, scale that up to a multimillion-dollar enterprise business decision affecting hundreds if not thousands of fellow employees and months of work. It shouldn't be surprising that many potential sales never happen simply because customer stakeholders struggle to reach consensus, not on what to buy but what to do. Lack of alignment on the most pressing problems worthy of attention stalls not only a purchase but organizational action altogether. It's very hard for customers to buy a complex solution if they lack consensus on the best course of action, let alone the underlying problem.

Yet, virtually every sales approach is built on the assumption that customers know—and agree on—what they're trying to do. So, when a deal dies, suppliers often assume it's because customers fail to appreciate the value of their solution to address an agreed-upon problem. But in the end, the primary obstacle to deal success often isn't customers' lack of appreciation for the "supplier's value"; it's customers' inability to establish broad-based agreement on what they're solving for to begin with.

Outcome Uncertainty

Even when customers completely agree on what to buy, why to buy it, and how it's valuable, they can still doubt their ability to actually realize that full value. And with good reason. It's not just hard to buy solutions; it's equally hard to *implement* them.

In today's intensely interconnected world, virtually every solution requires deep integration into everything else. Systems have to be connected, data have to be shared, log-ons need to be seamless. All that information needs to be secured against leaks, incursions, and crashes. Meanwhile, the actual users of those solutions have to be bought in, see the need, and integrate the solution into daily workflow. The same applies for physical products as much as technological ones.

Yet, even in a world of perfect integration, the solution might still underperform. Not only do suppliers have to prove accurate in the value they promise, but end users have to be sufficiently skilled to extract that value. After all, if someone buys a Ferrari but can't drive very well, the car will never deliver maximum performance even when built to spec. That's not Ferrari's fault, that's on the driver and their inability to extract full value no matter how good the car.

This is the world of outcome uncertainty, where customers often doubt supplier promises far less than their own organization's ability to realize the full value after purchase. It's the business equivalent of the famous breakup phrase, "It's not you, it's me." Customers believe the supplier but equally doubt their own organization: "We'll find some way to screw this up. We always do."

One theme threads through all four of these challenges to customer decision confidence. All of them are supplier agnostic. In fact, as a seller, you might think, "These aren't my problems to solve!" But what if they could be? For suppliers *that's* the opportunity—to unlock the growth trapped in B2B buyers' collective decision dysfunction.

When it comes down to it, we aren't just competing against the competition. We are competing against our customers' lack of confidence. And the primary goal of *The Framemaking Sale* isn't to help you steal a bigger piece of the pie in an ever-shrinking market, but to equip you as a seller or a sales team to expand the market overall by boosting customer confidence—to help you *sell* more by helping your customers *buy* more.

If we want to sell more in today's commercial environment, we have to make things *easier* for our customers. Not easier to buy from us, but easier to buy *irrespective* of us. To help customers believe they *can* navigate the spaghetti bowl of B2B buying such that they *do* want to do that again. And again. And that next time things will be easier.

A NEW WAY FORWARD

You'll remember at the heart of this book lies a simple question: What would a seller have to do to become the one seller—or sales team—that customers actually *do* want to talk to?

The answer? Become the one seller—or the one supplier—who helps customers feel a little less overwhelmed and a lot more confident in their own ability to take decisive action.

The way to do that is Framemaking, and we'll talk more about what it is and how it works in the next chapter.

CHAPTER 2

Introducing Framemaking

O ne of the simplest examples of Framemaking we've ever heard
came from Kevin, the head of sales at a large provider of
"human capital management" solutions (software designed to manage common HR activities).

Kevin had joined one of his top sellers (we'll call her Tara) on
an in-person visit to the head of HR at a large prospective customer.
While the deal was still in early-stage development, both its potential size and strategic importance made an in-person visit worthy of
their time.

After a brief wait in the office lobby, Kevin and Tara were ushered into the head of HR's office where they sat down, exchanged
pleasantries, and prepared to dive in. Just then, the door opened, and
the company's head of procurement stepped in, sat down, and apolo-
gized for the late arrival.

Kevin was perplexed. *"What in the world was the head of* procurement *doing here?! It's* way *too early to be talking about price! This
doesn't end well."*

But there was nothing to do now but follow the lead of his star seller as she led the group through what turned out to be an incredibly productive meeting. In fact, the group made more progress in that one conversation than most of Kevin's sellers achieved across an entire series of meetings. Even better, the head of HR and head of procurement were actually *looking forward* to collaborating on the project.

Back in the rental car on the way to the airport, Kevin shook his head in disbelief. "That was absolutely crazy when the head of procurement walked in! Most reps would have panicked, but you didn't miss a beat, just adapted and kept right on going! How the heck did he even find out about the meeting in the first place?"

Tara looked confused. "Well, actually, he was there because I advised the head of HR to ask him to be there. I even drafted the email, letting him know we were meeting to talk about the impact on both spending and cost by rethinking HCM, suggesting he might like to join us."

Kevin, who had been burned enough times in his career to know how badly procurement could derail a deal, couldn't believe what he was hearing.

But Tara kept going. "We both know that procurement is eventually *going* to get involved. And every time they get involved, they get involved last minute asking all sorts of questions that blow everything up. I'm tired of losing that way. So now I'm telling every customer, 'You need to get procurement involved early. Your life will be so much easier if you do. So, let's get them in early, figure out their concerns, align their objectives, and answer their questions from the start. That way, we'll know a lot sooner whether it makes sense for us to move forward or not.' Just like we saw today. Customers really appreciate the help navigating the dysfunction inside their own companies. It's such a mess. Half the time, they don't even talk to each other until we're months into discussion, and then it all falls apart. So, if they won't fix it, then I will. Otherwise, I'm never gonna hit target. And I'm not missing President's Club for that!"

WHAT IS FRAMEMAKING?

As a reminder, Framemaking is the act of making a complex task or decision feel more manageable, both by establishing clear, credible boundaries around its scope and by identifying key considerations and prioritizing best next steps.

The primary objective of Framemaking is to take something hard or overwhelming and make it easier, thus boosting the likelihood of productive progress and a positive outcome.

Now, if you're thinking, "But that's exactly what the best sellers do already!" you'd be right. That's precisely why they're the best sellers. Step-by-step they're helping customers identify the right questions, prioritize critical considerations, align organizational priorities, create collective consensus, and determine next steps, all in order to boost customers' confidence to make bigger decisions.

This is exactly why Kevin's star seller invited procurement to the meeting with HR. She was helping her customer champion frame the complexities of consensus creation. How, exactly? Kevin's colleague knew that every large HCM purchase requires input from procurement. She's also learned that you're far better off seeking that input very early in a purchase journey rather than late. That early involvement makes things so much easier down the road when it comes time for a final decision. As a result of her guidance to invite procurement to the meeting, the head of HR was far more confident in winning over the rest of his peers because he'd just won over one of the toughest. All thanks to Tara's guidance and coaching.

Alternatively, if procurement was going to block the deal for whatever reason, Tara wanted to figure that out as early as possible. Why waste time on a deal that's never going to happen?

FRAMEMAKING'S OBJECTIVES: EASE AND AGENCY

So how exactly does Framemaking work? The cognitive psychology behind Framemaking is both well-known and well-documented in academic research from giants like Amos Tversky and Daniel Kahneman.[1] But for our purposes in B2B sales, it really comes down to two key objectives: ease and agency.

Making Buying Easier

In 2016, CEB (now Gartner) research found 39 percent of B2B buyers reported feeling overwhelmed by the buying process. In 2018—just two years later—that number had nearly doubled to 77 percent![2] If we're going to boost customers' confidence in making large, complex decisions, then we need to find a way to make those decisions easier—or at least, *feel* easier—for customers.

Most B2B commercial executives would appear to agree. Seeing an opportunity for meaningful differentiation, many suppliers have invested heavily across the last decade in reducing the amount of "friction" customers encounter when interacting with their company. Often, these efforts are directed by a newly formed "customer experience" team and backed by company-wide training to become more "customer centric." Slogans proclaiming "Customer 360" and "The Year of the Customer" are featured at sales kickoffs led by senior executives urging colleagues to "put the customer at the center of everything we do." All in an effort to improve the ease of doing business across every possible touchpoint connecting customers to their organization.

So, in many ways, it feels like we're all focused on boosting customer ease already.

Except we're not. At the end of the day, most current customer experience efforts are little more than supplier centricity wrapped up in customer-centric clothing, as they're almost exclusively designed to solve for customers' experience *with the supplier*.

But that's not customers' primary problem. Remember, the vast majority of B2B buyers cite *their own organization* as the key cause of purchase difficulty. They're not struggling to buy from your company; they're struggling to make decisions inside their *own*.

Which is not to say that a laser focus on easing customer effort while interacting with your company is a misuse of funds. It's just a missed opportunity.

From a seller's perspective, it's the difference between a customer who says:

"Working with that seller was amazing! It was by far the easiest part of this process!"

versus,

"Working with that seller was amazing! They just made everything so much easier!"

The difference is subtle but significant, particularly in terms of scope. The seller in the first example is easy to work with. The seller in the second makes the rest of the work easier too. To be sure, the former at least doesn't *contribute* to purchase difficulty, but the latter actively *eliminates* it.

How do you become the one seller that customers actually *do* want to talk to? By helping customers address and eliminate purchase difficulty that you didn't create. Helping them navigate internal struggles that you can't control. Proactively mapping the minefield of customer buying difficulty and guiding buyers step-by-step to progress a decision more easily through their own organization. Simply put, by becoming an "engine of ease."

And improving customer ease is less about adopting a "customer-centric" approach than applying a "supplier agnostic" mindset to address buying decision difficulty. Especially when much of the pain of B2B buying has nothing to do with the supplier organization at all.

Amplifying Customer Agency

That said, effective Framemaking isn't just about ease; it's equally about control.

Remember, our ultimate objective in B2B sales is boosting customers' decision confidence. That's the North Star that dramatically increases the likelihood of a high-quality, low-regret sale. Yet, while reducing complexity may be necessary to increase customer confidence, B2B buyers are unlikely to make an expensive, large-scale purchase simply based on purchase ease alone. Customers need to feel confident they are making the *right* decision, not just an easy one. They've got to believe they've asked the right questions, conducted sufficient research, thoroughly considered alternatives. They need to determine the correct metrics, targets, and timelines to measure impact. They need to collectively agree on the underlying problem and the best course of action. These aren't decisions customers can delegate to a third party as the customers themselves are the ones on the hook for the outcomes those decisions produce. And when it comes to complex B2B solutions, the stakes of a bad purchase are simply far too high, including personal consequences to professional credibility and even job security.

Bottom line, in B2B buying customers' confidence in the supplier matters far less than customers' confidence in themselves.

Some have argued that things like service guarantees and shared ownership of outcomes offer effective ways to boost customer confidence, but their impact on confidence is weaker than one might expect as these tactics primarily provide a safety net against the consequences of making a bad decision rather than a practical means of boosting the likelihood of making a good one. Effectively, they're a kind of insurance policy against downside risk. Their primary posture is "just in case this turns out to be a bad idea, you're protected." But the fact remains, it was still a bad decision.

Framemaking, on the other hand, starts from a far more positive place: "Let us help you make the best decision possible." With so much riding on the outcome, it's critical that customers see these decisions as *their* decisions. That sense of agency is critical for decision confidence.

Framemaking provides sellers a practical means for dramatically improving purchase ease while simultaneously amplifying customers' perception of individual agency.

As an example, consider the travel agent working with the family planning their big vacation. A good travel agent will likely frame that purchase by saying something like,

> "Over the years, I've worked with a lot of young families planning the trip of a lifetime—especially for their kids. It can be really overwhelming. There are so many questions to consider and everything seems important! But what I've learned is, for the vast majority of families with young children it generally boils down to a simple checklist of a few critical questions—a couple of which most families often overlook."

At that point, the agent might review those dimensions, emphasizing criteria the family may have otherwise missed (maybe it's hotels with planned activities for children, dining options based on pickiness of children's appetites, or park-pass options based on scheduled naptimes) and then provide their clients guidance on how to determine where they stand on each attribute, leaving the ultimate decision up to them.

So, the agent frames the decision to make it more manageable. But equally importantly, they allow for sufficient latitude, or degrees of freedom, within that frame for customers to determine for themselves where they stand on each criterion. Ultimately, the choice is the buyers', not the seller's. The agent *simplifies* the decision but does not *make* the decision. After all, customers are far more likely to confidently make a decision—and then *feel good* about that decision—if they believe the decision was theirs to make in the first place. Without decision confidence, there is no decision.

Compare this approach to the agent who tells clients, "I've been working in the industry for twenty-five years, stayed at every hotel in the area, and been to all of these parks hundreds of times. I've seen it all. And based on my experience, here's what I think you should do."

Yes, this agent has simplified the choice—all the way down to a single choice, in fact. *But* this agent has also *robbed the customer of the chance to choose.* Instead, the agent is asking customers to rely on *someone else's* judgment rather than their own. *But how can customers feel good about their decision without the opportunity to make a decision in the first place?*

FRAMEMAKING'S ACTIVE INGREDIENTS: PROMPTING AND BOUNDING

There are many tools in the Framemaking toolkit, but chief among them are bounding and prompting—sort of first among equals when promoting ease and agency. For some, the terms may be self-explanatory, but we'll unpack both in detail and provide examples throughout the book as they describe the key mechanism by which virtually all Framemaking interventions function. If ease and agency are the ends, then prompting and bounding are the primary means. So, let's take a moment to briefly introduce each here.

For those times when customers are overwhelmed—with too many questions, too much information, too many stakeholders, possible outcomes, or potential metrics—Framemaking sellers can use bounding to suggest clear boundaries defining in very practical terms what matters most, and what matters much less. In some ways, it's like having a kind of purchase editor, stripping away extraneous considerations and bringing focus to what matters most, whether it's a decision, a process, a person, or a question.

In bringing focus to a challenge, Framemaking sellers might propose a specific, structured framework, for example, that organizes ideas, maps processes, prioritizes questions in highly structured ways. Even informal conversations can provide opportunities for bounding simply through the act of offering suggestions.

Prompting is essentially the act of suggesting. When sellers prompt customers' thinking, they're simply suggesting a certain question, course of action, objective, metric, idea, you name it. Prompting plays a critical role in Framemaking, as many of the best ways to address customers' key buying challenges aren't immediately clear to customers themselves. Perhaps there's a person they'd be well-advised to include earlier in a purchase that they hadn't thought of. This was the case with Tara suggesting the inclusion of procurement. Perhaps there's a helpful way to organize information or prioritize objectives customers haven't considered. Or maybe it's an easy way to improve the likelihood of a positive outcome. Really, the sky's the limit, and across the book we'll provide all sorts of practical examples of prompting in action across the four buyer challenges that undermine customer confidence. We'll also look at ways to prompt emotional reactions and why it matters for Framemaking. Finally, we'll take you through steps to determine what to prompt in the first place. After all, there are all sorts of things we might prompt customers to consider that could actually make buying feel harder, not easier. It's not prompting for prompting's sake, but prompting for the sake of making a previously confused customer feel in control and, ultimately, increasing customer confidence.

Equally important is what prompting is *not*. Prompting is *suggesting*, it is definitively *not* "telling." Remember, the primary goal of Framemaking is boosting customers' confidence in *themselves*. So, prompting, as suggesting, proves especially important as it leaves it up to the customer to decide whether to actually act on a prompt. The seller makes the suggestions, the customer makes the decisions, maintaining a sense of agency as a result.

In the context of Framemaking selling, both bounding and prompting are specifically designed, deployed, and intended to make buying easier while promoting customers' sense of agency.

We'll have a lot more to say about both prompting and bounding throughout the book, but bottom line, framing a decision makes it more manageable. By prompting consideration of critical dimensions within a frame, we boost customers' confidence that they've sufficiently weighed their options. By allowing for degrees of freedom within that frame, we empower customers to exercise agency and take ownership of their decision. All in the name of increasing their confidence to make bigger decisions rather than no decision.

Think back to Kevin's star seller, Tara, inviting procurement to the early-stage meeting with the head of HR. Tara didn't tell the executives what to discuss or how to decide. She simply suggested, based on lessons learned from similar companies, that if they want to make progress, they both need to be part of the discussion from the very beginning. She then facilitated that conversation, suggesting some of the topics for discussion but allowing the executives themselves to determine how to proceed with the decision. Ultimately, the decisions they reached were their own.

How can you become the one sales rep customers do want to talk to? By helping customers make a complex task or decision feel easier. First, by establishing clear, credible boundaries around its scope, and second, by prompting exploration within that framework while leaving sufficient space for customers to come to their own conclusions. Ease and agency through prompting and bounding.

A FRAMEWORK FOR FRAMEMAKING—ESTABLISH, ENGAGE, EXECUTE

Designing and deploying a Framemaking sales approach will always follow the same three steps: establish, engage, execute. The three E's of ease, as it were.

Establish

The first step in any Framemaking effort is to establish the frame itself. If customers are overwhelmed with too many questions, which questions matter most? If they're struggling with too much information, which content will prove most valuable? If they struggle to align stakeholders, which stakeholders are most important and what questions or issues are most likely going to cause friction?

Notice, in order to help make things easier for customers, we first have to understand what's hard. So, the first step in any Framemaking exercise is a kind of assessment or audit. We'll need to map customers' current behavior as accurately as possible to identify the specific points of pain or complexity that leave customers feeling confused or overwhelmed. We'll introduce specific means for making that happen throughout this book, but at a high level, a good starting point is always customers themselves, whether it's structured interviews or simply casual conversations. Maybe it's surveys, or some kind of benchmarking exercise.

However we gather that data on what's hard, we'll want to ensure we cast a wide net and remain supplier agnostic. We're not trying to identify "what's hard about working with us," but rather "what's hard about this aspect of a purchase?"

Once we've identified what's hard, we then need to prioritize. Which steps are most important? Which questions matter most?

What stakeholders have to participate? Which content is most helpful? The answers to these questions provide a basis for guidance—whether presented in a formal document like a maturity model or diagnostic tool, or through a conversational suggestion like, "In working with customers like you, one of things we often find is . . ." Effectively, we're establishing a boundary—or frame—defining what's in and what's out for customer consideration. We're bounding the decision.

How do we know where to set the boundary? One of the best ways to determine key criteria for a good decision is to ask customers who've successfully navigated something similar how they got there. We especially like questions like, "What's one piece of advice you'd give to another organization about to embark on a similar decision?" Or, "If you had to do it all over again, what would you do differently?" Again, all supplier agnostic. In fact, the best sellers often achieve the same outcome without ever speaking to a customer at all, simply by conducting a post hoc analysis of won and lost deals. This is exactly how Tara identified the critical importance of procurement's early involvement.

Either way, not only can you use the answers to help overwhelmed customers focus on the decisions that matter most, but you can also equally use them to prompt considerations that might otherwise get overlooked. For example, "We've talked to a few other customers who've told us there's one question everyone tends to overlook that turns out to *really* matter."

Whether knowingly or not, many top sellers are likely already prompting customers' thinking in a similar fashion. And in many cases, that existing organizational experience with other customers can be captured to scale Framemaking efforts already proven effective. For example, after Kevin's customer visit with Tara, you can imagine his next step was to suggest that the rest of his team consider involving procurement earlier as well.

The value of establishing a frame through the use of social proof cannot be overstated. Generally speaking, customers are far less interested in a seller's opinion, regardless of how many years they've been selling. What virtually every customer values most is insight into what other customers like them have done. After all, that's the next best thing to having done it yourself.

The whole idea here is to establish clear guardrails within which customers are most likely to make easy progress.

Engage

Once we've established a frame, we need to engage customers in a conversation applying that frame to their specific context. Here, the primary objective isn't simply to present the frame to customers but to have them interact with it.

If the frame is packaged as a formal assessment tool like a maturity model or a benchmarking survey, one can have customers complete the exercise collaboratively with colleagues and then participate in an interactive conversation where results are provided and compared to others. If Framemaking unfolds through a more informal conversation, the seller can nonetheless guide customers Socratically through a series of bounding and prompting questions:

> "We find just about every company struggles to determine the right way to do 'X.' Is that something you've struggled with too?"

> "In working with other organizations, we find it typically boils down to these three questions. Does that correspond to your experience? Is there one that especially stands out?"

Notice all these examples are designed to make things easier by "chalking the field," creating a manageable scope for consideration. Yet they all leave room for agency, allowing customers to determine for themselves how they prioritize criteria or consider the relevance of different dimensions with the frame.

The whole idea here is to win buy-in. Not for you, your company, your brand, or your product, but for the frame. Do they perceive your proposed frame as an effective means for organizing their thinking or progressing their decision? Have they taken ownership of the frame by aligning their thinking and activity to fit within its context? In the case of Tara and Kevin's sales call, did the head of HR actually follow through and invite procurement to the meeting, and did the head of procurement actually show up?

These are not only good indications of whether the customer is bought in to the frame, but they're also good predictors of whether the customer is likely to make progress in their decision. In fact, Framemaking proves to be a highly effective deal qualification tool, as customers who fail to engage with the frame are also far more likely to struggle to progress productively and efficiently through the purchase on their own.

Across the coming chapters, we'll examine a series of practical examples of customer engagement through Framemaking, some simple, some far more complex, but all designed to identify which customers are most willing to accept help and therefore move forward with greater confidence.

Execute

Now we're ready for the follow-through on Framemaking. You've established an effective frame to simplify a buying task, you've successfully engaged customers in its application to their purchase process, and you're ready to execute the plan.

Within the context of Framemaking, however, "execute" refers far less to the execution of a set of sales plays and far more to a seller's role in *enabling customers* to execute a plan derived from the frame itself.

So, if the frame suggests the inclusion of a specific stakeholder, the seller works with their customer contact to get that stakeholder involved. If the frame suggests that two pieces of content matter more than any other, the seller ensures customers have consumed that content and stands ready to prompt a discussion around its conclusions. If the frame identifies a number of dimensions in critical need of cross-function alignment, the seller works with their customer contact to set up and facilitate an alignment conversation, or workshop, much like we saw in the case of Tara.

In other words, winning customer buy-in to a decision framework is only the beginning. The sales rep still needs to play the role of coach, or sherpa, and guide customers step-by-step through that frame in a way that keeps them confident, preserves their agency, and reduces decision doubt. Sound difficult? It can be. But it's critically important, as it's the best, most predictable means to ensure customers progress with confidence through the purchase process.

Essentially, by assuming the role of guide or coach, you're assuming a certain proportion of the customer's buying burden—making it easier for them by taking on some of the work yourself. You're making it easier. But you're also setting them up for success. Just like an athlete who wins a tough race will thank their coach while now feeling far more confident in themselves, customers who employ your frame to successfully navigate a complex solutions purchase will thank you for your help while now feeling far more confident in themselves and their ability to make large, complex decisions on behalf of their company.

PUTTING IT ALL TOGETHER

Now that we've established the why, what, and how of Framemaking, we're ready to dive into the details. Across the next four chapters, we'll unpack each challenge to customer confidence in greater detail and then offer an antidote using the three E's of Framemaking, starting in Chapter 3 with decision complexity.

CHAPTER 3

Untangling Decision Complexity

A few years back, while exploring the rising challenge of stalled deals with a group of senior sales leaders, one chief sales officer shared the following story. They'd been working an eight-figure deal for the better part of a year. The biggest deal in the history of their company. After months of work on both sides, the deal was nearing the finish line, and everyone was excited. Sitting in the pipeline with a 95 percent likelihood to close this quarter, the deal represented the difference between the company dramatically exceeding expectations or missing target by a country mile. This deal was a big deal.

And all signs looked good. The deal had an enthusiastic customer champion advocating actively for the supplier among her colleagues. The deal had cleared IT, won end-user buy-in, and garnered cross-functional support. They were about as close to the finish line as you can get without actually crossing it. Everything was on track for a huge win and a champagne end to a killer quarter. All they needed was the call from their champion confirming they were good to go and a signed contract was on its way.

Except it wasn't. And the call never came.

Instead, they waited. And waited. No email. No phone call. Days ticked by, yet no sign of their champion as quarter end crept ever closer.

You can imagine, with two weeks to go, the sales team was sweating bullets, sending emails, leaving voicemails. By this point, they'd probably tried the old change of voice strategy, where the manager calls instead of the seller, or—everyone's favorite—even sent flowers to the executive assistant to recruit her help.

But still, nothing.

Until the call finally came. On the call, the once enthusiastic champion was now uncharacteristically reserved, even apologetic. "Unfortunately, I have some bad news."

The seller's heart sank. "What's up? How can I help?"

"Well . . . ," the champion hesitated, almost embarrassed, "it turns out that any purchase over $15 million has to go in front of our Capital Review Board for review. I'm so sorry. To be honest, I didn't know that was something we had to do. I'm so sorry, this is all new to me. I've never been involved in a purchase of this size before. This is *so* frustrating!"

Ugh. Don't panic, thought the seller. *This is bad, but salvageable. We've still got two weeks. That's a lot of time.*

"That's not a problem," he said. "How can I help? I'm happy to put together whatever documentation we need. We'll refresh the models, design a presentation deck for you, and if it helps, I'll hop on a plane and come out there to present with you. I could be there first thing Monday morning. Would that work? I want to make this as easy as possible for you."

"I really appreciate that, thank you," the champion replied. "But that's not the problem."

"Whatever it is, I'm sure we can help. Just say the word. Two weeks is plenty of time."

"The problem," the customer sighed, "is that the Capital Review Board doesn't meet next for another two and half months."

That dull thud you just heard was the seller's heart hitting the floor. His quota, the trip to Cancun, the company's quarterly performance, the potential impact on the stock price. Poof. All gone in a single, simple statement. Silence.

"Yeah, it's bad," said the champion. "I'm so sorry! This is not how I saw things going. I'm so excited to work with you guys, and I'm so frustrated that we're slowing things down. But you know what's *really* crazy?" asked the champion.

"What's that?" the seller asked, with visions of his imploding quota dancing in his head.

"I didn't even know we *had* a Capital Review Board," replied the champion.

As the chief sales officer shared this story with a roomful of his peers, the collective sense of familiar pain was palpable.

"The good news," he said, looking around, "is we eventually did manage to get the deal done. Just three months later than we'd hoped. But the biggest lesson by far for us? At the early part of every deal now, we ask customers, 'Do you have a Capital Review Board? If you're not sure, let's find that out first. And if you do, let's be sure to get on their schedule now. We can help prepare you for that meeting and make sure you've got solid answers to the questions they're likely to ask. We'd hate to see your plans get derailed in the final mile. We've seen it before, and it can be really frustrating.'"

He shook his head, lost in the memory, and said, "We're never falling in that trap again."

MANAGING PURCHASE COMPLEXITY

When we introduced the spaghetti bowl of B2B buying in Chapter 1, three powerful lessons jumped out:

1. Customers loop their way through a typical purchase journey in a complex, often unpredictable fashion.
2. That unpredictable, often illogical motion proves deeply frustrating, emotionally draining, and psychically exhausting to customers.
3. The vast majority of that frustration has little, if anything, to do with the supplier selling to the customer, and virtually everything to do with the customer's own company getting in its own way.

It's no wonder so many buyers have so little confidence and even less desire to face another purchase process. Successfully navigating the number and diversity of potential—often surprising—obstacles strewn across a typical B2B buying journey is enough to make Ferdinand Magellan uneasy.

But just because B2B buying has become increasingly difficult to navigate, doesn't mean it has to be that way.

In this chapter, we tackle customer decision complexity. Specifically, we'll look at ways sellers can apply Framemaking to proactively simplify the buying process, increasing customers' confidence to not only start a buying journey but see it all the way through once it's started.

As we dive in, it may help to think of the customer's purchase journey as a complex organizational project that needs to be managed with care and attention.

And if a complex B2B purchase is basically a large-scale organizational project, B2B buying arguably requires some kind of project manager—a purchase process project management office, as it were.

In sales, we often think of our customer champion as playing that role. We rely on them to shepherd the deal through their organization: mapping a consensus creation plan, identifying, connecting, and coordinating various stakeholders, specifying stage gates, ensuring timely execution, and delivering the "project" as specified within the time frame determined. After all, if we can't rely on the customer champion to navigate their organization, then who's going to do it? That's why we call them "champions," right?

But who the heck wants that job? That's hard. And there's no guarantee the customer champion has the experience, desire, capacity, or personal credibility to make any of that happen. From a supplier's perspective, all that effort is *absolutely* worth it as it likely represents the difference between a closed-won deal and an inextricably stalled one. But from a *customer's* perspective, playing project manager through the spaghetti bowl of B2B buying is often high effort, high risk, and low reward. In many cases the perceived benefits aren't sufficient to justify the personal risk and thankless effort necessary to steer a complex purchase to successful completion. Not when the status quo, while likely deeply flawed, may be good enough.

Truth be told, most champions are likely hoping sellers will assume much of the heavy lifting of purchase management without relinquishing control of the process, thus bringing the effort-benefit ratio far closer into balance. The key is to increase ease for the customer while maintaining their sense of agency.

But heavy lifting with what, exactly? And how? That's Framemaking. To understand how a seller might apply Framemaking to ease decision complexity, we must first understand what's driving all that decision complexity.

B2B BUYING BECOMES A TEAM SPORT

Perhaps the most obvious factor contributing to purchase complexity is the number of people now involved in a typical B2B solutions purchase.

If you've been in sales long enough, you might remember the days when sellers were trained to climb their way to the corner office and engage the senior decision-maker to get a deal done. After all, only senior leaders sat at a sufficiently high altitude to sign off on both the scope and expense of ever-expanding "solutions," especially those that involve integrating workflows across an increasing range of processes, functions, technologies, and teams.

However, as those very same expanding solutions came to touch ever more stakeholders across the customer organization, not surprisingly those individuals wanted greater input into purchases that directly impacted their daily work. And senior leaders quickly learned that stakeholder buy-in was critical for solutions success. After all, why buy a solution if no one was going to use it? In fact, starting as early as 2010, B2B buyer research identified "widespread support across the team" as senior leaders' number one criterion for choosing one supplier over another—outscoring all other attributes tested, including solution features, supplier brand, and even purchase value.[1] Clearly, today's world of B2B sales is a world of broad-based customer consensus.

But consensus among whom, exactly? That's where things start to wobble for both sellers *and* buyers, as the cast of characters typically involved in a modern-day B2B purchase has expanded dramatically.

As reported in *The Challenger Customer*, when we first measured the size of an average B2B buying group over ten years ago, we found a typical B2B purchase included an average of 5.4 customer stakeholders. At the time, that number was shocking to many heads of sales and marketing as it was well beyond the one or maybe two stakeholders most sellers were trained to engage beyond the senior decision-maker.

Today, however, 5.4 seems almost quaint. A distant memory of times gone by when buying groups were far more manageable. Over the last decade, the average number of stakeholders typically involved in a B2B deal rose dramatically until our most recent survey, where it topped double digits at just over eleven.

Funny enough, the very first time we presented that latest data to a large group of chief sales officers, the head of sales at a large trucking and logistics company raised his hand, stopped the meeting, and declared, "I don't believe it! That number is way too small!"

THE PAINFUL WORLD OF BIG BUYING GROUPS

He proceeded to tell the following story. Last year their company was working a deal with a big-box retailer. It was a multimillion-dollar deal—one of the biggest in the history of the company—and the team had been pursuing it for over a year. The deal ultimately got right up to the finish line, complete with buy-in from the customers' senior leaders, so members of the executive leadership team along with the account manager took the corporate jet to Minnesota to close the deal and sign the contract.

When they walked into the customer's corporate headquarters, they were ushered to a large conference room, where they sat down and set things up for what they thought would be a small meeting with senior leaders to work through a few final questions and sign the paperwork. As they waited for the meeting to start, they were surprised when several people they'd never met before entered the room and sat down. Minutes later, it was a couple more. Then a few more. By the time the meeting started, there were sixteen people there from the customer side! Some were familiar, but many were new, and almost none had been actively involved in the deal to that point.

What proved to be especially surprising, however, was not that the supplier team hadn't met most of them, but rather that most of them had never met each other either. They would come in, introduce themselves, and one of *their own* colleagues would say something like, "Oh, you're Bob from procurement! It's so good to put a face with the name!" (And this was prepandemic, before the shift to working from home.)

Not surprisingly, no sooner had the meeting started when the questions and objections started flying. "How come we've structured things like this? This won't work for our stores in the West." Twenty minutes in, and the whole thing had fallen apart, and the deal collapsed.

It was a painful, yet totally relatable story. And unlike the Capital Review Board story, this one didn't have a happy ending. Months later the deal still wasn't done.

One can only imagine the mood in the plane on the flight home. Brutal.

That experience highlights two new fundamental truths of B2B commerce: You know you're not closing the deal that day if the first item on the meeting's agenda is "Get more chairs from the room next door." And, you *really* know you're not closing a deal that day if the meeting starts with customer stakeholders introducing themselves . . . to *each other.*

At the time, the story was eye opening. These days, it feels uncomfortably common (swapping Zoom for the corporate jet, perhaps).

Several months ago, we were speaking to the president of an enterprise software company who told us they'd just lost an eight-figure deal because the twenty stakeholders in the customer's buying group not only had never made a collective purchase before, they'd never had to make a collective *decision* before. They literally couldn't figure how to navigate their own internal decision-making process because they didn't have one.

In large enterprise sales, it's even worse. In a recent conversation with a Fortune 500 software provider, an executive on the team pinned the average number of customer stakeholders in a large deal closer to sixty or eighty, and sometimes even more!

In the *Harvard Business Review,* Schmidt, Adamson, and Bird reported that purchase likelihood sinks from 80 percent to 30 percent when buying-group size increases from one to six people.[2] Today, most sellers we talk to would be excited to have only six stakeholders and a conversion rate of 30 percent. Not surprising that everyone, sellers and buyers alike, is feeling the frustration.

A BIGGER PROBLEM THAN BIGGER NUMBERS

But the real challenge with large buying groups isn't their size, it's actually their diversity—or, more technically, their heterogeneity.

Generally, we're huge proponents of organizational diversity for a host of reasons. But when it comes to B2B buying, this specific flavor of diversity can significantly slow efficient decision-making as each member of that growing buying group likely represents a different role, function, division, or geography. There's someone from HR, marketing, senior leadership, IT, data compliance, finance, procurement, legal (a.k.a. the Sales Prevention Department), you name it. In international deals, multiply those roles by region: Asia Pacific; Europe, the Middle East, and Africa; North America; South America. It's a lot. But more importantly, each of those stakeholders prioritizes a different set of questions and concerns specific to their role and responsibilities, often only marginally relevant to others on the team, and sometimes even in direct conflict.

Figuring out how to align these diverse perspectives is not an easy challenge, especially when the individuals involved see conflicts among themselves.

Generally speaking, across the last several years, each new addition to a typical B2B buying group has represented not only a new role in the purchase but a new role in the company altogether, a result of wide-ranging forces requiring companies to constantly evolve. One example we have been hearing about from many sellers is the CISO, or chief information security officer—a role that didn't formally exist in many companies just a few short years ago. For other companies, it might be someone in customer success, customer experience, revenue operations, ESG (environment, social, and governance), sustainability, diversity and inclusion, data integration, or AI ethics. All roles that weren't common when we first started collecting customer stakeholder data a decade ago. All bringing unique voices, perspectives, and priorities to the table.

Yet, despite—or perhaps because of—that increasingly broad range of stakeholders, most companies follow no prescribed order of operations regarding when or how any of these individuals should get involved in a complex purchase decision. Typically, that means anyone less familiar or less connected to central decision-makers is likely pulled into deliberations later rather than sooner, often forcing reconsideration of already-agreed-upon conclusions and causing frustration for everyone. This isn't just herding cats. It's herding two cats, a dog, three chickens, a bull moose, and an okapi. Good luck! Essentially, it's a large-scale, often high-stakes organizational project with little to no project plan.

It's no wonder that sellers have been trained to rely on a customer "champion" to navigate this mess. This stuff is really, really hard. But if it isn't easy for a seller to slalom through this collection of competing concerns, why would we assume it's any easier for a customer champion? The presumption that they're somehow more able to navigate their company's purchase process simply because it's *their* organization proves pretty problematic. And as that customer champion wends their way through their own internal complexity, cashing in favors, putting out fires, cajoling reluctant colleagues, dodging unanticipated obstacles, and still getting stuck wrangling with legal, it's no wonder buyers lose confidence in their ability to make high-quality, large-scale decisions on behalf of their company.

FRAMING THE PURCHASE PROCESS

The way those customer obstacles typically present themselves to the seller will feel very familiar.

Often, it's in the form of a phone call or email or even text message, late in the sales cycle, when the customer champion reaches out—sometimes chagrined, often perturbed, frequently frustrated—and opens the conversation with arguably the four worst words in sales: "It turns out that . . ."

Let's face it, any customer conversation that starts with "It turns out that" is like a relationship conversation that starts with "We need to talk." It's all downhill from there.

"It turns out that procurement needs to look this over, and they've got some tough questions I can't answer."

"It turns out that the European team is working on a similar project, and we'll need a few months to align everyone on a single path."

"It turns out that we've just announced a significant re-org, and all new purchases are on hold for at least six months."

Painful as it is, however, what's especially interesting when a customer utters, "It turns out that," is that they're often sincerely surprised. Whatever it is that it turned out to be, that particular obstacle wasn't something they saw coming. But more often than not, the seller isn't surprised at all. While the customer may be experiencing this particular challenge for the first time, the seller has probably encountered the same thing in similar deals *multiple* times.

And right there, that one small but meaningful moment of information asymmetry, represents the heart and soul of Framemaking. Because that asymmetry represents opportunity. Not only does the seller know something the customer doesn't; they know something potentially *helpful*. Which naturally raises the question, What if rather than waiting for customers to get stuck and struggle, sellers took it upon themselves to *proactively* help customers identify, address, or even avoid the purchase obstacles inside their own company that they didn't see coming? What if sellers effectively assumed the role of buyer coach or buyer's guide, helping customers navigate their own organization's purchase process and diverse buying group with decisive confidence rather than familiar frustration? That's powerful.

That's Framemaking.

However, the core objective of *The Framemaking Sale* isn't just to document customers' frustration, but to *reduce* it—specifically through differently designed sales interactions.

So, how can we use Framemaking to boost customers' confidence in their ability to successfully shepherd a complex purchase decision through their organization?

To do that, we need to find a way to make the purchase journey feel easier, more manageable, and less overwhelming. All while simultaneously reinforcing customers' confidence in *their* ability, not just our expertise. After all, they're the ones ultimately responsible for steering the purchase through their organization. Our job is to *enable* the journey to a purchase decision, not to make that decision on our customers' behalf.

So let's take it step by step—establish, engage, execute.

ESTABLISHING THE FRAME—MAPPING THE MINEFIELD OF B2B BUYING

Step one in framing a customer's buying journey is determining what makes that journey difficult. In some ways, identifying typical deal obstacles may not seem like a new idea. However, for most sales organizations, Framemaking requires a critical shift in perspective regarding "what's hard" about B2B sales. While most sales approaches focus almost exclusively on obstacles sellers face when selling, Framemaking centers entirely on the obstacles *buyers* face when buying, agnostic of sales interactions altogether.

Specifically, we need to identify the organizational obstacles inside the customer organization that buyers struggle to overcome on their own or, worse, fail to anticipate altogether.

Conducting an It-Turns-Out-That Audit

One of the best ways to identify potential obstacles customers might face along their buying journey is to conduct an "it-turns-out-that audit."

An it-turns-out-that audit is simply an inventory of the different problems, challenges, or questions that turned out to stall a past deal of similar size or configuration applied to the kinds of deals you're currently seeking to sell. If B2B buying is "landminish," this is a map to that minefield.

Effectively, it's similar to a loss analysis—a look back at past lost or stuck opportunities to determine what hung them up or prevented their successful close.

Unlike traditional loss analysis, however, an it-turns-out-that audit isn't focused on ways the supplier company has come up short—whether on price or an ability to deliver value. Instead, it's specifically designed to identify and prioritize the unexpected obstacles, unanticipated questions, and unaccounted for customer stakeholders inside the customer's *own* organization that ultimately proved insurmountable, or at least highly challenging, to completing a purchase. So, we're not just interested in lost deals but in any purchase where obstacles, stakeholders, or questions slowed things down materially.

In an it-turns-out-that audit we're not asking, "Where did we go wrong?" but rather, "Where did the customer get stuck?" After all, sticking points in one company are likely sticking points in another. And sticking points proving surprising to one buyer will likely prove surprising to another.

As the sales team conducts the audit, it helps to view deal stalls through three distinct lenses:

People: Which individuals, teams, or functions got involved unexpectedly, complicating or slowing the purchase process?

Perhaps their involvement was not planned at all, or the nature or timing of their involvement was not expected by your customer champion, creating delays or additional effort.

Questions: What unanticipated questions arose, and from whom, requiring additional effort, time, or evidence to answer? Did any questions prove to be actual deal-breakers?

Process: What process steps did customers themselves fail to predict, creating delays or inefficient rework (e.g., data compliance, regulatory risk, geographic localization)?

To be sure, as the audit evolves, some deals will prove stuck or lost for idiosyncratic reasons. But across enough deals, patterns will arise. Perhaps certain questions from procurement. Or certain information-security concerns on the IT team. Or, as a chief commercial officer related to us in a recent conversation, perhaps changing European data-protection laws have triggered certain legal and compliance requirements that many US companies are not yet prepared to meet without outside legal counsel. The potential obstacles are as diverse as they are numerous.

Yet, in aggregating those patterns to enable Framemaking, it's important to consider three key questions to ensure maximum value when engaging customers with the results:

1. Are we teaching customers something new?
For Framemaking purposes, not all purchase obstacles are created equal. We're especially interested in obstacles that offer an opportunity to teach customers something new. Maybe it's an obstacle they hadn't yet considered, or perhaps it's a known obstacle that can be addressed or avoided in a manner they've failed to identify on their own.

Either way, our goal is to come to the table with a unique and valuable perspective on how to navigate the customer's internal decision complexity in a way that materially boosts their confidence in their ability to shepherd a purchase to an easier, successful conclusion. For example, perhaps it's not just a view on who's likely involved in the purchase, but who *should* be involved—including when and how—to reduce delays further down the road. Or, maybe it's not just questions customers typically need to answer as part of a purchase, but questions customers easily overlook, increasing regret post purchase.

As a practical litmus test, the initial reaction we're seeking from customers in a Framemaking conversation is not affirmation but actually unease, or at least introspection. If their response to your guidance is "I totally agree!" chances are pretty good you haven't taught them anything new. On the other hand, if they respond with, "Huh, I hadn't thought of that. That's a really great point," chances are pretty good you've just offered a valuable perspective that helps them think more thoroughly or accurately about how they might advance the purchase decision through their organization.

2. Are we focused on a small number of obstacles with the greatest impact?
Not every decision obstacle, question, or stakeholder objection is created equal. It's probably best to focus on the 20 percent of obstacles that create 80 percent of the customer frustration. It's those predictable patterns that lend this exercise its value.

3. Are we finding early indicators of future problems?
That said, sometimes a unique purchase disruption at one customer organization may prove predictive of challenges soon to

be faced more broadly. These obstacles may represent a kind of canary in the coal mine anticipating purchase difficulty yet to appear in future decisions. Certain questions or concerns around generative AI, for example, might fall in this category.

In the end, whatever the patterns may be, the critical value of the exercise is the perspective generated from aggregate experience. By pooling perspectives across many opportunities, a team of sellers can tap into something incredibly valuable that individual customers can't access on their own: broad experience across multiple attempts to navigate similar decisions.

Learning from Customers Who've Gone Before

In addition to relying on sellers' direct experience pursuing past deals, commercial teams can naturally consult with customers themselves to complete the picture of decision complexity standing in the way of efficient purchase decisions—whether it's through individual seller outreach, "top-to-top" conversations, marketing-led customer interviews, or any other combination of means.

Insights gained from asking customers about the challenges they faced moving a complex decision through their organization can prove invaluable in coaching similar customers to avoid similar frustration. This is especially true for challenges sellers never see, as they occur behind closed doors—all the internal wrangling, budget debates, personal politics, staffing decisions that slow down decisions but never come up in seller conversations during the sale itself.

Yet these kinds of postsale examinations of "what was hard" rarely happen. On the one hand, the seller, happy to have closed the deal, has no interest in asking customers to recount the difficulties they encountered to get there, while customers have no real incentive—or likely desire—to recount the months of internal effort it took to get a deal done. Why risk opening a can of worms or unnecessarily reliving all that pain? Frankly, many customers may be glad to just have the decision made.

Meanwhile, marketers or customer experience teams conducting postsale surveys all too often focus exclusively on the customer's experience with the *supplier* organization throughout the purchase process. They collect customers' level of satisfaction *with the supplier*, their likelihood to recommend *the supplier*. It's useful data, perhaps, but it solves for a completely different problem—customers' experience with the *supplier* organization, rather than their experience within their own. It's understandable that selling teams typically don't gather this kind of insight. But they should.

So how do we do that? Tactically, it's powerfully simple. There are two questions we've found a small handful of companies using to elicit exactly this kind of insight from customers—whether through seller-led conversation shortly after a deal closes, or perhaps via a customer success team as part of deal implementation:

Question 1: Based on your experience, what advice would you have for companies about to embark on a similar purchase journey that might make their lives easier?

Question 2: If you had to do it all over again, what would you do differently to make your lives easier?

Note that we want to capture the entire range of potential missteps spanning both omission (what they didn't do but should have) and commission (what they did do but shouldn't have).

But either way, our sole focus is maximizing customers' ease and agency: What could *you do* differently to make *your life easier?*

Both questions are designed to identify customer actions, not seller behaviors, all from customers who've been there before.

Putting It All Together

So what exactly is the output of all of that input into customers' buying challenges? Conceptually, the answer is an ability to help frame the customers' journey through their spaghetti bowl of buying in a far more effective, efficient, and *easy* manner.

Tactically, the answer is far more prosaic: It's a framework. Maybe it's a spreadsheet. Or a PowerPoint slide. The form factor doesn't really matter, actually. The important point is simply that we build a map of the minefield—an "inventory" of ways a purchase might be delayed, stalled, or killed altogether—accompanied by two things:

Mitigating strategies: A strategy for overcoming each challenge based on a combination of team brainstorming and previous customer experience.

Prompting questions: A set of questions mapped to each obstacle designed to prompt customer consideration of the relevance of that obstacle and the best way to address its potential impact. Practically speaking, these are the exact words a seller might use to introduce the potential challenge.

Once it's built, this document represents an invaluable resource for framing customers' decision complexity. You've just established an unabridged frame for helping customers move far more easily through a purchase. You now have a step-by-step prompting guide of advice you might provide to customers at various points along their journey to help anticipate, mitigate, or even avoid potential obstacles.

Ultimately, as a kind of buying coach, we want to guide customers to navigate their organizational decision complexity better than they could on their own. That knowledge represents value that helps customers not just know or do something but more importantly *feel* something—specifically, confident in their ability to shepherd a purchase decision through their organization with fewer surprises, less effort, greater control, and diminished dysfunction.

ENGAGING CUSTOMERS WITH A FRAME—COACHING CUSTOMERS THROUGH DECISION COMPLEXITY

Imagine, you now have in front of you an inventory identifying the most common and surprising ways a customer buying journey might slow or stall. At this point, understandably, you might be pretty excited to share that inventory with customers in order to demonstrate your expertise, establish yourself as a trusted advisor, and most importantly, boost the odds of a successful purchase and closed-won sale.

But be careful.

The one thing you probably *don't* want to do at this point is put that entire list in front of a customer champion and say, "Here are all the things that could go wrong along your months-long purchase journey." Remember, at the end of the day, we're not solving for what the customer knows, but how the customer *feels*. And naturally, the last thing we want them to feel at the outset of a purchase journey is overwhelmed—especially when it's not too late to turn back to the peace and safety of the status quo.

To be sure, we do want them to understand—and address—critical obstacles, questions, and disconnects standing in their way. But at the same time, we want them to feel confident in their ability to navigate that minefield with low effort and high agency. So, just like a good coach doesn't give their athletes sixteen things to address at once, be sure to parse those obstacles into practical, manageable steps, prioritizing the one or two most urgent at any given point to immediately increase ease and ensure progress.

That means we need to identify an order of operations. Which obstacle or questions do we flag next for customer attention? Which do we hold back? How do we figure that out? This is where talking to other customers who've already navigated a similar purchase successfully, despite frustration, can really help. By discussing very openly what they'd do differently if they had to do it all over again, or asking them to provide advice to others embarking on a similar journey, we can craft specific, tactical advice for future customers. Perhaps we nudge a customer toward an action designed to more easily manage a challenging next step. Or maybe we prompt customers to rethink or reshuffle process steps altogether—for example, involving procurement far earlier in purchase deliberations.

Bottom line, while we may build a large, complex framework mapping the entire minefield of B2B buying, we don't necessarily need to share that entire framework all at once. The goal of Framemaking is to help customers buy, not impress them with our knowledge.

That said, once we've identified the best next step in framing customers' purchase journey, we also need to deliver that guidance in a compelling, empathetic, and believable way.

Engaging Customers as a Connector, Not an Expert

If there is one thing seemingly every customer wants to know, it's "What are other companies like us doing?" Or "How have other companies like us handled a similar challenge?" (Ironically, they typically ask this question directly after insisting that their company is completely different.)

In many ways, the question isn't surprising. Customers are looking for reassurance that they're not alone, that others have gone before. They're seeking a source of confidence—confirmation that they're addressing the right problem, applying the right solution, or selecting the best supplier.

What's especially interesting, however, isn't that they're seeking reassurance, but rather whom they're seeking reassurance from. Notice, language really matters here. They're not asking, "What do *you* think we should do?" or "How would *you* handle this situation?" They're specifically seeking perspective from other companies *like them*.

This is what behavioral psychologists call *social proof,* and it's deeply rooted in human behavior.[3]

This is why it's so valuable to document both other companies' struggles with decision complexity and their successful efforts to manage it. Not only does that experience help prospective buyers identify potential red flags—"If it can happen to them, it can happen to us!"—it also provides a credible source of collective confidence—"If they can do it, we can too!"

After all, one of the most powerful sources of self-confidence across all human experience is the simple belief that you're not alone.

To that end, one highly valuable role sales professionals can play in any sales interaction is connecting customers to common experience. To give customers exactly what they seek by sharing the past experience of comparable leaders and similar organizations. What surprising setbacks did they face? How did they successfully navigate them? What lessons did they learn? What would they do differently, if they had to do it again? How could their past experience make our current process easier?

Notice, this is exactly the kind of insight generated from an it-turns-out-that audit. In a Framemaking world, the value sellers provide customers isn't so much *knowing* these things as *sharing* these things after aggregating past experience into a small set of key lessons. With Framemaking, every seller can very purposefully do what the very best sellers do almost subconsciously: package customers' past experience into specific insights and actions that prospective customers can act on with ease.

Take a moment, however, to consider the powerful implications of this shift for most sellers. In a Framemaking approach, the source of a seller's value isn't what they know, but what they *do*. It's not your role as an expert, but as a connector that sets you apart. In a Framemaking approach, the value a seller provides customers isn't based on product knowledge, industry expertise, or years of experience, but on the time and effort the seller has invested in identifying and sharing lessons learned from other companies going on a similar journey. To be sure, the best sellers can articulate their solution's unique value, speak to industry trends, and highlight their capabilities to handle real customer problems and opportunities. But so can a website. Or a video. Or a PowerPoint deck. What the best sellers can *uniquely* do is create a connection. Not just between themselves and a prospect, or between their company and the customer company, but between a customer's aspirations and similar organizations' shared experience. Framemaking sellers are creating a community of collective confidence. That skill sets them apart not only from other sources of company and market insight but from most other sellers.

How do you become the one seller—or sales team—customers actually *do* want to talk to? By delivering the one thing customers want more than just about anything else: material help based on credible, objective evidence, including insight into what other companies like them are doing.

One of the most powerful tools a seller can use to establish their role as a connector lies in the language they use to engage customers in a Framemaking conversation.

Irrespective of the customer challenge you're seeking to frame, the idea is to ground that frame in credible evidence, based on social proof. The best way to reinforce that social proof is to acknowledge it directly through a phrase like:

"In working with other companies like yours, one of the things we've been surprised to learn is . . ."

. . . followed by whatever insight or process step you're sharing to guide the customers' thinking.

It's a powerful phrase, as it emphasizes your role as a conduit of experience rather than a source of expertise. Unlike most sales conversations grounded in an asymmetrical, almost adversarial, relationship between seller and customer based on a premise of "I know something you don't know," sharing the experience of other customers shifts the conversational dynamic from *convincing* to *collaborating*. We're not looking for customers to take our advice or believe our expertise, but to explore with us what we've seen elsewhere and determine its relevance for their organization.

That said, we want to ensure, of course, that they make a *good* decision, not just any decision, but one they feel good about. So whatever claim we append to this phrase has to be true, credible, and relevant. Your organization has to have actually worked with other customers like them, and whatever insight or experience you're sharing must merit their consideration.

To illustrate through an example, we can see a lot going on in this seemingly innocuous phrase that can deeply impact a Framemaking engagement. Consider the following two options for making a customer aware of a potential landmine:

Option 1: "In working with other companies like yours, customers often see deals this big require approval from some kind of 'Capital Review Board.' That can lead to lots of frustration as those boards typically meet only once a quarter. In fact, one company we work with got delayed six months waiting for an approval they originally didn't even know they needed. It was maddening! So, now we're seeing some companies involve their board much earlier. And it's been really interesting to see how much faster and easier things move when that happens."

Option 2: "We often see deals this size require approval from some kind of 'Capital Review Board.' If you have one, we'd strongly recommend involving them earlier to make things faster and easier."

If you're a left-brained, straight-to-the-point kind of person, you probably prefer Option 2. It's quick, efficient, and direct. You're making a clear, concise recommendation based on a brief statement of the problem.

Option 1, on the other hand, feels longer (because it is), less direct, and less prescriptive. So, let's all go with Option 2, right? That's certainly what traditional sales training would say.

But there's a method to the madness in Option 1. Notice, unlike Option 2, Option 1 makes no recommendation of an exact answer or discrete action. Rather, we're simply prompting. We're giving customers exactly what they want by sharing what other customers like them have learned while providing context to help customers see themselves in that situation. The point is to prompt options for consideration, not to solve a specific problem, allowing customers an opportunity to come to their own conclusions.

With respect to agency, counterintuitively, we're *removing* ourselves from the position of authority rather than assuming it—something deeply contrarian to decades of sales training. In a Framemaking approach customers should consult the Capital Review Board earlier not because we advise them to do so, or even because *other customers like them* experienced painful frustration when they didn't. Rather, they should do so because they *decided* to do so, based on clear evidence in the form of others' experiences. In Option 1, in other words, the ultimate decision is the *customer's*, not the seller's. We're simply creating a space for customers to come to that conclusion within a frame that we've established. In the end, we're framing to promote *their* sense of control, not to demonstrate our depth of knowledge. It's the difference between helping customers feel they're in charge and we're here to help, versus confirming that they're confused and we're super smart.

Don't forget, the goal of Framemaking isn't for customers to think more highly of the seller, but to think more highly of themselves. This increased confidence is what will lead to closing a deal, so we think of "In working with other companies like yours" as the phrase that pays.

Additionally, Option 1 provides four distinct advantages.

First, it's far more replicable. Option 1 significantly reduces the burden on a seller to demonstrate individual expertise. Notice, in Option 1, the seller serves more as a "messenger" than an expert. Providing value by sharing other customers' experiences naturally reduces the need to rely on one's own personal experience. As a result, newer sellers with less market expertise, or any seller who feels less confident that their knowledge matches or surpasses the customer's, is still able to add significant value by providing the one thing virtually every customer lacks: access to other customers like them. Even if an inexperienced seller lacks that kind of access individually, their team can aggregate that experience collectively. That's why it's so valuable to conduct an it-turns-out-that audit as a team rather than alone.

Second, it's fungible. More advanced sellers will quickly develop an ability to connect buyers to similar customers by proactively defining what "similar" means. For customers to see the value in shared experience from other customers like them, they naturally need to agree that the organization in question is, in fact, "like" them. That kind of connection isn't always obvious. Many executives will ask for insights or ideas from other companies like theirs, but then respond dismissively when provided examples because they're distracted by superficial differences. Buyers typically think of companies "like" them through a lens of industry, size, or product mix. However, successful sellers can usually find similarities that others easily overlook. Perhaps two companies are similar in terms of go-to-market model, leadership structure, corporate culture, or government regulation. Advanced Framemaking sellers often articulate these similarities proactively to ensure their target customer sees the connection and places value on the shared wisdom as a result. For social proof to work, customers need to perceive a common connection.

Third, it's inclusive. Not to get too grammatical, but the specific verb one pairs with the pronoun "we" in the phrase that pays really matters for ensuring a Framemaking posture and reinforcing customers' sense of agency. Pairs like "we believe," "we recommend," "we suggest," or "we'd advise" are verbs of *telling* rather than collaborative learning. They're meant to demonstrate the seller's knowledge and confidence rather than build the customer's. Instead, consider pairs like "we've learned," "we've seen," "we watched," or "we've heard." These are verbs of discovery and learning, conveying an invitation of collaborative exploration. Remember, our objective isn't to convince customers of our conclusions but to lead them to believe in their own.

Finally, it makes an emotional connection. When sharing stories from other companies, consider not only what you want your customer to know or learn but also what you want them to *feel*. Every good story has both a teaching point and an emotional point. Once you identify the feeling you're hoping to evoke, use specific language that conveys that emotion. In Option 1, for example, you'll find the words "frustrating" and "maddening." That's not an accident. Those are exactly the emotions that customer felt when they ran into that situation, and that's exactly the emotion we want our customer to feel "by proxy," as it were, when they hear the story. After all, that's exactly how they'll feel if they encounter the same obstacle in their own organization. Let's put them in those shoes now through narrative, so they can avoid that feeling down the road in reality. It's an incredibly valuable, classic storytelling technique as it helps customers *feel* the relevance and urgency of your prompt, increasing the likelihood that they'll act on it without you telling them that they need to. Essentially, you're using word choice to increase the odds that customers come to the "right" conclusion on their own, deepening rather than undermining their sense of agency.

Engaging Customers with Other Customers

Beyond channeling customer experience through sales conversations, we can also engage prospective buyers directly with other customers who've successfully navigated their own spaghetti bowl of buying. Sellers have relied on customer testimonials for years, but think of this as a customer testimonial for Framemaking.

We first saw this idea at a midsize tech company, but it represents a practice universally applicable to virtually any kind or size of company.

The company found it hugely valuable to identify happy customers that had already navigated an especially complex spaghetti bowl of buying and then connect them to prospective customers still early in their own purchase journey. However, in a surprising twist, sellers at the supplier company specifically coached current customers not to talk about the supplier at all—despite the fact that they'd have positive things to say if given the chance. Instead, the supplier sales team would explain to the happy customers that the goal is to pair a prospective customer with a kind of "purchase coach" or "buying mentor"—someone to help them anticipate questions, avoid obstacles, and identify critical decision-makers based on their experience inside their own organization.

In those preparation calls with the existing customer, the supplier sales team would prompt them to answer questions for the prospective customer, such as these:

"If you had to do it all over again, what would you do differently to make the whole buying process easier?"

"Who did you bring into the decision later that you should have brought in sooner?"

"What was the hardest part of the entire buying journey, and how would you advise similar companies to avoid a similar experience?"

The supplier's exclusive objective was to help buyers identify and prioritize the specific obstacles, questions, and steps most in need of careful attention. Not surprisingly, prospective customers found these conversations hugely valuable in managing organizational decision complexity. These were customer testimonials, to be sure, but specifically designed to help buyers frame their buying journey.

And unlike more traditional customer testimonials, notice that the fact that these current customers might be raving fans was largely irrelevant. To be sure, you likely wouldn't want to nominate grumpy, dissatisfied customers to play this role. But in the end, they're not testifying to how great you are as a supplier or a prospective partner. Their role isn't raving fan, but buying guide. So, their "testimony" is actually supplier agnostic. The incredible value these successful buyers play on your behalf isn't to build prospective customers' confidence in you as a fantastic potential partner, but rather to build prospective customers' confidence in *themselves* as effective decision-makers.

EXECUTING A FRAMEMAKING BUYER'S JOURNEY— VERIFYING CUSTOMERS' PROGRESS

Whether we engage individual customer stakeholders directly or indirectly in a Framemaking conversation, we need to ensure their confidence remains high as additional stakeholders join in and unanticipated questions inevitably arise across an unfolding purchase journey.

To successfully execute a Framemaking strategy across the many months of a typical B2B buying cycle, we're going to call on a powerful tool called customer verifiers.

A customer verifier is simply a specific, clear, predicable customer action that objectively demonstrates their progression through a purchase journey. To be clear, customer verifiers are not only customer centric, they're supplier agnostic. While a customer action may result directly from a specific sales activity, it's not the seller's action we're looking for, but the customer's *re*action.

For example, early in his career as a leading sales enablement professional, Mike Blanchette introduced to his team the idea of a sponsor letter, one of the simplest yet most valuable examples of a customer verifier we've ever encountered. Think of a sponsor as a kind of customer champion. They're your main point of contact into a customer opportunity—someone you engage early as part of a discovery conversation to identify customer needs and determine opportunity fit.

The idea of a sponsor letter was simply that a seller, after conducting an initial discovery call, would send an email to the customer champion summarizing five things from the conversation:

1. The business challenge or opportunity facing the customer
2. The potential actions the champion's company might take to address that challenge or opportunity
3. The specific ways the seller's company might help
4. A specific next step in the purchase process
5. A request that the champion confirm those four things were correct and the champion was ready to proceed to that next step

In many ways, it's simply good—but often overlooked—sales hygiene. After a discovery call, send a thank-you, summarizing the conversation and laying out next steps. But for Mike, the critical point wasn't that the seller sent the note; it was that the champion responded with a yes. *That* was the verifier. That was the crucial trigger logged in the CRM system signaling a move from sales stage one to two, not the seller sending the letter, but the customer's positive response.

In a world where sales activities are no longer predictive of purchase progress, that's the power of customer verifiers. They're specially designed to track a customer's movement through a purchase based on their actual demonstrated behavior.

The concept of customer verifiers appears in *The Challenger Customer* as an effective means to reorient suppliers from sales activities to customer outcomes and dramatically improve pipeline accuracy.[4] In the case of Framemaking, however, we'll reimagine customer verifiers as an equally potent means to boost customers' self-confidence while promoting purchase ease.

Designing Customer Verifiers

Specifically, what makes verifiers work is their design. Every good customer verifier meets four criteria:

1. **Customer centric:** Customer verifiers are completely supplier agnostic. It doesn't matter whether a supplier action caused a specific customer outcome or not. It's the outcome itself that matters.
2. **Behavior-based:** Customer verifiers aren't based on something a customer says, but on something a customer does.
3. **Objective:** That behavior isn't open to interpretation—the customer says either yes or no, a meeting happens or it doesn't, something is approved or it isn't.
4. **Documentable:** Verifiers create a paper trail of sorts, often in an email or other digital communication that can be logged in a CRM system and referred back to later.

In the case of the sponsor letter, the contents of that letter might be challenges, opportunities, and next steps that the customer volunteered or that the seller prompted. The source doesn't matter as long as the customer takes ownership. In terms of behavior, either the sponsor responds to the letter or they don't. Objectively, either their response is a yes or it isn't. And in terms of documentation, that objective response can be logged in the CRM system as clear evidence of deal progress.

Likewise, one might engineer similar verifiers across an entire purchase. For example, here's an illustrative list for a typical complex solution:

1. Sign-off on a "sequence of events"
2. Confirmation by key customer stakeholders to attend a "stakeholder alignment workshop" at a specifically scheduled time
3. The completion of a stakeholder alignment workshop including participants' documented agreement with the results
4. Buying group sign-off on solution design
5. Buying group sign-off on a business case for the purchase
6. Agreed-upon pricing, terms, and conditions
7. Procurement sign-off
8. Legal sign-off
9. Signed contract

Naturally, in certain industries and go-to-market models, this list might look somewhat or even substantially different, maybe even significantly longer. For simpler solutions, or perhaps for retention/renewal decisions, the list might be substantially shorter (though not necessarily).

Irrespective of how many a company employs, customer verifiers prove almost indescribably valuable for suppliers as they offer objective, documentable, behavior-based indicators *from the customer's perspective* as to where a complex purchase decision actually stands. In that respect, they serve as a "You Are Here" dot in the spaghetti bowl of B2B buying.

In fact, when we present customer verifiers as a concept, we often asked sales leaders a two-question thought exercise to demonstrate their value for pipeline visibility and forecast accuracy. The thought exercise goes like this: the next time you're speaking with a seller on your team about the status of a particular deal—perhaps as part of a weekly line-by-line or coaching session—after your seller shares where a particular deal stands along your sales process, ask them the following two questions:

1. *How do you* know?

   How do you actually *know* that's where that deal stands? What evidence do you have? And if their answer starts with something like, "Well, we had a call the other day, and it went really well. They're really excited about how we might help them," then consider the position of that deal immediately suspect. Likewise, if the answer is, "We just ran the demo, and everyone on the call was super excited! Really engaged," whatever your seller says next regarding the position of that deal should be treated as speculative at best.

   To be fair, that's not because sellers aren't trustworthy, or because they have poor judgment. Frankly, we're all prone at times to overly optimistic "happy ears." Even more to the point, their assessment might actually, in fact, be completely accurate. But how do you know? When it comes down to it, it's still *their* assessment, not the customer's. Which leads us to the second question.

2. *If I were to ask that customer the same question, what would they say?*
   Sometimes a seller might be all the way down the funnel in sales process stage six, when the customer is way back in buying stage two. Or, just as likely, different customer stakeholders might answer that same question in totally different ways, as their perceptions are all over the map. So, if we want to understand where a deal truly stands in our pipeline, then we need to know where customers stand in their actual purchase behavior.

That's the power of customer verifiers. They provide an unvarnished view of deal status through demonstrated customer behavior.

As a quick aside, we once shared these two questions with a group of sales leaders in New York City. Doug, a chief sales officer at a financial services company, told us he'd just implemented customer verifiers in his own organization and was horrified to discover that a full 70 percent of his pipeline was essentially based on wishful thinking. Doug looked around the room and said, "Do you know how hard it is to walk down the hall to the CFO, look him in the eye, and explain that your forecast is off by a full 70 percent?" You could nearly feel the oxygen leave the room as the entire room of CSOs mentally placed themselves in Doug's shoes as he walked down that hallway. After a beat, one of the other attending heads of sales asked aloud the question everyone was thinking: "Wow, what happened?"

Doug responded, "Oh, it all turned out OK. After I explained to the CFO how I'd reanalyzed our pipeline and gave him the accurate number, he looked at me and said, 'That's OK, I've been discounting your forecast by 70 percent for the last two years anyway. But the good news is, now I don't have to!'"

Rethinking Customer Verifiers for Decision Confidence—Framemaking with a Sequence of Events

Until now, we've looked at verifiers exclusively as a way to more accurately indicate to suppliers the status of a potential sale. As such, they represent an effective means to boost supplier confidence in both pipeline health and forecast accuracy.

But what if we were to think of customer verifiers not just as a means to help suppliers improve forecast accuracy, but equally as a means to alleviate customers' internal decision complexity and improve confidence in their ability to navigate their own organization as a result? What would that kind of customer verifier even look like? And how would it work?

We suggested earlier that a typical, complex B2B purchase is similar in many ways to any other organizational project that might be run through a project-management office. It requires careful planning, identification of stage gates, owners, influencers, and due dates for interim deliverables or outcomes. However, most B2B buying decisions aren't supported by that kind of organizational infrastructure—almost like a general contractor ensuring the buying "project" stays focused, moves forward, and finishes on target.

In fact, just the opposite—most B2B buying decisions are championed by whichever mid-level or senior leader is most vested in seeing its success. To be sure, central teams from legal, procurement, and IT are likely involved, but they are typically not responsible for efficiently advancing the deal. Effectively, the customer champion for any given deal becomes the de facto general contractor for that particular deal. Yet, chances are high that shepherding that decision to successful completion, while potentially important, represents at best a side-of-desk project to the leader championing that purchase; leading that purchase through the spaghetti bowl of B2B buying happens in addition to their normal day-to-day responsibilities. What's more, it's possible, even likely, that they're not only leading that type of decision for the first time—or the first time in a long time—but also that they have little or no formal experience or training in the complex project-management skills necessary to bend their organization to action around the complex purchase in question.

So, they're going to need some help—a step-by-step guide along the easiest, straightest, least spaghetti-bowl-y path possible through the thicket of internal consensus creation, problem identification, solution exploration, requirements building, and supplier selection. The best tool in the customer verifier toolkit to execute a Framemaking approach to customer decision complexity is known as a sequence of events. As the name implies, a sequence of events is a step-by-step list of necessary events or steps required to advance a sale efficiently and predictably to a closed-won deal. Only, in the case of Framemaking, we'll reimagine that document as a tool designed to support buying, not just selling.

One might capture a sequence of events in any number of ways: perhaps a shared document, slide, or spreadsheet, or possibly on some kind of shared platform potentially within a buying portal. But regardless of form factor, the document itself is actually rather straightforward.

Most importantly, it is the result of a deeply collaborative exercise of cocreation with customer stakeholders early in a sale. As part of that collaboration, we're not simply giving customers a blank piece of paper and asking them to map a journey they struggle to anticipate on their own. Rather we bring valuable insight to the table that helpfully frames their thinking while simultaneously allowing them the freedom to adjust as necessary. From there, the seller and customer can collaboratively combine the best of their collective experience to shape a formalized version of the sequence of events specifically tailored to the customer's unique needs and context.

As a result, a good sequence of events will lay out each step in a purchase process in order, identifying necessary stakeholders, opportunities for parallel processes, specific interim stage gates, owners for each step, and projected timing for each. A sequence of events specifically designed for Framemaking, however, has a very different use case. Traditionally, suppliers have used a sequence of events to gain visibility into where a deal stands, not to give customers confidence in how a deal should proceed. By guiding customers along their purchase, a Framemaking sequence of events is purposefully designed to make buying easier, while simultaneously preserving customers' sense of agency over the decision-making process.

This is where all the work we've done to establish and engage customers with Framemaking really pays off. Because now we're in a position to approach customers with an informed hypothesis of how they might best move a purchase decision through their organization. You'll remember, we don't want to share with customers the entire breadth of findings from the it-turns-out-that audit and your inventory—all of the many ways this kind of purchase might stall or go off the rails altogether—as they're likely to find that kind of unabridged compendium of potential purchase stalls completely overwhelming, resulting in a net loss of customer confidence. Instead, we want to lead a clear, manageable process of sequence-of-events design to ensure organizational buy-in and purchase progress with as little pain as possible—all based on social proof and the experience of other customers like them.

The result is an agreed-upon map of exactly how the decision will unfold, along with specified deadlines, interim deliverables, and a clear assignment of roles and responsibilities (evenly distributed between supplier and customer stakeholders), providing both clarity and transparency to everyone involved. That's not to say, of course, that the purchase decision will never deviate from that prescribed path. After all, no plan survives engagement with the enemy (where the "enemy" is the customer's own organizational reality of decision complexity). But now customers have not only a map that materially simplifies that spaghetti bowl of buying but also a kind of preliminary warning device to help them identify and address potential problems far earlier. This is exactly why Kevin's top sales rep invited procurement to the early sales meeting at the beginning of Chapter 2. Effectively, she was managing to a sequence of events before an actual sequence of events had even been established.

The real value of a sequence of events for Framemaking lies not in its creation but its acceptance by the customer organization. Ideally, once the sequence of events for a particular purchase is established, a Framemaking seller will ask the buying group to sign off on that sequence, almost like a nonbinding contract. Critically, that documented approval represents the actual customer verifier. It's supplier agnostic (after all, the customer is signing off on a map navigating *their* purchase journey, which they helped create, and not the seller's sales process). It's behavior-based. It's objective. And its approval can easily be documented in a short email exchange.

But just as valuable, each of the line items in the sequence of events becomes a potential verifier in itself. So, at any given point along a purchase journey, not only can a supplier verify the status of a sale, but just as importantly, a customer can verify the progress of their purchase. They have a clear framework and set of next steps for advancing the decision through their organization—a kind of constant reassurance that they're on the right track and making material progress. This kind of objective reassurance can act as a powerful means not only for creating customer confidence but for maintaining it as well when challenges arise. Now, the customer has a map to the minefield of B2B buying specifically tailored to their organization and can proceed with far more clarity to a place where they're back on track should they ever deviate from the planned progression.

Qualifying Deals by Verifying Customer Progress

That said, one might naturally wonder, what happens when customers wander too far off track to easily recover? Or, what happens when customers choose not to engage in mapping the journey at all, effectively refusing to cocreate a sequence of events?

In either one of those cases, the supplier now has far greater visibility into the likelihood of that deal ever crossing the finish line. Chances are high that if the customer opts to forgo signing off on a sequence of events, or chooses to map that sequence unilaterally ignoring both seller and colleagues' input, or struggles repeatedly to stay the course for whatever reason, then that purchase is highly unlikely to successfully close. Those are all warning signs suggesting this deal should either be treated with caution, put on hold, or disqualified altogether.

In this sense, engaging customers through a Framemaking approach not only helps customers feel more confident in purchase likelihood but also helps sellers feel more confident in deal qualification.

If we step back and look at the big picture, a customer's internal decision complexity is arguably the single biggest threat to B2B buyer confidence. Simply put, B2B buying is long, hard, and landminish. Ultimately, the ability of a seller to not only help the customer map that complexity, making it more predictable, but materially reduce it, making it more manageable, can significantly reduce the risk of stalled deals as customers are now far better equipped to avoid or navigate the underlying organizational dynamics leading to those challenges. That's the power of Framemaking.

Decision complexity is not the only source of buying difficulty, however. The path to decision confidence is fraught with a number of incremental challenges, each eroding customer confidence in its own way and each requiring its own antidote. The next of these challenges is information overload, which we'll tackle in Chapter 4.

CHAPTER 4

Reducing Information Overload

B ryan Smith, CEO of Expedient, a provider of cloud services, knew he had a problem. In 2018, Bryan was Expedient's chief sales officer, tasked with driving growth in a highly contested market dominated by a small number of major players. The shift to cloud computing was well underway, presenting Expedient with a potentially huge market opportunity. However, the company's relatively small size compared to market behemoths required punching dramatically above its weight to command attention in a marketplace crowded by both well-established brands and a vast array of service providers, analysts, consultants, and research firms all producing endless streams of guidance, advice, data, claims, and reviews. One can only imagine Bryan's strong sense of urgency to ensure Expedient's unique strengths cut through all that noise.

In fact, Bryan's thinking at the time was completely natural—and quite common: *If we're going to stand out in this crowded market, we need to demonstrate deep expertise establishing Expedient as an industry "thought leader." That means we've got to publish content with the same quantity and quality as companies many times our size.*

The problem, of course, was that standing out wasn't going to be easy. Expedient lacked the resources, people, and time to come anywhere near the aggregate coverage and quality of content currently available to potential customers. This wasn't just going to be hard, it was going to get really expensive. Bring on the content marketers!

However, that's when Bryan landed on a very different, far less expensive, far more effective way to engage customers and stand out.

In a move many commercial leaders might find surprising, Bryan ultimately chose to develop and publish as *little* new content as possible. After all, the industry was already awash in high-quality content from well-known competitors and third parties. Instead, Bryan instructed the Expedient sales team to lean on *already existing* content produced by competing sources as the basis of customer conversations. One way or another, customers were likely consuming that content already, and Bryan realized that a kind of quid pro quo content competition represented not only an uphill battle for customer attention but also a huge missed opportunity for his sellers to support customers along their *current* learning journey rather than seeking to start a new one altogether.

So, Expedient sellers shifted from providing customers even *more* content to providing valuable perspective on the content they were already consuming, including content produced by top competitors. Effectively, Expedient's primary customer engagement objective shifted from demonstrating industry expertise to helping customers categorize, analyze, synthesize, and prioritize existing information into a set of practical conclusions and organizational decisions that best suited their specific needs. It was a powerful form of Framemaking. In a very clever way, Expedient had outsourced the expense of content creation to their competition while using that same content to completely differentiate their customer engagement strategy.

From their customers' perspective, the positive effect was powerful. Expedient sellers assumed a posture of *making sense* of information rather than providing even more information to consider.

Bottom line, Bryan converted a problem into opportunity by carefully crafting an approach to information that positioned Expedient sellers as a *solution* to information overload rather than a contributor to it.

Picking up on a term broadly recognized in the business literature at the time, we called this posture "sensemaking" (we still do), but more specifically in the context of B2B buying, it's a form of Framemaking tailored to information. Now Expedient's CEO, Bryan stands by the decision more than ever, as it's borne out for Expedient the central premise of this book: the best way to improve customers' confidence in you is to engage them in a way that boosts their confidence in *themselves* and their ability to make large, complex decisions on behalf of their company.

So, what led Bryan down this counterintuitive but powerfully effective path? Let's take a look.

THE RISE OF THE SMARTNESS ARMS RACE

When CEB first started researching the impact of online information on B2B commerce in 2010, the story at the time was largely one of customer empowerment.

With a dramatic rise in online content, B2B buyers were suddenly empowered like never before to learn on their own. In fact, in a widely cited statistic first published in the *Harvard Business Review*, B2B buyers were, on average, 57 percent of the way through a typical B2B purchase prior to proactively reaching out to a supplier sales rep to get their input into whatever it was they were seeking to do.[1]

Essentially, sales professionals were getting shut out of customer conversations as customers were now conducting on their own many of the activities sellers had traditionally relied on for decades to gain access and skew a purchase in their favor. With online information, customers could now identify a need, prioritize that need relative to others, explore possible solutions, select an appropriate course of action, determine purchase requirements, narrow the set of considered suppliers, and largely settle on everything but price prior to reaching out to a supplier sales rep. For customers, it was simply a matter of working through online content to separate signal from noise, identifying the most relevant insights that represented the highest potential return for their specific business needs. At that time, most supplier content was still heavily skewed toward listing capabilities rather than solving customer problems, so that kind of independent learning journey was not only effective but also rather efficient.

Fast-forward to today, however, and the world of online learning looks completely different. Across the last decade and a half, not only has the amount of online content exploded exponentially, but customers' ability to draw clear, confident conclusions from that content has eroded dramatically.

Case in point, in a 2019 study of B2B buying conducted at Gartner, 89 percent of B2B buyers agreed that the information they'd encountered as part of a recent complex B2B purchase was generally of high quality. A year later, that number had climbed to just over 90 percent.[2] Customers were still finding quality information, useful and engaging, relevant to their needs, backed by data, conveyed in a compelling manner, and supported by leading industry experts. But now they were finding high *quantities* of high-quality information. Which meant separating signal from noise was no longer nearly as easy, or often even as possible. How do you decide which information to believe, when it all seems believable and the quality of the information itself is no longer a viable criterion for separating good from bad?

So, what happened? Suppliers happened. In the early 2010s, recognizing customers' shift to online learning, suppliers saw both a need and an opportunity to follow along. Not with just any content, however, but content that demonstrated a supplier's deep expertise and superior skill.

It's almost as if every CEO woke up one morning in 2012, looked in the mirror, and said, "We need to stand out and build greater customer trust. I've got it! We'll become a [wait for it . . .] *thought leader.*" (We imagine them squinting into the distance as they whisper those words like a magical spell. *Thought leader . . .*)

The logic was simple: If we can demonstrate to the market that we have deeper expertise and more quality advice than anyone else, then customers will naturally trust us with their toughest business challenges. We'll become customers' "partner of choice" in their "greatest time of need" to help them address their "mission-critical priorities." Sound familiar?

Meanwhile, seeing an opportunity to demonstrate greater value and generate broader demand, marketers enthusiastically picked up and ran with that mandate, developing an entirely new kind of marketing called content marketing.

Simultaneously, new technology from companies like Hubspot offered marketers better, faster ways to produce, distribute, manage, and track all that content, creating a new technological category called marketing automation—all designed to support a completely new go-to-market model, inbound marketing.

And we were off to the races. Since then, most B2B suppliers have installed sophisticated technology to produce and place high-quality content in front of customers at tightly targeted moments of high receptivity. At the same time, virtually every supplier has better data, improved analytics, and more evidence than ever to sway customer opinion with compelling evidence and a strong story. And, of course, the channels through which suppliers can deliver that kind of high-quality insight are now seemingly endless—their own website, the broader Internet, and traditional media, through search, over mobile, via social platforms, at tradeshows, you name it. In aggregate,

B2B suppliers have built a massive machine to develop and deploy huge amounts of high-quality information at massive scale. Spamming the world with "insight," ironically, in an effort to stand out.

We call it the smartness arms race. And the result—while completely foreseeable—wasn't what anyone wanted, especially B2B buyers.

A BAD ENDING TO THE SMARTNESS ARMS RACE

Perhaps not surprisingly, in the smartness arms race the only real losers are B2B buyers. In a 2021 Gartner B2B buyer survey, we found that 55 percent—*over half*—of B2B buyers found the amount of information they encountered as part of a recent purchase to be trustworthy but simultaneously overwhelming.[3] The information was great; it was relevant, backed by evidence, and largely credible. But there was just so *much* of it. That 55 percent speaks volumes to any executive hoping to win on thought leadership. More is not better. In fact, *better* isn't better, either. From a customer's perspective, the quality of supplier content isn't the problem. It's the *quantity*. The world of B2B buying is so awash in quality "thought leadership" that incremental investments in yet more content are just as likely to exacerbate customer confusion as reduce it, no matter how much smarter, more insightful, or thought-leader-y it might be. For the vast majority of customers, another data-backed, insightful infographic, video, slide deck, or white paper isn't helpful; it's exhausting. Today's customers struggle to simply consume it all, let alone make sufficient sense of it to ensure decisive action.

Worse still, over half of B2B buyers—55 percent—struggle to see sufficiently meaningful differences across content to help them make informed tradeoffs—whether they're weighing one problem over another, comparing a possible solution versus another, or selecting a particular supplier ahead of another.[4] Over time, supplier content all starts to sound the same—addressing the same topics with similar insights backed by familiar data, all while claiming to offer fresh and unique perspectives on the market. A problem exacerbated by a host of advisory firms, consultants, trade associations, media outlets, and would-be podcasters all seeking to stake a claim on deep expertise and a unique ability to provide custom help.

Let's face it: in a world where customers are already drowning in high-quality information, providing yet more quality information delivered by a crack team of well-trained sales reps and expensive support specialists isn't going help suppliers stand out so much as blend—no better and no worse than the top two competitors equally armed with their team designed to do the exact same thing.

Bottom line, today's B2B buyers are drowning in a sea of sameness. Just as customers struggle to differentiate supplier *solutions*, they equally struggle to differentiate supplier *information*, making it increasingly difficult to make informed tradeoffs.

Yet, the seemingly obvious answer—to provide a more differentiated perspective—appears to offer little relief either, for buyers or suppliers.

When we presented an earlier version of these data a few years ago to a group of chief sales officers in Palo Alto, California, it was at this point in the story when a head of sales named Sean interjected, saying, "But we're OK. This doesn't apply to us because we did exactly what you told us to do!" (Uh oh. This rarely ends well.)

Sean went on to say, "We've worked hard to build the kind of unique insight you talk about in your book *The Challenger Sale*. So, while all of our competitors are out there telling our customers to *zig*, we're challenging customers' thinking, showing them that they really need to *zag*. So I'm struggling to see how this 'sameness' problem really applies to us."

To be fair, Sean was right. In *The Challenger Sale* and *The Challenger Customer*, we laid out a step-by-step content approach specifically designed to generate what we call "commercial insight," demonstrating why insight is far more effective than thought leadership.[5] But remember, at the time (2008–2013) we were solving for selling in a completely different information landscape, where supplier information that taught customers something new about *their* business was still relatively novel. But today's information landscape, built as it is on top of suppliers' collective desire to demonstrate thought leadership, is dramatically different. Here's how we responded to Sean:

If I show up to the customer telling them to *zig* and I've got robust data, compelling evidence, expert advisors, and happy customers willing to testify to the value of my unique perspective, that's fantastic. But what happens when my top one or two competitors show up at the customer, telling them to *zag*, and *they've* got robust data, compelling evidence, expert advisors, and happy customers willing to testify to the value of *their* unique perspective? Whom is the customer supposed to believe? How are they supposed to choose? While it may be true that you're showing customers a completely different path, the fact that your story contradicts your competitor's equally compelling story doesn't tip the balance in your favor nearly so much as it simply leaves customers confused at a higher level.

Indeed, in our surveys 44 percent of B2B buyers told us not only was the information they encountered as part of the purchase trustworthy, but it was also *contradictory*.[6] It's all compelling. It's all believable. But it suggests conflicting courses of action. Now what do I do? How are customers supposed to make a confident choice when the best possible options appear equally valid but nonetheless mutually exclusive? This is when customers will tell you, "You know, maybe we need to look at this a little bit longer. We're going to go back and look at our options. Why don't you call us back in about six months." All in the hopes that a little more research will offer a lot more clarity.

Plot twist: it doesn't. And the price suppliers pay is dramatically high.

THE HIGH COST OF HIGH QUANTITIES OF HIGH-QUALITY INFORMATION

Customers' frustration with an abundance of high-quality information comes at a high cost, especially to suppliers looking to close a high-quality, low-regret deal. Customers who find the amount of trustworthy information to be overwhelming are 54 percent more likely to play it safe, to settle for a smaller purchase with a narrower scope, probably at a lower price, requiring less disruption.[7] Meanwhile, customers struggling to see meaningful differences between similar vendors are an additional 33 percent less likely to buy a high-quality, low-regret deal. And, most dramatically, customers finding supplier information to be trustworthy but *contradictory* are 66 percent less likely to take the chance on a bigger, broader deal. Their struggle to easily reconcile the dissonance between equally believable but contradictory perspectives leads them to struggle to make a decision. And just to be clear, statistically, these effects are cumulative, leaving many customers, in aggregate, over *one and a half times* less likely to make a high-quality, low-regret purchase.

This is where the smartness arms race has landed us. In suppliers' efforts to win with thought leadership, they've measurably diminished customers' confidence and dramatically impaired their ability to buy anything but the safest of solutions, significantly decreasing the likelihood of their own commercial success at the same time. Bad consequences from the best of intentions.

So now what? If providing ever more quality information only gets us into deeper trouble, surely the answer can't be to provide *less*. It's unrealistic to imagine any supplier willing to unilaterally disarm in the smartness arms race.

To find an answer, we need to understand how we as humans respond to information overload.

THE VICTORY OF HUMAN BIAS

To be fair, as learners all of us generally benefit from each incremental piece of information, content, data, or research up to a point. It makes us smarter, more decisive, and more confident. But at some point, we hit our maximum capacity for learning and struggle to effectively process incremental inputs.

At a meeting of marketing leaders in Chicago, we once asked attendees to speculate on how long it took for their customers to hit that specific moment where online learning flips from helpful to overwhelming. Some said weeks, a few said days, and a couple answered in hours. But when a CMO in the second row blurted out, "Two seconds!" everyone turned and looked with surprise. "Two seconds?! Why two seconds?" we asked.

"Because that's how long it takes to hit enter on an Internet search and get ten thousand results back," he responded. He wasn't wrong.

At some point relatively early in a customer's learning journey, additional information doesn't make things easier, but measurably harder as each additional insight, perspective, or data point just makes it that much more difficult for customers to take decisive action.

So how do customers make a purchase decision when the quantity of information is overwhelming? Or when their online research finds an avalanche of "helpful" information from suppliers that appears trustworthy but ends up being contradictory? Or when, even with all of this information, the tradeoffs between vendors remain very difficult to make sense of?

At this point good decision-making gives way to bad as informed choices become best guesses, rational decisions become gut feel, and clear logic falls victim to human bias.

Indeed, years of behavioral psychology research have identified that when logical, methodical consideration falls short, this is exactly where well-documented human biases take over.[3] Here is a small sampling of such biases:

Anchoring: Customers overwhelmed with too much information fixate unproductively on a single perspective or piece of information to make a decision, despite sometimes clear evidence for a better, alternate path.

Belief perseverance: The strange but well-documented phenomenon where convincing, contrary evidence strangely reinforces a view rather than upending it. So, presented with clear evidence to the contrary, one chooses to hold on to one's original view even tighter rather than adjusting to accommodate new information.

Selective exposure bias: A fancy term for cherry-picking specific information simply to support one's preferred position, ignoring or discounting everything else.

Status quo bias: The common decision, in the face of overwhelming information, to choose not to choose. (This is that moment when customers say, "We've decided to study it more. Call us back in six months.")

Sound familiar? These are like a rogue's gallery of deals gone bad. How many of us have watched a good deal die, shrink, or shift against us, simply because our customers fell back onto one of these biases?

In fact, if you think about it, these kinds of biases aren't really about buying nearly so much as they're about *coping*. Specifically, they're natural, well-documented coping strategies for making some kind of sense out of the overwhelming amount of information suppliers are throwing at customers every single day. Of course, each of these biases represents a *possible* response by decision-makers, not a guaranteed one, but we'll need to find a means to reduce the likelihood that customers fall back on any of them.

Unfortunately, human biases in the face of information overload aren't the only challenge to decision-making that makes B2B selling so difficult. B2B buying behavior is also unpredictable because the human psychology driving that behavior is highly variable. In fact, behavioral psychologists have identified a continuum for information management that is important to understand if we are going to help customers overcome information overload and make a confident buying decision.

NOT ALL CUSTOMERS ARE CREATED EQUAL— MAXIMIZING VS. SATISFICING

Among Nobel Prize winner Herbert A. Simon's contributions to fields including artificial intelligence, economics, and cognitive psychology, his seminal work on human decision-making stands out.[4] When facing potentially overwhelming amounts of information, humans typically resort to one of two competing strategies in pursuit of resolution:

Satisficing: A decision-making strategy where individuals seek to meet a relatively small set of criteria in order to identify a "minimum viable solution" rather than an optimal one. The result of a satisficing strategy is a "good enough" outcome.

Maximizing: Individuals pursuing a maximizing strategy eschew "good enough" and seek instead the best possible outcome by exhaustively evaluating all available options. Maximizers strive for an optimal solution, not just a satisfactory one, often leading to decision paralysis and dissatisfaction due to the high standards they set.

The fundamental difference between satisficing and maximizing is why some consumers have hundreds of items "saved for later" on Amazon.com, while others have none at all. Satisficers get in, collect a bare minimum of information, make a relatively quick decision that they believe will be good enough, and move on. Their mantra might be, "Don't let perfect become the enemy of the good—or the good enough." Maximizers, on the other hand, often worry they might have missed something important to the quality of their decision. They typically prefer to conduct exhaustive research (which can also easily become exhaust*ing*) in order to make the best choice possible, often returning repeatedly to the decision for further consideration without achieving actual closure. Their mantra is closer to, "Only the best will do."

That's not to say, of course, that an individual is necessarily born exclusively a "satisficer" or "maximizer." Satisficing and maximizing are *behaviors*, not identities. So, while individuals might naturally gravitate toward one end of the spectrum or the other by default, it is equally true that one's tendency toward one or the other proves highly contextual. For simple, straightforward decisions, most of us gravitate to satisficing purely as a matter of efficiency. As the stakes increase and decisions become more complex or less familiar, the natural pull toward maximizing behavior typically becomes more dominant.

Why does any of this matter for B2B buying? First, of course, because B2B buyers are human beings (at least, for now) and therefore subject to hardwired human behaviors even in business settings. So, the dynamics of satisficing and maximizing are equally at play in company contexts as they are in personal ones.

Second, most large-scale B2B purchase decisions, of course, are moderately to highly complex, often involving some degree of financial, operational, or reputational risk. As a result, even when individual decision-makers might gravitate toward satisficing on their own, they're far more likely to lean toward maximizing as part of a more complex buying group, as that group seeks to establish common ground and mitigate risk. What's more, larger groups will often struggle to reach decisive conclusions as maximizers advocate for more time to study the problem and more options to consider.

Finally, in many cases, individual members of a buying group fear making mistakes, exacerbating maximizing behavior as they seek to cover all the bases so they aren't blamed for missing something important.

Either way, whether a buying group leans toward maximizing or satisficing, the results can be troublesome for suppliers seeking to sell complex solutions. Buyers who lean toward maximizing behavior will need help reducing their fear of messing up, of overlooking key criteria, or of failing to identify important considerations. For these customers, Framemaking sellers can bound customer deliberations, helping them determine when they've asked the right questions and done sufficient research to take decisive action. In these cases, the alternative is to simply stand by and watch customers spin through months and months of additional "learning" without ever reaching an actual purchase decision. We've personally watched a respected sales professional—and a good friend—allow this very thing to happen to a multimillion-dollar deal for over three years without ever closing it.

Too much satisficing can also be a problem. If the buying group tends toward satisficing and makes a "good enough" decision for either the status quo, a smaller solution, or an inferior competitor, then sellers will need to prompt customers to expand their thinking to accommodate a bigger, broader solution at a higher price point. This is a buying group that might need to be challenged to consider a broader course of action, a wider set of decision criteria, or alternate means of pursuing a decision.

Either way, Framemaking provides a powerful way to drive improved commercial outcomes by helping customers manage information and make better, more confident decisions as a result. Just as sellers can use Framemaking to help customers navigate organizational decision complexity with increased confidence, Framemaking enables sellers to boost customer confidence in the decisions they make based on the information they choose to consume.

FRAMING INFORMATION

The solution to too much information isn't more information. It's helping customers organize, prioritize, and analyze information in a more productive manner. To do that, we first need to understand what information customers consume already. Then we'll need to help connect that information to their specific context in a way that feels easy and manageable.

To that end, applying a Framemaking approach to information requires sellers to have a carefully considered information strategy—something relatively uncommon in sales. While most sellers approach traditional sales activities such as needs analysis, discovery, objection handling, and negotiation with a clear set of principled tactics, it's far less common for sellers to employ an equally disciplined approach to managing customer information. Traditionally, information was simply something sellers wanted to either acquire or deliver. But what if we were to treat information as something requiring careful, active management, particularly with a view toward helping customers consume content more productively to boost decision confidence? That's our objective here.

So, what does a Framemaking strategy for information look like? Let's take it step-by-step—establish, engage, execute.

ESTABLISHING THE FRAME—CONDUCTING AN INFORMATION AUDIT

The first step in helping customers navigate information with greater confidence is to identify which information they're most likely to consume.

In reality, sellers often engage customers long after their online learning journey has begun, so our ability to proactively steer early-stage learning is admittedly limited. But we want to be able to engage customers at whatever point—whenever that is—from a position of experience and empathy rather than one of inexperience and interrogation. To do that, we need to be able to predict not only which content customers are most likely to consume, but the questions, concerns, conclusions, and opinions they'll likely land on as a result, especially with a view toward where they'll get stuck, confused, or overwhelmed. Imagine a sales conversation that starts with something like, "We talk to a lot of companies in a similar position, and we find just about everyone is sort of stuck on at least one of three questions based on everything they've read so far. Do any of these sound familiar to you?" This kind of approach dramatically decreases the time required for sellers to adopt a framing posture, proactively coaching customers to organize their thinking in a way that helps them make better, more confident decisions. Regardless of whether it's new logo acquisition, customer retention, or account expansion, Framemaking allows sellers to start from a position of empathetic guidance rather than needs discovery.

So, how do we accurately predict which information customers are most likely to consume before they ever consume it? We use an "information audit." An information audit is simply an exercise whereby a seller, or sales team, identifies the following as accurately and completely as possible:

1. The **specific information** customers are most likely to encounter as part of the purchase of their solution (e.g., websites, videos, white papers, webinars, trade articles, podcasts, community forums) to better predict their likely degree of both expertise and confusion prior to direct engagement

2. The **relative resonance** of individual pieces of content to determine which information is most likely to capture customers' attention and disproportionately influence their thinking (e.g., due to credible evidence, persuasive rhetoric or visuals, industry-specific relevance)

3. **Extraneous information** that's too broad, too technical, or too vague, leaving customers simply overwhelmed trying to process it in a useful, organized fashion equally indicating potential Framemaking opportunities

4. The **unanswered questions** customers struggle to answer despite—or possibly because of—the information they consumed, indicating potentially high-value Framemaking opportunities

5. Any **contradictory perspectives**—backed by believable evidence—likely leaving customers struggling to choose between two seemingly viable options to predict places where Framemaking might prove most helpful

6. The **confident decisions** customers still struggle to make in spite of—or possibly because of—the content they've consumed

How do we find any of this out? One way is to ask marketing. However, most B2B marketing organizations do not collect this kind of information or package it for sellers in a way that enables Framemaking. So, barring that, one might approximate a buyer's learning journey on one's own, pretending to be a buyer, conducting an online search in a manner approximating likely buyer behavior. At the very least, this option will reveal the specific pieces of content customers will most likely encounter. That said, this kind of do-it-yourself approach is less helpful in identifying customers' likely questions, emotions, or points of confusion upon consuming that content.

Instead, the best way to conduct an information audit is to ask customers themselves. Of course, customers who haven't yet embarked on a purchase journey can't accurately know which content they're likely to encounter. But customers who have already completed (or attempted) a similar purchase can serve as an accurate proxy for those who have yet to begin. In that regard, the design principles of an information audit are comparable to those laid out in Chapter 3 for an it-turns-out-that audit, in terms of the following:

1. **Whom we ask:** Ideally, gather input both from customers who have successfully navigated a similar purchase already and from those who became stuck or ultimately opted for the status quo or a competing supplier.

2. **How we ask:** Most effectively, use person-to-person conversation, conducted by sales, customer success, or perhaps marketing. For greater scale, one might supplement individual conversations with surveys, win-loss analysis, focus groups, or other forms of data, including from third parties.

3. **Who does the asking:** While some leaders may prefer not to distract sellers with such nonselling activities, conducting (or at least participating in) these kinds of customer conversations serves as a powerful learning tool for sellers seeking to understand the mind of the customer. After all, an information audit isn't meant to merely catalog the information customers consume. It's designed to identify the range of emotions associated with that information (helpful? confusing? reassuring? overwhelming?). That matters because, at the end of the day, we're primarily solving for how customers *feel* as they navigate a complex purchase decision, not just what they learn. Listening to customers describe those

feelings in their own words—whether in live conversations, panel discussions at sales kickoff meetings, or in recorded interviews—can prove invaluable for Frame-making sellers seeking to demonstrate deeper empathy and construct closer connections.

So, exactly what do we ask in an information audit? To keep things simple, limit the conversation to some version (or subset) of the following list of questions, with follow-up as needed for either elaboration or clarification:

1. **Specific information:** Did you find the information you needed to help you through this purchase?
2. **Relative resonance:** Which specific pieces of content did you find most (and least) helpful?
3. **Extraneous information:** Was the amount of information available on this topic insufficient, about right, or overwhelming?
4. **Unanswered questions:** Which questions did that information best help you answer, and which questions remained despite (or as a result of) your research?
5. **Contradictory perspectives:** Did you run into any contradictory information that made decisions more difficult?
6. **Confident decisions:** Did the content you consumed increase, decrease, or have little impact on your ability to make a confident decision?
7. **Outcome:** What did you ultimately decide to do, and how confident were you in that decision?

Of course, out of conversational context, these questions can sound a bit academic or mechanical. In a live interview, a seller would want to convey them far more conversationally. This isn't meant to be an interrogation, but an exploration, steeped in curiosity and empathy, not self-interest. The goal is to anticipate the likely experience with the information future customers will encounter. After all, it's hard to coach customers through their information journey if a seller has never really considered the potential impact of the information their customers encounter.

As a side note, for those concerned that sellers going through this customer information journey will have decreased time on selling activity, keep in mind this kind of effort isn't required on every deal. It scales, as most customers' learning journeys will ultimately look relatively similar. And let's not lose sight of our ultimate objective: to be the one seller, or sales team, that customers actually *do* want to talk to. Chances are, customers won't see a great deal of value in speaking with a seller who hasn't seen fit to familiarize themselves with the research and information most relevant to their potential purchase.

ESTABLISHING THE FRAME—CONTEXT OVER CONTENT

Once we've mapped customers' most likely experience with information, we're in a far better position to provide help. That help might fill a gap in understanding, clear up confusion, or provide guidance on which questions matter most. Almost never, however, will it be to simply provide customers more content without connecting it to all of the other information they've consumed already or are still likely to encounter—no matter how well designed that content might be. That's simply not helpful, as it leaves it to customers—55 percent of whom are already struggling with overwhelming amounts of trustworthy information—to figure out on their own how to integrate yet another perspective with all the other content they've already seen.

That's the aspect of information most sellers overlook when providing customers a point of view: connecting it to context. It's simply a reality that the information or content that suppliers provide customers isn't consumed in a vacuum, but alongside a huge amount of other information. And it's really the interaction effects across all that content that impact both what customers learn and how confident they feel as a result. So rather than avoiding addressing others'—even competitors'—content, Framemaking sellers run right at it. Not with an intent to refute or criticize it nearly so much as to help customers organize, prioritize, and analyze *all* the information they're likely to encounter across a typical learning journey. All in a way that eases customers' learning and promotes their sense of control.

Bottom line, the primary goal in framing information is to *escape* the smartness arms race, not to win it. The best way to stand out in today's crowded information landscape often isn't to provide more information and exacerbate customers' tendencies toward maximizing, but to help customers make sense of the information everyone's already provided.

Engaging Customers with Information—Giving, Telling, and Sensemaking

If Framemaking is the act of making a complex task or decision feel more manageable, then it stands to reason sellers need a carefully considered approach to information when engaging customers overwhelmed with high quantities of high-quality information. In *HBR's* "Sensemaking for Sales," we identified three statistically distinct, meaningfully different seller approaches to information, based on buyer perceptions: giving, telling, and sensemaking.[8]

Giving: Sellers adopting a giving posture to information can best be summarized by the motto "more is better." They're very generous in sharing data, collateral, product specs, you name it, because they believe any information they provide to customers—especially at the customer's request—will move the deal forward in a material manner. It's a good-faith effort to advance customers' learning and be a helpful contributor to the buying process. Besides, if we don't provide that information, then someone else will. As a result, it's not uncommon for giving sellers to frequently press the rest of their organization for even more information to give. They're looking for something new to share, as the very act of information provision itself represents a demonstration of supplier value, naturally leading to deal progress.

Giving sellers might tell customers, "Just tell me what you need to know, and I'll get you all the information you want."

Telling: Telling sellers are the individual experts on a sales team. They typically demand far less of the rest of the organization as they've already got everything they need based on years of experience and deep subject matter expertise. Typically, that information is stored in their head or in a spreadsheet or slide deck they've created on their own. Given telling sellers' expertise, sales organizations often rely on them to drive deals because they're just so darn convincing. They've got experience, wisdom, and a certain amount of gravitas.

Telling sellers might tell customers, "Trust me, I've been doing this for nearly thirty years. Let me tell you everything you need to know."

Sensemaking: Sensemaking sellers are perceived by customers as less focused on providing information, and more on helping to prioritize perspectives, quantify tradeoffs, and contextualize or even deconflict competing perspectives. They often do so by emphasizing simplicity over comprehensiveness. Their primary engagement strategy is to cut through information clutter rather than add to it. But just as important, they do so not by telling customers what to think and believe, but by suggesting a framework or set of cognitive boundaries, within which customers can determine for themselves what's best to believe. Sensemakers engage customers by exploring and cocreating rather than informing or instructing.

Sensemaking sellers might tell customers, "There's a lot going on here, and it all seems important. Let's see if we can make some sense out of all of this."

From the perspective of customers already overwhelmed by too much quality information, one can imagine how these three approaches impact sales interactions. Across over 1,100 B2B customers we surveyed, 87 percent were skeptical of giving sellers, and 72 percent were skeptical of telling sellers. Sixty-one percent reported they were *not* skeptical of sensemaking sellers.[9] And if you think about it, that actually makes sense, as sensemaking sellers aren't actually making any direct claims at all other than the following:

1. "There's a lot of information out there," which is indisputable.
2. "I'd love to try to help you make sense of it," which is backed up by action.
3. "Other companies like yours have found these questions to matter most," which is based on social proof.

To be sure, all sellers face a certain level of skepticism simply by being a sales rep. But if you want to be the one seller a customer actually wants to talk to, a good first step is to be a sensemaker, as nearly two-thirds of customers were able to get past their potentially misaligned incentives. Customers' willingness to openly engage sensemaking sellers with a high degree of belief is a remarkable testament to the value customers place in this very different engagement approach.

Customers working with a sensemaking seller are nearly four times more likely to feel confident in the information they're considering compared to customers working with a seller using a telling approach. This probably shouldn't be surprising, as telling can easily undermine a customer's sense of agency, and we've seen the critical importance of agency in customer confidence.

Perhaps not surprisingly, sensemaking sellers are far and away more likely to win high-quality, low-regret deals. In fact, of those customers perceiving the seller selling to them as engaged in giving, only 30 percent managed to make a high-quality, low-regret purchase. Meanwhile, customers identifying the seller selling to them as telling were a coin flip at 50 percent. However, customers working with sensemaking sellers successfully completed a high-quality, low-regret purchase an astonishing 80 percent of the time. Whether it's helping customers to reduce decision complexity or make sense of information, this is why Framemaking matters. In a world where the primary obstacle to break-out commercial success isn't so much sales reps' struggle to sell but customers' inability to buy, it makes sense that sellers who help customers feel more confident about the information they consume along their learning journey perform far better.

ENGAGING CUSTOMERS WITH INFORMATION— THE SENSEMAKING PLAYBOOK

So, how are sensemaking sellers framing information for customers? Based on the customer data, we can categorize the behaviors that set them apart into three broad buckets: *connecting* customers to carefully curated information, *clarifying* that information by explaining, simplifying, and deconflicting, and *collaborating* with customers to help them construct knowledge for themselves.

Connecting

First, sensemaking sellers curate the information they share for utility and clarity, including only what will help customers advance along their purchase journey with increasing confidence. That information might corroborate or undermine a customer's earlier thinking, but in either case it is chosen and deployed with a view toward purchase progress. Depending on the situation, Framemaking sellers may seek to prompt customers to consider information, topics, or questions they might have otherwise overlooked, or they may find it necessary to bound the questions or considerations that matter most for their customers' particular context. Either way, the goal is never "connect to more," but "connect to (only) what matters most."

Sensemaking reps readily admit the limits of their knowledge. Because skepticism of sellers can be so damaging, there's clear value in simply saying, "I don't know," rather than manufacturing a half-truth that can be easily fact-checked. Admitting one's limitations can also forge powerful connections with buyers, who probably don't know either. That moment of personal authenticity creates an opportunity for collaborative discovery and learning, which sensemaking sellers leverage by offering select additional information. In the end, their role isn't to have all the answers, but to lay out a frame providing a practical path toward them.

Clarifying

In many ways, a sensemaking seller's key to success is helping customers feel confident they've asked the right questions, understood competing perspectives, and accounted for potential contingencies. As a result, sensemaking sellers are particularly good at clarifying complex problems, explaining technical information, and turning abstract concepts into understandable, shareable, compelling insights. They give customers just enough information, bounding the conversation to what matters most and then helping them meaningfully interpret and simplify that material to create a consistent, coherent, convincing narrative that bolsters customer confidence.

Collaborating

A sensemaking seller ensures that the conclusions customers reach are their own. Remember, all Framemaking is based on ease and agency. So, sensemakers' primary objective is to guide buyers on a learning journey rather than to tell them what to do. Interestingly, sensemaking sellers often encourage customers to independently verify seller-provided information and give them an easy way to do so. They offer a framework for learning that makes customers feel in control to construct their own ideas; that confidence increases the chances that buyers will make a quality purchase decision rather than delay or make no decision at all.

A MASTERCLASS IN FRAMING INFORMATION—EXPEDIENT REVISITED

So, what does a world-class Framemaking effort around information look like? Let's return to the story of Bryan Smith at Expedient for a practical example. When Bryan and his sales team conducted an information audit, they were able to determine the specific content customers typically encountered as part of their learning journey into cloud computing, the most common questions and points of confusion where customers felt most uncertain taking decisive action, and the specific ways in which all that content either distracted customers from Expedient's unique strengths or led them to undervalue those strengths altogether.

One might assume, of all that insight, that last point was the most important, as it enabled Expedient sellers to refute competitor claims and clarify Expedient's unique value proposition in their own customer conversations. And there's no question that insight proved extremely valuable. But not as directly as one might assume.

Instead, the team's attention was primarily drawn to something else—the specific content customers were consuming and questions they still struggled with as a result. After all, Bryan reasoned, if customers felt overwhelmed and confused, their typical human status quo bias would kick in, and it wouldn't matter whether Expedient stood out from the competition. The company was still likely to lose to no decision if customers recognized Expedient's unique strengths but nonetheless remained insufficiently confident about which solution to pursue, if any at all.

The first thing Expedient sellers learned was virtually every customer had watched the same video series from a top competitor. Not just any competitor, mind you, but a massive one. The kind of competitor no one ever gets fired for buying from. And that video series was deeply influencing customers' thinking. In many ways, the series was helpful, thorough, and easily understandable, so it was no wonder buyers mentioned it. Problematically for both Expedient and potential cloud computing customers, however, the series failed to raise some of the most cutting-edge issues in a rapidly changing industry, leaving customers partially uninformed and Expedient at a distinct disadvantage given their particular capabilities.

As a result, Bryan made a bold decision. Expedient's information audit clearly told them that customers were going to encounter the competitor's video series one way or another—it was practically unavoidable. So, if Expedient couldn't encourage customers to run away from the competitor's content, then Expedient was going to run right at it, proactively recommending to customers they seek it out. After all, not only was that going to happen *anyway*, but the video series was actually pretty helpful in laying out the fundamentals to cloud computing.

That said, in running right at it, Expedient sellers didn't simply advise customers to watch the videos and leave it at that. Instead, they adopted the role of content coach, providing customers a helpful framework to think through the best questions to ask themselves as a result of watching the videos.

Practically speaking, a conversation with an Expedient sales professional might sound something like this:

Have you seen this video series yet? If you haven't, it's really worth a look. We find virtually everyone comes across it sooner or later, as it's really helpful in cutting through the noise and laying out the primary considerations in developing a cloud strategy.

Something to watch for, though, customers tell us, it sometimes raises as many questions as it answers. Especially as the technology has evolved pretty rapidly since it first came out.

In fact, in working with other companies like yours, we've found it's helpful to really boil things down to three questions, where these videos can really help, and then two more considerations that are a little bit newer.

We'd be happy to share some more on those points if it would help, but primarily what we've learned is, there are certain questions you'll want to focus on to determine what's right for you.

Notice this kind of customer engagement does a few things simultaneously.

1. It reassures customers that they're looking at the right information and asking the right questions (especially if a seller from a competing company is suggesting it).

2. It makes customers' learning journey just a little bit easier by providing focus on the few pieces of content that matter most.

3. It establishes a clear, practical framework for engaging with that information by bounding customer attention to a small number of key considerations or questions, nudging buying groups toward satisficing behaviors.

4. It taps into social proof (e.g., "other companies like yours") to boost customers' confidence that they're focused on the "right" questions.

5. It promotes customers' sense of agency that they're the ones making the decisions. To be sure, Expedient sellers have staked out a small number of key criteria that they would argue matter most. But they leave it to customers themselves to determine where they land respective to those criteria, based on their specific organizational context.

6. Expedient sellers offer further help and reassurance should the customer feel the need for more prescriptive guidance. They don't simply say, "Check out this information," and leave customers to muddle through on their own.

7. While less obvious, Expedient is naturally skewing that frame to include the criteria where Expedient shines. To be clear, they're not directly selling the value of Expedient per se, but they are ensuring that the criteria that set the Expedient solution apart are at least part of customers' consideration. This type of prompting is especially important if the customer is prone to too much satisficing.

So just as a company might seek to "get ahead of the RFP," Expedient is seeking to "get ahead of information," encouraging customers to consume information through a lens that increases the likelihood they will appreciate Expedient's unique strengths without having to resort to a review of specific features and benefits. But first and foremost, Expedient's goal is to reduce the likelihood that customers become overwhelmed altogether and simply choose not to choose. They are helping customers to be less prone to maximizing by competing against status quo bias first and competitors second. So, rather than leading *with* Expedient's unique strengths, Expedient sellers establish a framework for information consumption that naturally leads *to* Expedient's unique strengths.

From a strategic perspective, one of the most interesting aspects of Expedient's experience is the fact that the company is using existing content to engage in Framemaking, rather than creating all new Framemaking content and thus adding to customers' learning burden. Bryan and the team have not only opted out of the smartness arms race, they've effectively outsourced the cost of new content creation to the competition. At the same time, they've dramatically increased the "surface area" for competitive differentiation not by redesigning what they sell but by rethinking *how* they sell. They've distanced themselves from the competition—in a highly competitive market—by improving the Expedient *sales* experience rather than (or in addition to) the Expedient product experience. And they've done that by solving for the way customers perceive *themselves* rather than the way they perceive Expedient—specifically boosting customers' confidence in their ability to wade through an increasingly overwhelming amount of information and make effective decisions based on their specific organizational needs.

None of that would be possible without first establishing a deep understanding of customers' current relationship to information.

This is why conducting an information audit really matters. It helps sellers identify customers' most acute pain points when it comes to information and enables them to then boost customer confidence to take an action other than no decision.

EXECUTING A FRAMEMAKING APPROACH TO INFORMATION

As important as sensemaking is for building customers' confidence across the many months of a typical purchase journey, it is equally true that neither customers' specific information needs nor a seller's best-bet approach to framing information remains completely consistent across that time. This is where the information audit proves especially valuable in helping sellers better identify customers' highest priority information needs at various points along a purchase process so they can offer the most helpful and relevant guidance as a result.

Early in a purchase journey, for example, customers may be unsure which questions to ask. They're often dealing with a high number of unknown unknowns contributing to a sense of confusion, exasperation, or overwhelm. Symptomatic of this challenge are customers lamenting, "Where do we even start?" or "I'm concerned we're missing something really important." In these situations, a highly structured framework like a maturity model or performance diagnostic can prove especially helpful to customers in laying out key questions or dimensions for consideration. These kinds of frameworks are especially effective when built on research sourced from similar companies and designed to provide companies believable benchmarks to their current performance.

That's not to say we'd expect individual sellers to build such frameworks on their own. That's likely a bad idea for a number of reasons (e.g., lack of scale, expertise, time, access). But it's not uncommon for star performing sellers to have cobbled together something similar on a spreadsheet stored on their local C drive, and this can be adapted and adopted by other sellers in the organization.

From the Framemaking seller's point of view, this kind of diagnostic tool is equally powerful for both bounding customers' exploration of a purchase to a more limited set of dimensions—promoting ease, saving time, and possibly leading to unique strengths—all while prompting customers to consider questions or opportunities they might have otherwise overlooked. To be sure, customers will likely understand this is part and parcel of a seller's motivation, so the framework absolutely must be credible—based on evidence, data, benchmarks, and social proof, and delivered from as neutral position as possible, agnostic of outcome or specific supplier. The primary goal must be to help customers arrive at a confident assessment of their position, not an automatic purchase of your solution. If the framework has even a whiff of self-interest, it's suspect at best and likely fails to deliver on your primary objective—building customers' decision confidence.

When executed correctly, however, a diagnostic or maturity framework can provide customers significant help not only early in a purchase journey, mapping the boundaries of their purchase decision, but across the remaining journey as well. It is a practical means to keep members of the buying group on the same page—often, quite literally—as team members can use the tool to bound, prompt, or reengage colleagues. Think of it as a plan on a page. Maturity models, for example, are excellent tools to prompt questions or criteria that customers may have never considered, all while bounding their thinking to a finite set of considerations. For example, consider a maturity model with, say, four levels of development (e.g., beginner, intermediate, advanced, and world-class) arranged in columns, and seven dimensions for considerations laid out in rows across those columns. Each of those columns and rows—along with each of the resulting twenty-eight cells—offers an opportunity to prompt customers' thinking in some fashion as they seek to pin-point their current status across the model. It engages them in a discussion as they compare themselves to that standard, leading to a self-assessment. At the same time, the fact that the model has only seven rows and not, say, ten or twenty, bounds their thinking to those specific criteria as the ones that matter most—at least for the sake of completing that particular assessment.

All that said, should customers use that assessment to determine that the best course of action for them is not ultimately the purchase of your solution, that's not necessarily great news, but it's also not the worst news either. Now you know, and you found out early. In that sense, diagnostic frameworks are a powerful tool for both boosting customer confidence and improving customer qualification at the same time.

Case in point, based on their market research, Expedient identified customers' highest-priority questions regarding cloud transformation and then developed an assessment tool to provide customers a practical means to answer those questions for themselves, all while identifying hidden costs and unforeseen savings they had failed to identify on their own. Critically, the tool wasn't designed to provide customers with Expedient's assessment of their business, but instead to provide customers an easy, practical means to confidently conduct that assessment for themselves. The framework allows customers to organize, analyze, and prioritize information and then move forward confidently with bigger, broader decisions. In fact, Expedient found that buyers who take its assessment converted at a rate of 80 percent, whereas those that did not converted at 30 percent. Effectively, customers are repaying Expedient with their business for the value they see in feeling more confident in themselves.

The real opportunity of an effective information-framing strategy is not just in helping customers consume more information, but in finding common ground on which and how much information matters. At the end of the day, Framemaking sellers help customers organize, analyze, and prioritize information in such a way that they're confident they've asked the right questions, conducted sufficient research, and thoroughly explored the most relevant alternatives so that they feel more confident in proceeding with a purchase.

That said, information isn't the only dimension along which customer stakeholders may struggle to find alignment. There's the bigger picture of agreeing on what they're even trying to do in the first place to drive company performance. Without that kind of consensus, there is no purchase at all.

Let's turn to that challenge next in Chapter 5.

CHAPTER 5

Addressing Misaligned Objectives

Of all the Framemaking stories we tell, the one we come back to most often is the parking garage story. Alas, it doesn't have a happy ending.

Chris was the head of sales for a medical-device company selling large scanning machines to hospitals, typically at a price of several million dollars apiece. Recently, they were pursuing a deal valued over $15 million. It was one of those deals that would make or break the quarter, and the entire team had invested countless time in the deal—senior leaders, subject matter experts, deal-proposal teams, implementation specialists, you name it. The team had run the playbook to perfection. Not only had they gained access to the target hospital's senior decision-maker, the chief of surgery, but they'd laid out a highly compelling case for the value of their scanning machines relative to their top competitors: higher efficacy, greater accuracy, fewer repairs, easier to use, less training required. And all that value added up to saving more lives, quite literally. The chief of surgery was sold. There was no question in their mind, this was the superior solution, delivering the greatest value, and offering the best outcomes for overall patient care. For both the head of sales and his entire team, it felt like a slam dunk; the deal was in the pipeline with a 95 percent likelihood to close.

There was only one final step standing between the team and a champagne end to the current quarter. Given the deal's size, the purchase required final approval from the hospital's executive leadership team, made up of not only the chief of surgery but also, among others, the hospital's chief administrative officer, the heads of finance and procurement, and the hospital's chief marketing officer. Of course, as it was an internal meeting, no one from the supplier organization was invited to attend, but the team had prepared their champion well. The chief of surgery had everything necessary to put forward the supplier's superior value, including a compelling business case denominated not only in improved productivity, decreased costs, and increased revenue but in actual human lives as well. So, yes, the deal stood in the balance behind closed doors, but things looked good. The team had done everything right.

When the decision came, it was devastating. The chief of surgery fought hard for the deal, but the decision ultimately "didn't go their way." The entire hospital leadership team agreed the business case was clear and compelling, but in the end, the supplier lost the deal anyway. So, what happened?

"The crazy thing is," Chris told us, "we didn't lose that deal to the competition. We lost it . . . to a parking garage. It turns out that this particular hospital had a serious parking problem."

So, while the chief of surgery did a great job laying out the business case for saving more lives with better scanning machines, the chief marketing officer countered with an arguably even bigger problem: poor patient experience. Families arriving at the hospital in emergent-care situations would drop a loved one off at the door, placing them in the care of hospital staff, but then be forced to drive around for twenty minutes looking for parking while their loved one was in the hospital alone, afraid, and possibly in need of a medical or even legal advocate. It had become such a problem that it was showing up in the hospital's "volume" numbers. When possible, patients were choosing alternate nearby hospitals to avoid the parking problem. It's hard to save more lives, the head of marketing argued, if there are fewer patients in need of care in the first place. And the team agreed. The scanners could wait. The parking problem could not. So, they chose the parking garage.

Several years later, we shared this story with a group of commercial leaders at a meeting in Denver, including Tim, the general manager for a large division of an enterprise software company. When Tim heard the story, he exclaimed, "That exact same thing just happened to us last month! We were by far the best choice, and the customer knew it, but they decided to do something completely different instead. It cost us millions of dollars."

In sales, it is profoundly painful to be the number one choice for your customer's number three problem.

THE PROBLEM WITH SELLING VALUE

Across 2022–2023, prevailing economic uncertainty driven by rising inflation meant B2B customers were trimming budgets, cutting costs, and canceling monthly subscriptions at an alarming rate. For companies built on a recurring revenue model—whether quarterly, monthly, or consumption based—the pain was especially acute, as the lack of long-term contracts made it far easier for customers to walk away. Especially across the software-as-a-service (SaaS) industry, built, as it was, entirely on a subscription-based model, the message was inescapable. In a world where customers have no contractual obligation to stick around long term, it is critically important that they maintain a deep and abiding appreciation of your solution's unique value.

Customers' perception of supplier value becomes the primary glue that makes relationships stick over time. Without it, customer retention drops, expansion stalls, and growth rates crash.

Today, company leaders continue to exhort sellers to embrace a customer value mindset as foundational to success. Untold annual reports, CEO investor conversations, and CRO pep talks sound a familiar refrain: *Everything* comes down to our ability to demonstrate value. Without it, customers won't buy, won't stick around, and won't grow with us over time. If customers can't see our value, we can't win. As a result, many organizations' sales training investments have swung heavily toward selling value, as the value mindset has come to infuse virtually everything we do in B2B sales and customer success. It all makes sense, really. What chief executive or revenue officer wouldn't emphasize a need to "sell on value," "convince customers of our value," or "ensure customers see our value"?

Every company has its own custom recipe for business-case building, of course—including its own unique name (e.g., impact assessment, solution brief, value plan)—but the business case typically spans a pretty common set of materials. Beyond an extensive review of the company's unique features and benefits, for new customers, there are industry benchmarks demonstrating how similar companies have realized huge value from the supplier's solution. There are testimonial videos of senior leaders from well-known companies speaking to someone just off camera, preferably supported by dramatic music. For existing customers, there's user feedback data demonstrating widespread support based on customer satisfaction or net promoter scores, along with utilization reports demonstrating the degree to which happy users are highly engaged and deriving massive value from the supplier's solution already. And for every kind of customer—the crown jewel of the entire business case—there's the ROI calculator (a.k.a. financial impact assessment, cost-benefit calculator, value calculator) taking customers step-by-step through each dimension along which the supplier's solution provides value and building a compelling quantitative case for the supplier as the best option to provide what the customer cares about most.

For large companies, the business case can easily cost well into six figures and require input from an entire team of people, possibly including a centralized deal desk or value team dedicated exclusively to this kind of support. For smaller companies, the sales enablement or marketing team lends a hand, along with sales engineers, presales executives, and other subject matter experts. And in many cases, star performing sellers will have their own version, cobbled together from years of countless customer encounters, scattered across scores of folders, buried deep on their laptop's C drive. Wherever one might fall on this continuum, the business case, in whatever form, is considered by most commercial leaders as one of the most important, powerful tools for winning customer buy-in, building stakeholder consensus, and ultimately securing closed deals. Articulating business value sits right alongside effective discovery and skilled negotiation as a core competency required of every effective sales professional and sales organization.

But current approaches to value selling fail to address an underlying problem with modern-day B2B buying. No question, convincing customers of your solution's unique value is important. It just might not be of *primary* importance. The problem with a value-centric approach isn't its intention but its timing. There's an order of operations to customer value that really matters, yet most customer engagement strategies, by design, fail to follow that order.

THE MATH IS LAST

In many ways, CEOs and CROs have it right: conveying value in a clear, compelling manner is absolutely critical for closing a deal. With few exceptions, customers won't buy your solution if they can't see your value. However, while value articulation is a critical step for deal success, it's not the best *first* step.

Let's recall what we're solving for. The single biggest factor boosting the likelihood of a high-quality, low-regret deal isn't whether customers are confident in your ability to deliver value; it's their ability to collectively agree on a definition of "value." In other words, it's whether members of the buying group feel confident they're aligned with *each other* on their highest-priority problem or opportunity, along with the best course of action to address it. And that matters, because it's hard. Sometimes, *really* hard. The simple reality is, customers are juggling many different questions well beyond whether your solution might be helpful. Questions like "What are we even trying to do?" and "How are we trying to do it?" Without common conviction around what to *do*, customers will naturally struggle to feel confident in what to buy. Yet if we look at most suppliers' efforts to convey customer value, they're seeking to solve almost exclusively for the latter: what to buy—or, perhaps more precisely, why buy from them. But building customers' confidence in supplier capabilities in the hopes that confidence will prove sufficient to ensure customers' collective buy-in to a problem represents a deeply supplier-centric mental model, which completely overlooks the broader organizational context within which that purchase decision unfolds.

So, what's the alternative to leading with supplier value? In a Framemaking approach, supplier value is far less an *input* to customer confidence than an *output*. While suppliers typically build business cases in order to *generate* customer confidence in their solution, in reality, customers' collective belief in the value of a supplier is a far better way to *demonstrate* their confidence in a course of action leading to that solution in the first place. Perceived value doesn't generate customer confidence, but demonstrates it.

The first thing a buying group needs to agree on is their objective: "What are we trying to do?" Depending on where in the company the decision sits, that objective might be very broad (e.g., expand our market share in Europe, the Middle East, and Africa), somewhat narrower, for example an internal initiative (e.g., improve employee engagement and retention), or possibly highly targeted inside a single function or team (e.g., increase inbound marketing qualified leads). In our parking garage story, the hospital leadership team ultimately chose between two competing high-level objectives: "Increase patient traffic" versus "Increase quality of care."

One step down from objectives are tactics (see Table 1). If objectives represent *what* we're trying to do, then tactics answer the question, "*How* are we going to do it?"

Objective (What are we trying to do?)	Tactic (How are we trying to do it?)
• Improve employee engagement and retention	→ • Through improved employee coaching and mentoring
• Expand market share in EMEA	→ • Through the acquisition of 1–2 regional players
• Increase inbound marketing qualified leads	→ • By producing significantly more thought leadership

Table 1

Of course, objectives and tactics are closely connected as they cascade through an organization. Indeed, objectives are often simply the output of asking "how" against a tactic located one level higher in organizational scope. In that respect, tactics in many ways reflect the well-known five-why exercise associated with root-cause analysis, just reimagined as a five-how exercise. So, just as we might with a five-why exercise, we can start at one level of objectives and tactics (e.g., "improve employee engagement and retention") and either ladder up to higher-order organizational objectives or dig deeper into ever-more-tactical detail until we land at a place suitable for practical execution given current resources, capacity, and competing organizational priorities (see Table 2).

Objective (What are we trying to do?)	Tactic (How are we trying to do it?)
Control growing staff costs due to wage inflation	By increasing organizational productivity by 3 percent
Increase organizational productivity by 3 percent	**By improving employee engagement and retention**
Improve employee engagement and retention	By increasing employee coaching and mentoring
Increase employee coaching and mentoring	By upgrading coaching training for frontline managers
Upgrade coaching training for frontline managers	By using newly available technology to provide customized feedback

Table 2

From a strategic perspective, this is why most suppliers are keen on developing broader solutions to meet a wider scope of customer needs. They're effectively trying to climb the tactics ladder, as higher-level tactics are typically associated with bigger, broader—and hopefully more differentiable and profitable—solutions. In the HR services space, for example, virtually every provider has evolved from payroll or benefits-management services to far broader "human capital management solutions," encouraging customers to outsource a far larger basket of tactics in one fell swoop. Addressing customers' higher-order needs captures greater proportions of value.

Be that as it may, from a *customer's* perspective, regardless of whichever tactic they pursue, customer stakeholders then need to agree on the specific results they're seeking to achieve. So, if the first two questions they're asking are,

Objective: "What are we trying to do?" and,

Tactic: "How are we trying to do it?" then the next logical question is,

Result: "How will we know when we get there?"

Notice, this is different from "*Will* we get there?" or "How likely are we to get there?" This is about *defining* the destination first. And if the struggle for customer consensus wasn't sufficiently fraught already, this is where things can really run off the rails. Various stakeholders may agree on what to do and how to do it but strongly disagree on other things:

- "What does 'good' look like?"
- "How much is enough?"
- "How long should it take?"

Using our example above, imagine a meeting called to discuss the results of the effort to boost employee engagement and retention. Perhaps things have gone well, and at the conclusion of the project, the team lead, filled with a certain amount of pride, guides peers through a series of bar charts demonstrating real improvement in both engagement and retention. Success! Yet, upon concluding the presentation, the questions and comments start flying (each preceded, of course, by hollow affirmation):

- "This is great, but why aren't we measuring engagement based on the newer version of our engagement survey? I thought we all agreed that thing needs an overhaul."
- "I'm sure we're all excited to see the numbers go up, but I would have thought the jump would've been higher. Especially with our younger staff."
- "It's great to see these results, but why is it taking so long? With the current labor market, we gotta move faster."

Ugh. These kinds of meetings are etched in our collective memory. One doesn't read these quotes so much as *feel* them, almost

viscerally, deep in one's psyche. Because we've all been there. Whatever the project was in your organization, there's always that one
person. The skeptic. They're there just to second-guess everything, it
seems, or to just plain rain on everyone's parade. Every. Single. Time.
And woe be unto us all if that person is the boss's boss or a person in
power. To be fair, sometimes they're actually *right*. But that doesn't
make it any less exhausting—particularly for the project team who
spent months seeking in good faith to drive real results. Yet, this is
often what happens when large groups pursuing diverse priorities
seek to make collective decisions.

For those who've played a starring role in this movie more
than once, they've learned the hard way that the best way to nip
soul-crushing, post hoc second-guessing in the bud is to settle *in
advance* on the specific metrics, targets, and timelines the group
will use to judge whether a project—or a purchase—has been successful. Simply put, to define what "success" looks like. After all, it's
hard to move forward on a large-scale decision if the group making
that decision cannot say with confidence exactly what they're trying
to accomplish to begin with. In fact, more emphatically one might
argue that a large-scale project or purchase *shouldn't* move forward
if the group making that decision cannot say with confidence exactly
what they're trying to accomplish. When embarking on a project or
making a large purchase, getting clear on results means there are
actually three things it's imperative for you to clearly, collectively,
and *confidently* define in advance:

Metrics: How will we measure our progress?
Metrics might be quantitative or qualitative, denominated in currency, volume, or any number of options,
so long as stakeholders agree on the metrics' efficacy.
Of course, as part of that agreement, additional discussion around both data sourcing and quality may be

necessary to ensure everyone believes whatever outcome those metrics eventually represent. Often it can be equally important to specify which metrics will *not* be used and why, simply to minimize questioning results once they're available: "I can see the improvement according to *this* metric, but what about this other metric?"

Targets: How will we know when we get there?

If metrics represent the path along which results are measured, clear, agreed-upon targets are critical for establishing a finish line for success. Across the execution of a project or implementation of a purchase, stakeholders will naturally ask, "Is it working?" "Did we make a good decision?" or "Are we seeing value?" Without established targets, these questions have no clear answer, and confidence in the future results of a current purchase consideration is necessarily tied to the clarity of the target. Like metrics, targets may be quantitative or qualitative as they are denominated in terms of the metrics already agreed upon.

Timeline: How long is it going to take?

From a purely logical point of view, one could argue that timelines are no different than any other metric, whether measured in hours, weeks, months, years, or something else. Likewise, any metric of time will require a specific target (e.g., in three weeks, before end of quarter, or across the next five years). So what might justify isolating timeline as a stand-alone dimension? Nearly all other metrics and targets will require some sort of time dimension to be meaningful. So, yes, we might want to improve efficiency by 3 percent, but over what span of time exactly? Weeks? Months? Years? Defining a clear time dimension for each metric and target dramatically diminishes post hoc second-guessing through questions like "Why did it take so long?"

Applying our example might look something like Table 3.

Objective	What are we trying to do?
Tactic	How are we trying to do it?
Result	
Metric	How will we measure progress?
Target	How will we know when we get there?
Timeline	How long is it going to take?

Table 3

Ideally, to make a high-confidence purchase decision, a buying group needs not only a clear answer to each of these five questions but also a clear, agreed-upon understanding for *why* those answers are the best for that particular decision.

We refer to these five questions using the simple shorthand OTR—objectives, tactics, and results. Or, if you want to look fancy, OTR_{MTT} for objectives, tactics, results (metrics, targets, timeline) (see Figure 2). It's a simplification, to be sure, but it nicely captures the five key dimensions critical for any high-confidence purchase decision in B2B. Effectively OTR frames the customers' perception of value. And without customer consensus across these five questions, the value of a supplier's solution may be absolutely indisputable in the abstract but completely irrelevant within the customer's organizational context if that context hasn't been sufficiently clarified in a way that very specifically leads to the supplier's ability to provide unique value. Ultimately, it doesn't matter how many lives your scanning machines will save if those machines can't relieve a patient parking problem in urgent need of attention. The question every B2B buying group must answer, therefore, isn't, "Is the value of the supplier's solution clear?" but rather, "Is the value of the supplier's solution *relevant*?" And if stakeholders can't agree with a high degree of confidence on each dimension of OTR in a way that leads to your solution's value, then the fact that your solution delivers value to a long list of similar customers (as demonstrated proudly on your website through a long list of logos) doesn't really matter. Your solution must deliver value *in context.*

This is why we think of supplier value as an output rather than an input. As one commercial leader told us from years of similar experience, "The math is last." To sell complex solutions, we need to lead *to* our company's unique value rather than lead *with* our company's unique value.

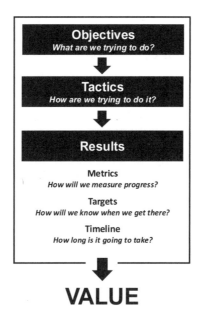

Figure 2

VALUE FRAMING

From a supplier's perspective it's especially important to ensure customers' confident consensus across OTR for two reasons: first, to prevent a deal from stalling either temporarily or completely due to customer stakeholders' inability to align around a common vision, and second—worse still—to prevent a deal from actually closing *despite* a lack of confident consensus across OTR. To be sure, a supplier might celebrate that closed deal in the short run, but they'll likely incur significant collateral damage when that buying group later realizes they can't effectively assess the outcome of their purchase because they never fully agreed on some dimension of OTR at the outset. In that case, chances are pretty high that any blame for unclear results will land in the lap of the supplier, as the exact parameters of performance were never fully defined.

So, how in the world can sellers ensure customer confidence across OTR_{MTT} prior to a purchase? Especially when so many of these deliberations happen over the horizon, behind closed doors inside the customer company?

Step one is to diagnose the degree to which customers have achieved confident consensus across each level of OTR (see Table 4). A lack of confident consensus often appears in customer statements

Objective	"We love what you guys do, but we've got a lot on our plate right now."
Tactic	"If it were up to me, I'd buy it tomorrow, but the other regions are pushing for a different approach."
Result	
Metric	"We see the value, but we're still thinking through how to maximize the impact we deliver to our teams."
Target	"You've made a compelling case, but we're still trying to define a realistic goal for improvement."
Timeline	"We love the fact it's a proven solution, but we're feeling a lot of pressure to get some quick-hit wins."

Table 4

beginning with familiar but painful phrases like, "We love what you guys do, but . . ."

The problem, of course, is that when we hear such statements, more often than not it's late in a sales cycle after we've invested months of time, money, and effort to ensure customers are excited about our solution. Worst-case scenario, it's only after the final customer meeting that we discover we've lost to a parking garage. If we want to avoid the pain and cost of customers' late-stage second-guessing, then we have to determine their alignment across each dimension of OTR as concretely as possible in advance. Using the OTR framework not only provides a structured means to identify dangerous customer disconnects sooner, but it also enables a far more accurate means to diagnose the nature of those disconnects and determine their potential impact on customers' collective confidence to make a purchase decision.

Even more importantly, however, OTR provides sellers an opportunity to help. Remember, Framemaking is the act of making a complex task or decision feel more manageable. First, by establishing clear, credible boundaries around its scope. And second, by identifying key considerations and prioritizing best next steps within those boundaries. As such, it's hard to imagine a better, more powerful role for Framemaking than helping customers establish consensus across objectives, tactics, metrics, targets, and timelines. From a customer's perspective, establishing confident consensus at each level of OTR is hard enough on its own. But in aggregate, the five intertwined layers of OTR represent arguably the single highest hurdle customers must overcome to establish a high degree of confidence in any organizational decision, let alone a large-scale purchase. It's no wonder that 40–60 percent of B2B deals end in no decision. This stuff is hard.

From a seller's perspective, customers' internal struggles to achieve alignment across OTR might represent the single biggest reason why so many sellers naturally fall into what one sales leader recently described as "RFP harvesting," or prioritizing deals where customers put out a tender or request for proposal because they "already have it all figured out." Essentially, many sellers see themselves as takers rather than makers when it comes to customer alignment across OTR, assuming there's little they can do to influence this kind of internal wrangling. And if they were right, it might actually make sense to delay engagement until this process is complete. It's as if they instinctively recognize that customers' lack of confidence in their own alignment across OTR indicates a sales opportunity less worthy of their valuable time. *Let's let them figure all that out, and they'll call us when they're ready.*

Yet, customers' struggles to align across OTR represent a both productive and powerful way for sellers to play a far more proactive and valuable role in driving deals by serving as a helpful guide in aligning buyers. That's the opportunity for Framemaking—less about framing customers' perception of supplier value and more about framing customer alignment on objectives such that the supplier's value comes into sharper focus. Framemaking sellers have an incredible opportunity to provide customers helpful guidance that materially improves their alignment around what to do such that they're more confident in deciding what to buy as a result.

We refer to this version of Framemaking as value framing, prompting stakeholders to consider alternative objectives, tactics, metrics, targets, or timelines they might have otherwise overlooked, or bounding that exploration in ways that help customers progress more quickly and confidently through the frequently fraught debate around defining OTR such that they arrive at an actual purchase with a high degree of decision confidence. Like all Framemaking, value framing is about boosting ease and ensuring agency, in this case specifically applied to OTR.

So, how exactly does that happen? Let's take it step-by-step: establish, engage, execute.

ESTABLISHING A FRAME FOR OTR WITH INTERPERSONAL PERSONAS

Similar to decision complexity, the first step in ensuring customer stakeholders are aligned around objectives, tactics, and results is to determine which stakeholders matter the most when it comes to OTR alignment. Unlike framing to reduce decision complexity, however, when framing value we're less concerned with the step-by-step process by which a purchase decision advances through an organization, and far more concerned with the priorities motivating each stakeholder across the buying team. And here, we'll want to cast a wide net, accounting not only for full-time members of the buying committee who must say yes to the purchase but also for the wider range of occasional stakeholders who play a more limited role in the purchase but still wield sufficient influence to either slow the decision or veto it altogether. For example, stakeholders in finance or IT teams may not make the purchase decision, but they certainly can stop it, stall it, or kill it if it fails to meet requirements aligned with their OTR. Likewise, senior executives will often defer to their team to make the best-fit decision for their priorities and only get involved if it becomes necessary to overrule all or part of a decision. Either way, in value framing we'll need to account for both groups—the smaller one that must say yes and the larger one able to say no.

How do we accurately inventory such a broad and varied group? One way, of course, is to ask the customers, "Who on your team will likely be involved in this purchase process?" Far from making things *easier* for customers, however, that question places the entire burden of buying-group identification on the shoulders of customers. That may be fine for highly experienced buying groups—which do exist, of course—but may prove unhelpful to customers who might not be sure, especially if they're making this kind of purchase for the first time, or the first time in a long time. To that end, reminiscent of the it-turns-out-that audit introduced in Chapter 3, the most effective

Framemaking sellers will review recent or even current deals with similar customers to better predict not just who is involved but who *should* be involved. One might imagine, for example, in the future the sales team selling medical scanners to hospitals will absolutely suggest to customers that the hospital's chief marketing officer be more directly involved. That CMO may not need to approve the deal, but the experience with the parking garage has shown they certainly can derail it. Painfully so, in fact.

Having conducted an it-turns-out-that audit and created as complete a list as possible of stakeholders involved anywhere along the purchase, the critical step in value framing is to consider how those stakeholders relate to each other. Ultimately, the goal isn't to cut them out of the deal but to ensure their productive collaboration. To do that, Framemaking sellers seek to predict where those stakeholders are most likely to do the following:

1. Align with each other across objectives, tactics, and results
2. Conflict with each other across objectives, tactics, and results
3. Fail to connect at all with each other across objectives, tactics, and results
4. Lack confidence in their alignment across objectives, tactics, and results
5. Collectively fail to consider an objective, tactic, metric, target, or timeline altogether that would help them align more easily, with greater confidence, and simultaneously come to value the supplier's unique strengths with greater conviction

To be sure, the very best sellers do this almost instinctively, possibly without even realizing they're doing it. For the rest of us, it helps to organize this thinking into a logical framework we like to call "interpersonal personas."

Like more traditional stakeholder personas, interpersonal personas capture various customer stakeholder characteristics spanning things like role, priorities, typical concerns, maybe personal aspirations. For our purposes in aligning customers across each dimension of OTR, Framemaking interpersonal personas also captures the typical objectives, tactics, and results for each customer stakeholder as accurately as possible, ideally specified in terms of concrete metrics, targets, and timelines when available (possibly sourced, for example, from company financial reports, online interviews, guest spots on industry podcasts, or simply earlier conversations). Of course, if these things aren't known for the stakeholder in question, especially in advance of actual customer engagement, experience with similar past deals can go a long way in equipping sellers with a relatively close approximation. At least early in a sale, the aim of interpersonal personas is not 100 percent accuracy, but rather a relatively defensible approximation that allows a seller to engage customers in a value framing conversation in a credible and helpful manner. Think of it as a form of hypothesis-based selling, where the hypotheses are tuned less to a customer company's overall business problem and more specifically to the top-of-mind objectives, tactics, metrics, targets, and timelines of each stakeholder involved in the purchase.

Unlike traditional stakeholder personas, however, interpersonal personas place these individuals within their organizational context, mapping the interaction effects across stakeholders' OTRs, with an especially strong focus on points of likely alignment and potential misalignment across each OTR dimension. This unique interstakeholder perspective equips sellers to help customers anticipate and even avoid disconnects or disagreements that could slow purchase progress or stall it all together.

For example, we once worked with a global producer of industrial cleaning supplies and safety equipment that sold through long-term contracts into large manufacturing facilities. In mapping their customers' frequent struggles to reach efficient purchase decisions, they determined that a facility's head of operations and its head of safety often worked at cross-purposes, frequently slowing or stalling collective decision-making to an absolute crawl. The plant manager prioritized operational throughput, uptime, and efficiency above all else. The safety engineer was more than willing to shut down production in order to address potential hazards or out-of-spec safety gear. To be sure, the plant manager cared about safety, and the safety manager cared about efficiency, and both cared deeply about overall company performance. But each approached those common goals through the lens of their specific roles, which then determined their primary objectives, tactics, metrics, targets, and timelines. That disconnect often led to frustrating delays as the two leaders struggled to find common ground. Clearly, the supplier needed a way to proactively help them reach agreement by making an otherwise fraught OTR alignment process easier.

Interpersonal Personas

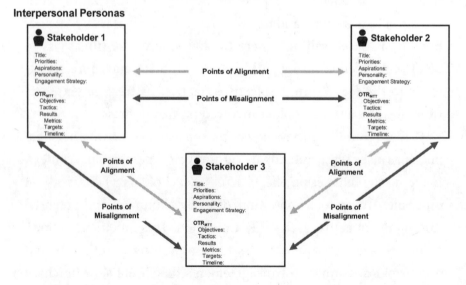

Figure 3

Using the OTR framework baked into interpersonal personas, the Framemaking seller can work with customers to better identify the specific "altitude" at which they're most in danger of misalignment based on the experience of other companies who've pursued a similar purchase (see Figure 3). It can work reactively as a diagnostic when customers' "check consensus" light starts blinking on their purchase-progress dashboard. Or, even better, Framemaking sellers can use it proactively to help customers avoid objective misalignment in the first place, greatly diminishing the risk of exhausting second-guessing down the road.

For example, in the case of the supplier of cleaning and safety supplies, both the plant manager and the safety engineer are seeking to maximize worker productivity. So they agree on the objective. They disagree, however, on tactics. The plant manager believes the best way to improve productivity is by maximizing uptime, while the safety engineer seeks to boost productivity by preventing employee injury that necessitates downtime, sick leave, overtime for replacement labor, and possibly a drop in employee morale. Who's right? Yes. It's sort of a Mars-Venus problem, where there isn't really a right answer. The only productive way to overcome stakeholder misalignment is to establish some sort of common ground.

Yet, what often happens instead is the hard work of creating confident consensus across all five dimensions of OTR_{MTT} is simply sidestepped by a handful of stakeholders seeking to make progress. Many times, stakeholders more central to a purchase decision will define clear metrics, targets, and timelines without confirming broader stakeholder agreement around higher-order objectives. After all, it's their decision, right? But in doing so, they often overestimate their ability to eventually win over colleagues to their proposed purchase as they fail to appreciate the broader organizational context within which that purchase takes place. For a seller assessing a handful of stakeholders' apparent confidence in metrics, targets, and timelines, but failing to recognize their lack of connection back to broader organizational objectives, this is exactly how one loses to a parking garage.

These kinds of customer disconnects are especially common when other members of the larger buying group are preoccupied with any number of equally pressing decisions at the same time. With the rest of the buying group distracted by day-to-day reality, it becomes easy for a smaller group of eager stakeholders, anxious to act, to skip steps in order to feel a sense of progress, leaving a full resolution of OTR until much later in a purchase when a lack of confident alignment reveals itself in an often painfully tense meeting where someone finally speaks up and says, "Wait a minute. Why are we even doing this?" or "I get it, but why are we doing it *this way*?" or "Why are we doing this *now*? Can't this wait until next year?" What happens next? More often than not, either by group consensus or senior-level mandate, a decision is made to step back and take more time to look at things more deeply. This is exactly the kind of "progress theater" Framemaking sellers seek to avoid by predicting where things might go wrong using interpersonal personas, ensuring customer stakeholders are more than simply superficially aligned at every level of OTR.

At a meeting of chief sales officers where we were discussing an early version of this idea, a head of sales joked, "This sounds more like couples therapy than a sales technique!" To which we'd reply, "You're not far off, actually." If that feels strange, it shouldn't: what we're solving for isn't so much complex solution sales, but complex human interactions.

ENGAGING CUSTOMERS TO DIAGNOSE AND OVERCOME MISALIGNMENT

Equipped with interpersonal personas, Framemaking sellers are in a far better position to prompt customers to consider potential misalignment across OTR that they might have otherwise inadvertently—or perhaps willfully—overlooked and to help them understand the consequences of failing to address that disconnect. Maybe they even start with, "Have you ever heard the parking garage story?"

Traditionally, stakeholders' points of misalignment might represent the very topics most sellers seek to avoid. How many of us, in preparing to support a sales call, have heard a seller say, "Now, there's some real debate around this point, so whatever you do, don't bring that up." But more often than not, avoidance begets only disappointment as that disconnect will continue to simmer and eventually threaten to derail the deal altogether much later in the sale. Everything's fine until it isn't. In the end, it's far better to run right at stakeholder disconnects than run from them, by proactively assessing the buying group's depth of agreement across OTR_{MTT} as early as possible in a sale.

The best way to initiate that assessment is through a series of what one might call discovery questions. However, this isn't traditional sales discovery designed to identify customers' needs, priorities, or preferences. Rather, value framing discovery is meant to determine stakeholders' level of collective confidence in OTR alignment. For example:

1. **Medical equipment:** We recently did a similar deal where the chief of surgery was excited to move forward, but things got hung up when the hospital CMO advocated instead for allocating those funds to a parking garage. Crazy as it sounds, have you talked to your CMO about how this purchase might support her marketing strategy?

2. **Capital equipment:** I know everyone will be excited about increasing throughput while decreasing defects, but if we were to ask your IT team about the data connectivity side

of things, or your HR team about potential headcount reductions, do you think they'd be on board? In working with other companies, we've learned how important it is to sync up with those two functions in particular.

3. **Business services:** I know you're excited about the potential reduction in operating costs—we are too—but if we were to ask your finance team, where would that metric be on their list of top three targets for improvement next year? Would it make the list? We've learned from other customers, it's always good to make sure we're all aligned on just how valuable these benefits might be given everything else you're trying to do. Your "need-to-have" may in fact be finance's "nice-to-have."

If we consider in turn each dimension of objectives, tactics, metrics, targets, and timelines relative to each potential stakeholder interaction across interpersonal personas, the number of discovery questions one might imagine are nearly endless. But these should give you a sense of not only how Framemaking sellers engage customers in a value framing conversation but also *why*.

From a supplier's perspective, the answers to these questions are absolutely invaluable in qualifying an opportunity, as they provide critical insight into arguably the single most important deal attribute of any complex B2B sale: the degree of customer consensus across OTR. That's why it's especially important to engage customers in value framing conversations early in the sales process. Customers exhibiting a high degree of misalignment—or a low degree of confidence in their current level of alignment—can be managed more proactively to establish that alignment, or pursued with less energy and fewer resources if alignment appears unlikely, up to and including complete disqualification altogether.

From a *customer's* perspective, it's the questions themselves that prove valuable, as they prompt critical reflection they might otherwise easily overlook or even willfully postpone. To be sure, for many customers this kind of nudge may feel more frustrating than helpful as it possibly exposes a point of tension or decision difficulty they'd rather not consider—especially if they're excited to move forward with a purchase. But the forcing mechanism of value framing questions, frustrating as they may be, ultimately proves helpful to buyers seeking to navigate the difficult process of stakeholder alignment.

That said, to increase the likelihood of a positive reception to value framing conversations, Framemaking sellers should consider a number of design principles when formulating these questions.

1. **Prioritize purchase ease:** The primary objective in Framemaking is to improve customer confidence by reducing purchase difficulty. To that end, sellers should be careful not to overwhelm customers with too many alignment questions at once. As good or important as any individual alignment question might be, ten of them delivered in rapid-fire succession would almost inevitably do more harm than good, leaving customers feeling more overwhelmed rather than more confident.

2. **Provide social proof:** In the hypothetical questions above, one can imagine the Framemaking seller is ready to elaborate by providing concrete examples of similar companies that have addressed comparable questions, including what they did and whether it worked. In cases where a more cautionary story lacks a happy ending (e.g., the parking garage story), sellers can speculate with customers what might have worked better instead while projecting that lesson to the customer's own organization.

3. **Preserve customer agency:** The objective isn't to *tell* customers where they might be misaligned, but rather to prompt them to assess for themselves their current risk of objective misalignment, including its most likely source. Ultimately, the goal is to *guide* customers to better alignment rather than *present* them with better alignment.

4. **Project real humility:** As we've seen elsewhere, Framemaking sellers adopt the role of connector rather than expert when framing value. The goal isn't to demonstrate one's expertise, but to connect customers to the shared experience of other companies like them. As a result, Framemaking sellers can lean far more heavily on the language of surprise and curiosity grounded in a spirit of collaborative learning instead of demonstrating personal expertise, experience, and opinion. Pointing out potential points of stakeholder misalignment can be a bit painful for customers, so Framemaking sellers deliver that message with empathy, curiosity, and a genuine desire to help. Their tone isn't "Here's what you need to do," but rather "Here's something that might help."

5. **Promote urgent action:** As important as it is for Framemaking sellers to ultimately boost customers' confidence, when it comes to framing value, the immediate emotion Framemaking sellers seek to evoke is closer to concern or discomfort. Value framing discovery questions are designed to make customers feel a bit uneasy about their colleagues' current level of collective consensus. Not to undermine their confidence per se, but to lead them to take action to ensure that their confidence is more than simply superficial.

The whole idea here is to prompt customers to stop for a moment and reflect on the broader organizational context of the purchase they're currently considering: Does it actually align with organizational priorities? Will other stakeholders agree at each level of OTR_{MTT}? Do we know? Have we asked? At the end of the day, no large B2B purchase decision occurs in a vacuum. It must compete against any number of equally important decisions for company resources, time, attention, and support. And if customers aren't willing or able to do the sometimes hard work of winning buy-in to this purchase relative to other competing decisions, then Framemaking sellers help them make that happen—or possibly qualify out when they can't.

Having raised the topic of potential misalignment across one or more dimensions of OTR, of course, it is now incumbent on a Framemaking seller to help bolster customers' confidence in their collective alignment. How, exactly? Arguably the best way we've seen is through something called a stakeholder alignment workshop.

EXECUTING VALUE FRAMING—
THE STAKEHOLDER ALIGNMENT WORKSHOP

Over the years, we've encountered a number of companies conducting variants of stakeholder alignment workshops spanning a diverse range of industries including financial services, SaaS, facilities management, and agricultural products. We first introduced this practice in *The Challenger Customer* as a means to unite stakeholders around a commercial insight leading to a supplier's unique capabilities.[1]

In many ways, the mechanics we described there apply equally well in a Framemaking context. However, there are a number of subtle differences worth noting. Here, our primary objective is to pull forward in time the meeting or exchange where customers realize they're not fully aligned across OTR and guide them to more productive agreement on (1) why they're considering a purchase in the first place, (2) how they'll assess the impact of that purchase, and (3) the specific results they hope to realize as a result.

The goal of the workshop is to unify customers on what they're going to *do*, not necessarily what they're going to buy. To be sure, the occasion of the workshop will likely result from one or two stakeholders expressing direct interest in our solution (likely a customer champion), but the workshop itself doesn't start from that expression of interest in our solution and move downstream from there, with us seeking to demonstrate our capabilities to a wider network of additional stakeholders. Rather, an alignment workshop shifts further upstream, taking a significant step back from the supplier solution altogether to establish collective consensus around an objective and tactic that our solution could eventually address. In this sense, like so many other forms of Framemaking, stakeholder alignment workshops are really designed to be supplier agnostic. The whole idea is to establish collective, confident alignment around the organizational *context* in which our solution might eventually be deployed, as customers' collective confidence in that broader context represents a critical prerequisite for ensuring the clarity of our value.

Should the workshop fail to generate that kind of confidence—perhaps because stakeholders struggle to agree, or agree on something completely unrelated, or possibly refuse to participate then that deal can be qualified accordingly, with a low likelihood of closing and an even lower likelihood of eventually renewing or expanding.

In its most basic form, a stakeholder alignment workshop is simply a meeting. Depending on the scope, complexity, and stakes of customer problems that a company's solution addresses, it might last sixty minutes, several hours, or even multiple days. It might be virtual, in person, or some combination of the two. For in-person meetings, a seller might travel alone or with a team to the customer to run a workshop, or customer stakeholders might join the supplier in their corporate office or dedicated solutions center purpose-built for exactly such occasions.

Depending on the size, complexity, and stakes of a company's offering, one end or the other of this spectrum will feel almost comically absurd—either ridiculously overengineered or dangerously underresourced. But in the end, neither is inherently right or wrong. The operational logistics of the workshop should correspond to the scope of the deals you're seeking to do. On one end of the spectrum, we've seen world-class sellers run similar workshops over one-hour Zoom calls. On the other, we've worked with a food-ingredients company that runs customer alignment workshops spanning upward of twenty people, in person, across at least two and a half days. To some, that level of commitment might sound crazy until you learn the customers invited to these workshops are each worth multiple billions of dollars in revenue to the supplier.

Some companies employ dedicated teams of presales experts, or even contract with outside facilitators to run these sessions, especially for highly complicated solutions. However, individual sellers are not only capable of leading most versions of an alignment workshop themselves, but they should run them whenever possible, as this sort of Framemaking activity is exactly the kind of customer engagement most likely to set them apart in customers' eyes as the one sales rep they actually *do* want to interact with. To be sure, value framing conversations require sellers to adopt a posture of facilitating rather than selling as the goal isn't to close a deal with your company but to align customer stakeholders inside their *own* company. But the best sellers are likely practicing those skills already, often without realizing it. And for everyone else, they're completely accessible with purposeful practice.

There are two key steps that will determine the value of a stakeholder alignment workshop to both the supplier and the customer:

winning customer buy-in to participate and conducting the workshop in a manner designed to create confidence around OTR.

Winning Customer Buy-In

The first challenge in conducting a customer stakeholder alignment workshop is getting customer stakeholders to show up. This is where the work of establishing a clear interpersonal persona in advance really pays off. Equipped with at least a viable hypothesis of who should be involved and the dimensions along which they're most likely to disconnect, the Framemaking seller can explore with his or her customer contact potential points of misalignment across relevant stakeholders, prioritizing them according to their potential impact on the buying group's ability to proceed with confidence. The types of questions we explored above will prove especially useful for demonstrating the downside risk of allowing misalignment to fester deeper into a purchase process, building urgency for the workshop while still engaging customers as a helpful connector rather than a supplier-centric expert.

In requesting a meeting with those stakeholders, the Framemaking seller should emphasize to invitees—either directly through email or indirectly via their customer contact—that the goal of the meeting is to establish alignment across objectives, tactics, metrics, targets, and timelines, *irrespective* of specific supplier solutions. The meeting is emphatically *not* a product demo of any kind. As always, it's important to share an agenda and set expectations in advance, including timing, the meeting objective (OTR alignment), and ground rules for participation (everyone leans in respectfully to the conversation with candor and transparency), and the role of the seller solely as a facilitator. Of course, the tone should be professional, but also upbeat and optimistic. To be sure, there's a hint of, "If we don't get aligned, things will go painfully off the rails," but the mood going into the meeting shouldn't be a war room mentality.

Instead, it should be an exploration of what's possible when everyone's on the same page. It's a careful balance between mitigating downside risk and maximizing upside potential, with the emphasis on the latter.

Of course, should efforts to organize the meeting prove unsuccessful, regardless of reason, that deal should be placed on probation and treated with skepticism regarding its likelihood to advance along a productive path, or to close in a timely fashion.

Running the Alignment Workshop

Logistically, sellers can run the workshop in any number of ways regarding location, length, number of breaks, breakouts, and so on, depending on deal complexity, customer preferences, past experience, and simply what's feasible given everyone's busy schedule.

But in terms of workshop content, the objective is to complete the meeting with a clear articulation of objective, tactic, metric(s), target(s), and timeline that everyone agrees on that may—or may not—lead directly to the purchase of your solution. Again, *that* conversation comes later. The workshop is meant to create a viable context for that consideration down the road (or not, as the case may be). Success isn't defined by stakeholders exclaiming, "Take my money!" in unison upon its conclusion, but rather by their collective acknowledgment that they're now on the same page with respect to what they're trying to do, how they're trying to do it, and how they'll measure results.

To that end, the Framemaking seller takes off their sales hat and puts on a facilitator one.

For sellers who've never considered their potential role as facilitator, think of value framing facilitation as a kind of dance, where your role is to lead in a way that makes following feel nearly effortless. The idea is to move participants step-by-step to a clear, confident outcome, but to do so in a way that feels very organic, so they don't feel directed at all, but simply encouraged to move in whichever direction they choose, within the agreed-upon framework. Perhaps it goes without saying, but this matters as it dramatically increases the chances that, in the end, stakeholders feel collective ownership for whatever they come up with. Remember, in Framemaking, we're not solving for their confidence in us, but for their confidence in themselves.

So how does the dance work? It follows a rhythm of prompt, explore, bound, prompt, explore, bound as it moves methodically from an agreed-upon objective through tactics, metrics, targets, and timelines (see Figure 4).

To warm up, the facilitator asks stakeholders to discuss a current business objective everyone agreed to prior to the workshop. Agreement in advance on this specific objective ensures the conversation falls within the broader scope of business challenges the supplier's solution is actually designed to address. After all, it doesn't make sense to run a stakeholder alignment workshop on a set of objectives completely unrelated to the kinds of challenges your solution seeks to solve. The idea here is to confirm that the objective is unanimously considered worthy of attention and in need of attention. It's helpful at this early stage to inventory some of the challenges the group is facing in achieving the objective now—both to get the discussion going and to set the tone for active participation from everyone. Those challenges will also prove valuable in brainstorming tactics momentarily.

The one thing the facilitator must guard against here is simply an effort by customers to divert to a different objective altogether, especially one completely unrelated to the supplier's solution set. This is why it's important to secure participants' approval for this particular objective in advance of the workshop as part of setting expectations. Should participants digress, the Framemaking seller can diplomatically reestablish the frame for the conversation by reminding the group that they themselves chose to scope the meeting around that particular objective.

The Stakeholder Alignment Workshop

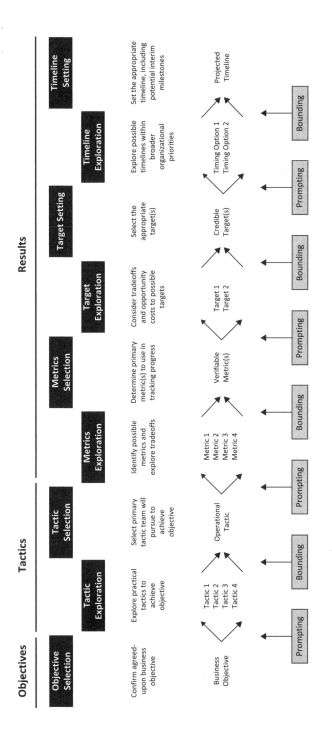

Figure 4

Having level set on what's hard about the targeted objective, the group is then ready to explore possible tactics meant to overcome those challenges and achieve that objective. Beyond simply documenting the team's suggestions, the seller can actively prompt the group to also consider tactics more closely associated with their solution using examples from similar companies as social proof. That said, the seller should be careful to focus solely on the solution, not the supplier. The tactics discussion isn't an exploration of what to buy, but of what to do. This is all supplier agnostic.

Once those tactics are on the table, participants are invited to discuss, compare notes, and successively narrow the list to one they can all agree on, guided by the seller, whose sole purpose here is to get them to settle on a single course of action, irrespective of what that action might be. To be sure, the seller can gently nudge the group toward a specific tactic more likely to lead to their solution, but they must be careful here to maintain their posture of tacit neutrality. It's likely no one would be surprised by a seller's attempt to bound the exploration of tactics in a way advantageous to them, but they can't do so in a way that supersedes their primary goal of simply providing helpful guidance toward OTR alignment. And should that alignment break in a way that doesn't naturally lead to the supplier's solution, despite the seller's best efforts to guide the decision in a better direction, then that too is a victory for the supplier. Yes, they're far less likely to win the eventual deal, but now they know and can proceed accordingly, shifting their attention to other higher-potential opportunities.

Whether the seller at this point exclaims, "Oh, would you look at that! We're out of time!" and ends things there or guides the group through the ultimate conclusion of the workshop is a bit of a judgment call, to be sure. But remember, Framemaking sellers' primary goal is to help build customers' self-confidence. And that act bears significant intrinsic value that, while it may not pay off today, can easily pay off down the road as customers remember who was most helpful in navigating decision difficulty.

Assuming things break in a more positive manner, the balance of the workshop then follows the exact same pattern of prompting, exploring, and bounding across metrics, targets, and timelines. So, step-by-step, Framemaking sellers systematically tighten the conversation more closely to their solution all without mentioning their solution by name. After all, the point of the meeting isn't to sell a solution. Indeed, if the meeting ends in a sales pitch, you're doing it wrong. Instead, the meeting should feel to customers that they're there to find alignment with each other on a business problem/ opportunity, not a potential purchase, because they are. That's actually the point. It's not a "Sell Something to Stakeholders" workshop or a "Let's Align Stakeholders on How Great We Are" workshop. The workshop, in fact, is designed to be supplier agnostic. It's about *their* alignment around OTR. To be sure, it's a bounded conversation, but one allowing customers a great deal of agency as they're prompted to expand and explore at each stage.

So, by the end of the workshop, customer stakeholders share a common vision of what they're trying to do, how they're trying to do it, and how they'll know when they get there. And should they ever lose their way, there's always the workshop to look back on to remind everyone what they agreed to. A buying group that successfully completes an alignment workshop is now in a better position to proceed with confidence through an actual solution purchase, as they now have a clearer sense for the parameters that solution will have to meet. Effectively, the output of an alignment workshop is a more precise articulation of the value the solution must provide.

For any seller thinking this entire thing sounds kind of hard, you're right. But consider for a moment. Not only might this process seem daunting to you, but arguably it feels even more daunting to your customer. After all, while you can opt out and wait for them to establish objective alignment on their own, they have no choice but to muddle their way through. It sort of makes you wonder, if 40–60 percent of purchase processes end in no decision, how many never get started at all, as would-be customers, still burned out from their last attempt at organizational alignment, simply choose to live with the status quo rather than run the OTR gauntlet yet again.

If our goal in Framemaking is to make things easier for customers, that often means we must assume some of that purchase burden ourselves, proactively adopting the role of guide rather than waiting for customers to successfully achieve alignment on their own. This is the kind of incremental effort star performing sellers typically embrace, not because they're more disciplined or hungry or they just want it more, but because they've learned the best way to sell more predictably is to help customers buy more confidently. Framemaking sellers find ways to shift the buying burden from customers to themselves while preserving customers' sense of agency at the same time.

At this point, we've solved for "What are we trying to do?" and "What does success look like?" But customers still face the challenging question of "Will it actually work?" (i.e., outcome uncertainty). Even with a very clear OTR roadmap, customers can doubt their ability to achieve their destination. So, that's the last dimension of customer confidence we need to address with Framemaking in Chapter 6.

CHAPTER 6

Mitigating Outcome Uncertainty

We were running a meeting with senior sales leaders in Southern California a few years ago when the conversation turned to solutions implementation. The discussion started where it often did, with attendees looking for better ways to improve the handoff from sales to account management to ensure customers had a more seamless experience working with their company. Too often, information was lost, customer concerns fell through the cracks, and promises made in sales conversations weren't communicated to the rest of the team. Generally, there was broad concern across the group that these implementation slip-ups were creating a negative customer experience at the worst possible time, unnecessarily undermining customer confidence in whatever they'd just bought.

Naturally, we spent time exploring possible solutions: better customer relationship management (CRM), better communication, formal protocols for hand-offs, team structure, even sales incentive plans. It was all pretty familiar stuff, if not always executed effectively. Of course, everyone duly made a few notes for incremental improvements once back in the office, but no one felt particularly excited about any one of the ideas. Honestly, there was a sort of nagging feeling in the room that we were somehow collectively missing something.

That's when Mark, a veteran sales leader at a global logistics company, who'd been quietly reflecting at his seat, jumped in with something completely different. "Actually," he said, "my problem is a little different. Is anyone starting to see this?" Mark proceeded to share a different kind of implementation challenge rapidly emerging across his teams. And his observation flipped the entire conversation on its head.

As a well-known global provider with decades of experience, he explained, their team had overcome many of the implementation challenges others were still seeking to address—they weren't perfect, but challenges were isolated, not systemic. That wasn't the problem. Even better, customers sensed the same thing. By and large, customers believed Mark's company would support both implementation and long-term value realization effectively, professionally, and more or less exactly as proposed. The problem, Mark explained, wasn't that customers lacked confidence in *his* company; rather they lacked confidence in their own, telling his teams things like, "We know you guys will come through, but we'll find a way to mess it up anyway." This was especially true for larger, more complex accounts where customers had to adapt technology, modify processes, and retrain personnel to take full advantage of the new solution. Especially troublesome, however, this lack of confidence wasn't slowing down implementations, it was slowing down *sales*. Customers who were worried they were going to fail post purchase were increasingly reluctant to make the purchase in the first place. Especially in those deals, Mark and his team realized they needed to spend just as much time and effort across a sale reducing customers' fear that their own company would not *achieve* full value as they did on reducing their fear that his company would not *deliver* it.

Bottom line, Mark told the room, when it comes to reducing customer concerns about smooth implementation and long-term value realization, this early trend made him wonder whether he actually had a problem with customers' perceptions of his company, or, in fact, he was facing a rapidly increasing problem with customers' perceptions of their own.

He was right to wonder.

IT'S NOT YOU, IT'S US

Addressing customers' outcome uncertainty proves especially challenging as it stems as much from human psychology as it does from process complexity. To be sure, there are undoubtedly steps suppliers can take to boost the likelihood that customers realize greater value from a purchase. But equally important are suppliers' efforts to boost customers' *belief* that they will realize greater value from a purchase. The two are absolutely related, but definitively not the same. In addressing either, however, sellers will first have to stop focusing on their ability to *deliver* value and instead build customers' belief in their own ability to *extract* value.

To demonstrate, let's use a B2C sales example many of us will know—considering a gym membership. Perhaps it's the new year and you've resolved, New Year, New You. You're going to eat better, sleep better, start yoga, build some muscle, and finally lose those extra pounds. So you put on your best athleisure and go tour the local big-box gym. You're a little wary, of course, as you want to avoid getting locked into a long-term contract, but you have to admit, you're impressed. This place has everything! Great equipment, clean locker rooms, endless classes, friendly staff. But as you take the tour, you're still stuck with nagging doubt: "But will I actually *use* it?" It's not that you doubt the gym; you doubt yourself. And in the end, you choose to pass not because you're afraid that the gym will disappoint you, but that *you* will disappoint you.

Now, if you're on the big-box gym corporate team selling memberships, you see this problem and think, we've got to do something! But what, exactly? Clearly, we've got to do everything we can to show potential members all the ways we can help them meet their goals! So we set about demonstrating to customers just how serious we are about helping them meet their goals. New membership contracts: "Cancel anytime!" New locations: "Right in your backyard!" More convenience: "Classes when you want them!" More support: "Personal trainers!" And most of all, new amenities! Olympic-size pools! Day care! Rock-climbing walls! Splash pads! Juice bars!! No doubt, gyms are doing everything they can to de-risk the purchase. There's no way customers wouldn't be confident in making this choice. It's got everything!

No doubt, for some prospective new members, the gym has won the battle of customers' confidence in their facilities. But for others, they haven't won the equally important battle for customers' belief in their own ability to take sufficient advantage of those facilities. And to be fair, many of us are right to be concerned. The fact that gyms thin out dramatically after the first two months of the New Year isn't because the gyms are doing anything different. The juice bar is still open, but there are dramatically fewer members there to enjoy it. The rest are home beating themselves up for believing yet again that this time was going to be different. This was going to be the year they stuck with it. And then it wasn't. Probably best to not even try next time. Pass the Tostitos.

Let's face it. That's real life.

But it's also real business. After a couple hard lessons spending millions on a new solution that your company never fully leverages, you begin to collectively think twice about buying the next one—no matter how much value the supplier can legitimately claim to have generated elsewhere, even in similar circumstances. After all, that was at other companies, not this one. We're different. We'll find a way to mess it up. It's not you, it's us.

MANAGING THE PHYSICS OF FEAR

Our friends Matt Dixon and Ted McKenna document a version of this phenomenon in data-driven detail in *The JOLT Effect*.[1] In contrast to FOMO, the fear of missing out, Dixon and McKenna introduce the idea of FOMU, the fear of messing up. In B2B buying, that fear can be a great motivator for sticking with the status quo—for choosing not to choose. After all, while it is absolutely true that no choice is still a choice, it is equally true that a choice for the status quo is a choice for the known over the unknown. Safety over risk. At least in the minds of customers afraid they'll mess things up.

But fear is a funny thing. In certain contexts, fear can *motivate* change as much as discourage it. Across our two *Challenger* books, *The Challenger Sale* and *The Challenger Customer*, we introduce the concept of commercial insight, which sellers can use to challenge customers' thinking by showing them new ways to make money, save money, or mitigate risk in a manner they'd either underappreciated or overlooked altogether.[2] The whole idea of commercial insight is to incite customers to abandon the status quo and embrace organizational change by demonstrating convincingly (and diplomatically) that the cost of maintaining their current behavior far outweighs the price and pain of embracing a new capability or course of action. We frequently describe this process as convincing customers that "the pain of same is greater than the pain of change," where fear (or unease, or discomfort) of the status quo is a *motivator* of change, enabling customers to willingly embrace an alternate course of action (one that ideally leads to the purchase of your solution).

The problem is, while commercial insight serves as a powerful way to disrupt customers' current behavior by breaking their mental model, the practical reality is, the more disruptive the idea (and the behavior change it entails), the higher the risk that customers' fear of messing up will ultimately drive them back to the very status quo you just pried them out of. In the end, many companies find themselves motivated to change, but simultaneously struggling to relinquish the status quo out of fear their organization will prove unable to execute change effectively, possibly leaving them actually worse off than where they started. So, they're sort of stuck between fear of missing out and fear of messing up.

This kind of tension not only leads to organizational paralysis—or, at the very least, decision sluggishness—but it can also cause individual exhaustion and a deep-seated sense of resignation. In our gym analogy, think of someone who's become convinced—maybe by a doctor or a health scare—that they need to lose weight, but they are equally convinced that, for whatever reason, that challenge will be insurmountable. So they're left stuck somewhere in the middle knowing they can't keep doing what they're doing, but struggling to know how to move forward without failing. It's a miserable place to be, regardless of whether you're on a personal journey or an organizational one.

At this point, what you need is someone to take you by the hand—figuratively in the business world, at least—and guide you step-by-step not just through the decision but along the journey beyond, to ensure you stay the course and realize the promise of the change you've chosen. Someone to make it easier, building your confidence that, yes, you can—whether it's reducing your BMI or swapping your CRM. Whatever that change may be.

Bottom line, when it comes to managing outcome uncertainty, think of Framemaking as a fear-reduction toolkit.

TWO TYPES OF OUTCOME UNCERTAINTY—PROCESS VS. PSYCHOLOGY

Very much like the other three challenges undermining customer confidence—decision complexity, information overload, and objective misalignment—reducing outcome uncertainty has a strong process component to it. Central to each of these challenges is some sort of organizational activity—decision-making, information gathering, strategy setting—that's become overly complicated or difficult, leading to confusion, frustration, and frequent exhaustion. Outcome uncertainty is no different with respect to value realization.

At the same time, more so than with any other force undermining customer decision confidence, outcome uncertainty presents an especially tough psychological obstacle, given its speculative nature. For any B2B deal, but especially a complex one, a relatively accurate understanding of the eventual performance of that solution is critical to justify its purchase. Yet, along the purchase journey itself, prior to solution acquisition and implementation, customers can't actually *know* the outcome of that purchase decision. Instead, they must guess—or estimate, if you prefer. And by necessity, guessing (estimating) is an inexact science. Typically, it's a complex mixture of hard evidence and directionally accurate data, spackled together by a slurry of gut feel, past experience, current perspective, and raw skill, all blended by a finger in the wind. It's that nexus of rational thought and subconscious instinct known as behavioral economics. And in many ways, it's remarkable how much of B2B buying rests on its application, especially when solving for outcome uncertainty.

What exactly does all this mean for customers' decision confidence? And how exactly can Framemaking help? Let's briefly examine each dimension—process and psychology—in more detail, and then we'll look at how we might address each through the lenses of establish, engage, and execute.

A Process View of Outcome Uncertainty—Providing Implementation Guidance

When we first discovered the incredible impact of B2B buyers' decision confidence on the likelihood of winning a high-quality, low-regret deal, we naturally spent months testing ways one might impact that confidence. One especially successful approach was for suppliers to ensure customers realized maximum purchase value through effective integration. Dramatically, customers scored nearly three times higher on decision confidence when they perceived suppliers as supporting their implementation efforts across three dimensions.

The first dimension is all about planning support. Customers' self-confidence climbs dramatically higher when the supplier selling to them not only lays out a clear implementation plan *prior* to purchase but also ensures that relevant customer stakeholders involved in—or impacted by—that plan understand and agree to their role in its deployment. Irrespective of new customer acquisition or existing customer expansion, tasks are set. Owners are assigned. Orders of operation and necessary contingencies are identified. Timelines are clear. And buy-in is documented. Essentially, it's an end-to-end project plan laying out both supplier activity and customer activity. Though, to be clear, the impact on decision confidence arises not so much from the existence of the plan but stakeholders' *alignment* around it. To that end, sellers who think, "Yeah, we do this already. We provide customers detailed guidance on implementation already. In fact, I sent that deck to the prospect just yesterday," are likely missing a huge opportunity to significantly boost customers' decision confidence by ensuring customer stakeholders actually engage with it, provide feedback, and collectively agree to both the overall proposal and each stakeholder's role in it. For many sellers, that kind of effort lands squarely in the big bucket of "not my problem." But the data clearly indicate, while it may not be their problem, it absolutely is their *opportunity*. Sellers who help to align customer stakeholders on postsale integration prior to deal close can dramatically boost customers' belief that their organization is implementation capable and therefore purchase ready.

The second way suppliers can boost decision confidence through integration support is all about offering customers actual tools to help support that integration as it happens. Of course, depending on the nature of the solution being sold, integration tools could range anywhere from tech support, on-call experts, computer code, mechanical assistance, or any number of tutorials, videos, or other content. Really, the sky is the limit (as long as it's actually helpful). It's whatever customers might find useful to materially increase their chances of successfully installing and extracting value from their purchase.

That said, with these data, remember, we're specifically focused on the potential impact of these attributes on customers' decision confidence (i.e., the degree to which they feel sufficiently confident to make a large-scale purchase). For these attributes to impact customers' decision confidence, then, customers must perceive them *prior* to making a purchase. That means that sellers who overlook—or even purposefully avoid—a conversation about solution implementation, perhaps worried that it might distract customers from the sale or unnecessarily give them something else to worry about, are missing a huge opportunity to boost customers' confidence in making that purchase to begin with. Indeed, we've seen a number of companies, including Mark's, introduce implementation teams directly into the sales process, beginning to guide customers step-by-step through implementation long before the deal is ever done. They're doing so not simply in an effort to get a head start on implementation, presuming the deal closes. In fact, just the opposite. They're presuming nothing. Rather, they're bringing integration support and guidance into the sale to increase the chances of winning the deal in the first place by framing customers' efforts to ultimately realize value. They're giving customers confidence that integration will prove easier than anticipated, reducing their fear they're simply setting their money on fire because their team will find a way to botch the implementation.

Finally, suppliers that connect prospective buyers to a robust community network significantly boost decision confidence by reducing outcome uncertainty. Across the last several years, customer communities have risen dramatically in popularity among B2B suppliers. Of course, some of the biggest and best known have been around for decades, including the Microsoft Partner Community and the Salesforce Trailblazer Community. But with widespread use of social media and virtual communication, it's hard to imagine an industry, category, or even company that doesn't either maintain or directly support some sort of user or customer community. And from a Framemaking perspective, it's easy to see why. The value to customers of learning from other companies like them seems nearly boundless, no matter whether they're seeking help on what to buy, how to buy, whom to buy from, or, in this case, how to ensure maximum value from the purchase once it's bought. Customers can learn a great deal from others' implementation efforts, whether effective or failed. Even better, in a community setting, that information is likely available in any number of ways, depending on how the community operates—through in-person events, virtual meetings, archived content, online videos, one-on-one interactions, you name it. Better still, community members can access that insight prior to a purchase, not just after, providing a great deal of reassurance. It's sort of like, "Before I jump off this cliff for the very first time with my hang glider, let me ask other beginning hang gliders like me what they wished they'd done differently once they were in the air." Those are not only great things to know before you take off; they're great things to know to help determine whether you take off at all. To that end, suppliers would do well to reserve a corner of community activity specifically for implementation advice—the Dos and Don'ts of Value Realization, as it were. Even better would be to focus a significant portion of that content on supplier agnostic advice, taking prospective customers methodically through the necessary steps inside their own organization to ensure they're ready to realize value. That kind of value realization framework could prove invaluable, especially to customers buying a particular kind of solution for the first time, or the first time in a long time.

That said, we're not suggesting, of course, that individual sellers set up their own customer community. While it's not inconceivable to do so—especially online—for most it isn't very practical, particularly at scale. Instead, when we turn to our three E's momentarily, we'll examine how sellers might leverage existing communities to diminish outcome uncertainty and promote customer confidence. But first, we need to dive into the psychology of expectations and outcome uncertainty.

A Psychological View of Outcome Uncertainty

Undoubtedly, providing customers clear guidance on navigating their internal minefield of implementation complexity can dramatically reduce their outcome uncertainty, but it can't eliminate it. Certainly not for everyone, as different stakeholders will see the exact same organizational purchase from completely different perspectives. In fact, stakeholders in the same company—sometimes on the same team—can have wildly divergent expectations regarding the likelihood of a purchase paying off as planned. Note, unlike in Chapter 5, where we focused on "What are we trying to do?" and "How will we know when we get there?," here, we're asking, "How likely is that to actually happen?" And when it comes to an answer, some stakeholders are naturally going to be more optimistic, while others prove more pessimistic (we're looking at you, finance). We might think of this as outcome-uncertainty variability.

What's more, individual stakeholders' personal expectations may vary as well—either as circumstances change across a purchase journey, or simply as a result of any number of reasons for uncertainty. Those expectations might vary a little or a lot—anywhere from "We might be off by a few points one way or another," to "We're either gonna be heroes or looking for a new job!" Yet, this kind of variability typically isn't accounted for in most B2B sales strategies or opportunity qualification scores.

Does it matter? Emphatically, yes. Variability in outcome expectations is an absolute killer of confidence. In their book *Noise: A Flaw in Human Judgment*, Daniel Kahneman, Olivier Sibony, and Cass Sunstein discuss how higher variability in judgments (referred to as "noise") can make decision-making more difficult. They explain that when there is a lot of variability in how different people assess the same situation, it can lead to inconsistent and unpredictable outcomes, making it harder to make clear and confident choices.[3]

This is exactly why all the hard work of stakeholder alignment introduced in Chapter 5 matters so much. However, even when fully aligned around objectives, tactics, and results, different stakeholders are still likely to apply different discount rates to the expected value realized from that purchase. As a result, it becomes especially important to identify each stakeholder's disposition toward purchase outcomes to determine the level of overall variability in expectations across a buying group. That will allow us, in turn, to assess and ultimately improve customers' level of decision confidence.

Putting it all together, if we want to address flagging customer confidence arising from outcome uncertainty, we'll need to provide customers clear, supplier agnostic implementation guidance while addressing residual variability in expectations.

How do we do that? Let's return to the three E's: establish, engage, execute.

FRAMING CUSTOMERS' EXPECTED OUTCOMES— RETHINKING VALUE REALIZATION

In many ways, the discipline of value realization is an already well-established, mission-critical component of many companies' customer success efforts. That's no surprise as the entire customer success function is grounded in an effort to ensure customers realize maximum value from a completed purchase in order to drive retention and secure the groundwork for future expansion. With Frame-making, however, we're seeking to achieve something different. Our goal is to boost the likelihood of a purchase in the first place, meaning we need to pull value realization conversations forward from postsale to presale, using them to create with customers a clear, more certain path to value long before they commit to stepping onto that path to begin with.

We'll need to invent a new kind of value realization altogether—effectively an anticipatory form of value realization so that customers feel sufficiently confident to set forth on a purchase journey. After all, our primary objective in boosting customers' decision confidence isn't to help them feel good about a purchase they've already made, but to feel confident in a purchase they have yet to make.

ESTABLISHING A FRAME FOR REDUCING OUTCOME UNCERTAINTY

As the two dimensions of outcome uncertainty—procedural and psychological—are related but distinct, we can develop parallel tactics for addressing each.

The Process for Value Realization

In many respects, the process by which one might establish a frame for guiding customers through solution implementation will look very similar to the it-turns-out-that audit introduced in Chapter 3. The primary difference between the two isn't how you conduct the audit, but rather what each audit is trying to discover. When solving for decision complexity (Chapter 3), we're focused on the specific steps customers might take to reduce effort and avoid landmines along a purchase journey. When solving for outcome uncertainty (in this chapter), we're focused on the specific steps customers might take to reduce effort and avoid landmines along a postpurchase implementation journey. In both cases, however, we're seeking to increase and sustain customer confidence as early as possible in the actual sale.

One of the best ways to help customers identify where they might struggle with implementation is to ask similar customers who've been down that path already. The insight they can provide in those conversations is absolutely invaluable. No question, there are a multitude of more formal or scalable ways to gather this information through centralized teams in sales enablement, marketing, customer success, or customer experience, using tools like customer surveys, focus groups, and AI-powered data analytics. But there's no reason why individual sellers can't gather at least some of this information on their own through simple, old-fashioned one-on-one interactions.

In fact, there's a strong case to be made that individual seller conversation leads to better results than anonymous organizational surveys—perhaps not in scale or scope, but in terms of customer connection and authenticity. Compare a sales conversation about implementation that starts with, "I was speaking to a senior executive in your same role just a week ago about their experience rolling out this approach, and she told me that one of the things she really wished they'd done differently is . . ." versus a conversation that begins with, "We've collected data from two thousand customers across every major industry rolling out this approach, and 83 percent agreed that the number one thing they wished they'd done differently is . . ." Which one do you prefer? For many, the research orientation and depth of data in the second option is undoubtedly compelling. However, there's something powerfully appealing about the first option. It just feels more human and real. As a customer, I'm not sure whether I'm like two thousand companies collected in a random sample. But I do relate to senior executives in the same role. The point being most sellers could likely generate 80 percent of the value of larger organizational initiatives simply by chatting with a few customers already down the integration path.

Again, the same two questions from Chapter 3 can also prove invaluable here in establishing a value realization frame sharable with others:

1. If you had to start completely over implementing this solution, what would you do differently (and why)?
2. If you were speaking with a peer executive about to embark on the same journey, what advice would you give them, to make their lives easier and help them avoid potential landmines?

At a more advanced level, a seller might aggregate the input from those conversations into a framework enumerating implementation challenges, along with possible solutions, designed in a way to help customers feel more ready rather than more overwhelmed when it comes to actual implementation. That kind of framework could take on any number of different form factors: a graphic-based map, an integration-readiness benchmark, an implementation diagnostic exercise, or perhaps some sort of red flags guide containing early warning signs of endangered value realization. Ideally any of these tools (or others) could be produced by a central team and broadly distributed, possibly even through digital channels. In fact, that might indeed be the more efficient way to produce this kind of value realization framework. However, in the absence of organizational support, most sellers could likely mock up a simplified version based on how current customers navigate implementation obstacles.

The Psychology of Managing Variability in Outcome Expectations

But how might we simultaneously address variability in stakeholder expectations in a way that builds sufficient collective confidence to proceed with a purchase? In other areas of business management (e.g., strategy, finance, management) scenario planning is often used as a powerful means for managing effectively while still embracing—or at least acknowledging—a relatively high degree of outcome uncertainty. Scenario planning is particularly effective as it allows for clear, confident action despite unclear or unpredictable business conditions. For our purposes in B2B buying, we can adapt this approach to help customer stakeholders align around a complex purchase decision despite variable expectations by offering insight into both a range of likely outcomes from that purchase and the concrete steps they can take to increase the chances of one outcome over another. How exactly? Scenario planning as Framemaking follows four steps:

1. IDENTIFY THE RANGE OF POSSIBLE OUTCOMES.

The first step is identifying the most likely range of purchase outcomes based on the documented, real-world experiences of similar organizations operating in comparable contexts that have already made an equivalent purchase. It is important to note, however, that this isn't simply the collection of customer success stories that every company posts proudly on their website. The emphasis here isn't on celebrating success but on defining a likely range of results. Oftentimes, this is exactly the kind of information suppliers seek to suppress, as they want to convey the impression that every purchase of their solution is an unmitigated success. But that's simply not realistic. And customers know it. "Everyone lived happily ever after" may be a common fairytale ending, but it's by no means a guaranteed business ending. So, what are other possible endings? Document those as well. Yes, the incredible successes, but also the minor disappointments. What does it look like, exactly, when things don't go completely to plan?

That's not to suggest, of course, that suppliers should publicly air all their dirty laundry. After all, nearly every supplier has at least one unmitigated disaster under their belt that they're hoping never sees the light of day, usually the result of a pretty unique set of circumstances. But that's not what we're after here anyway. The upper and lower outliers aren't nearly as helpful as the middle of the bell curve. What does an average/typical outcome look like? What about just below average, and just above? How much of a delta in outcomes might one actually expect should things go slightly better or worse than plan? Let's face it, this is exactly what various stakeholders are trying to understand anyway in predicting results for their own organization. So why make it hard to find that information and undermine decision confidence as a result?

Now, lest you're thinking it sounds completely bonkers to admit to customers that sometimes companies don't always realize maximum value from your solution, we're going to turn that admission into an advantage across the following three steps. As we move through them, remember our primary goal isn't to convince customers that we're great, but to boost customers' self-confidence by acknowledging, addressing, and then reducing outcome expectation variability.

2. DETERMINE THE ROUGH LIKELIHOOD OF EACH OUTCOME.

Once we've identified a range of possible outcomes from the purchase of our solution, we'll want to weigh them according to probability and articulate them as possible outcome scenarios. For now, we'll call those outcomes x–baseline, y–exceeding expectations, and z–improvement needed, but as a seller, when you share these scenarios with customers, it's important—when possible—to denominate them in terms of the specific metric(s) customer stakeholders have aligned on as part of the OTR exercise introduced in Chapter 5. For example, "Eighty percent of customers saw results ranging from the baseline of x to exceeding expectations of y, while 10 percent achieved a slightly lower result between the improvement needed level of z and the baseline of x. The remaining 10 percent achieved exceptional results outside the normal range."

Notice how different this language is relative to a traditional customer success story. In fact, some sellers might be breaking out in hives reading this and thinking, "Why in the world would I ever want to show this kind of information to a customer? It's just going to cause doubt!" But actually, we're solving for the exact opposite effect. And sharing ranges like this can prove extremely valuable for two reasons.

First, the goal in providing a range of outcomes is to cast a sufficiently wide net to capture as many stakeholders' expectations as possible. If customer stakeholders are going to apply different discount rates to the likelihood of realizing value from the purchase of your solution, we want to make sure that whatever outcome they expect to see after applying that discount falls somewhere within this range. That matters because we're ultimately going to provide practical guidance on how they can improve their chances of landing in a better scenario. However, that kind of guidance feels relevant and valuable only if customers see their original expectations within one of those scenarios to begin with. Otherwise, it'll feel like we're helping them repair a window to keep out the rain in a house with no roof—essentially irrelevant.

Second, this range of outcomes creates helpful boundaries for customer expectations. If we simply show customers the single best-case scenario, they'll recognize it as such—the best possible case—and absent any helpful guidance from us, they'll fill in the blanks regarding the kinds of returns they believe are more realistic, which they may in fact presume to be much lower (we'd call this a false negative problem). By sharing data-driven ranges, we essentially set a lower bound to their expectations while providing a more realistic outcome for their organization. Without this kind of bounding, in other words, we may either fail to address customer outcome uncertainty at all, or fail to reduce it, as the results they imagine for their own organization are so wildly divergent from the results we shared from our raving fan. By focusing on telling the best version of *our* story, we've completely missed an opportunity to build customers' confidence in *their* story, putting a high-quality, low-regret deal at greater risk as a result.

That said, for those still scratching under their collars furiously, fear not, the goal here is not to simply share the less varnished truth of potential outcomes from our solution and then leave customers to figure out on their own how to optimize those outcomes. The whole point of scenarios is to create context for offering help.

3. DIAGNOSE THE DRIVERS OF EACH SCENARIO.

Step 3 is to determine why specific customers realize different levels of value. Those reasons are most likely related to people, process, or technology. Essentially, it's a root-cause analysis to explain variable levels of value realization from the purchase of essentially the same solution.

Should that sound like a complex task, fear not, as much of this knowledge already resides in your own organization among the implementation teams, customer success reps, and account managers who share a front-row seat to customers' solution integration efforts every single day. Typically, even a few brief conversations with members of those teams will reveal a relatively complete list of reasons why some companies succeed where others struggle. In the tech space, for example, the implementation team might have uncovered a little-known but highly disruptive software compatibility issue that can be easily addressed as long as one knows what to look for. Or in business services, implementation teams may have learned how to win over frontline managers to greatly increase the successful rollout of a new training initiative.

That said, we're especially interested, of course, in nonidiosyncratic drivers of value. Or, as we like to say, the exportable lessons that can apply broadly across a wide range of diverse organizations. While the lessons we seek come from companies who've already made the purchase, of course, the primary objective in sharing those experiences is to help companies still navigating the purchase to see themselves in that story. Ultimately, our goal is to be able to prompt their awareness around future implementation obstacles and opportunities such that they feel more confident now in their own ability to maximize value from the purchase down the road.

4. IDENTIFY THE ACTIONS MOST LIKELY TO PROMOTE A PARTICULAR OUTCOME.

The final step is to translate those implementation stories into specific actions prospective customers can pursue post purchase to mitigate downside risk while maximizing upside potential. So, if the lessons learned from step 3 resonate with a customer, the Framemaking seller can prompt the customer buying group to identify the specific actions they'll take (along with owners, influencers, and timelines) to ensure that lesson is applied as part of their implementation process. In many ways, the best sellers do this almost instinctively, helping customers anticipate implementation problems and identify means to maximize returns prior to purchase in an effort to ensure customers feel more confident in their ability to realize maximum value once that decision is made.

The goal here isn't to present customers with a fully formed implementation plan that they simply need to follow step-by-step. Remember, the key to effective Framemaking is not just ease, but also agency. And when it comes to reducing customers' outcome uncertainty, our goal isn't to simply solve for customers' confidence in their ability to follow our instructions. Rather we're solving for their confidence in their ability to manage solution implementation as it unfolds inside their unique organizational environment. We're teaching them to fish rather than giving them fish.

Our primary objective in presenting customers with various outcome scenarios is to connect and align them with each other, aligning otherwise divergent stakeholder expectations as best we can to create as unified an answer as possible to their collective question, "Is this going to work?"

ENGAGING CUSTOMERS BY FRAMING EXPECTATIONS

Let's face it, many of us in sales tend to think in extremes. The entire profession is sort of wired to work that way: For quota, it's either hit or miss. For President's Club, you either made it or missed it. For deals, it's either won or lost. And for colleagues, you're either helping me advance a deal, or you're completely dead to me (as at least one of us has heard numerous times from our dear friend and sales savant, Christian).

But in the complicated reality of complex B2B deals, not everything in sales represents a rounding error between zero and infinity. There's a lot of gray area between all that black and white. And that's where B2B buying both lives and dies. It's funny, sellers are frequently told they need to meet customers where they are, without much further elaboration. But when it comes to outcome uncertainty, that means meeting your customer somewhere in the ambiguous gray area where nothing is nearly so cut-and-dried as the amazing results we're all sharing in the carousel of Fortune 50 logos scrolling across the front page of our websites. From a customer's perspective, the far more likely reaction to those kinds of outcomes is probably a mixed bag at best.

Given the way they're wired—supported by the way they're trained—most sellers seek to paint an unambiguous picture of hugely positive customer impact. No exceptions. Everyone succeeds! Yet, especially in deals with a high degree of variability around outcome expectations, this kind of Pollyannaish messaging simply rings hollow, if not completely untrue among those stakeholders with more tempered expectations.

"But those claims are 100 percent true!" you might argue. And to be fair, you might be right. But are they true for everyone? Can your company legitimately claim that past performance at one organization guarantees future results for all others? Unlikely. And yet, by leaning exclusively on our best customer success stories, we're essentially signaling exactly that, an unbelievable truth. And while our credibility may take a hit in the process, that hit likely isn't too damaging, as every other B2B supplier is doing the same thing. The greater damage, arguably, isn't an error of commission, but an error of omission. We're purposefully walking right past an opportunity to reduce the "noise" around customer stakeholders' outcome expectations, leaving them to overcome on their own the reduced confidence that noise creates.

Simply put, our over-the-top, optimistic messaging around customer outcomes fundamentally fails to reduce either the outcome uncertainty or the expectation variability eroding customer decision confidence.

What's the alternative?

To be clear, we're not suggesting that Framemaking sellers refrain from sharing stories of customer success. But imagine if they followed them up with this:

"Sometimes this doesn't go as well as we'd hope. And you can imagine, we lose right along with our customers when that happens. So, we've spent a huge amount of time assessing the range of outcomes most customers can realistically expect to achieve, and then diagnosing exactly where things can go wrong. I'd love to share with you what we've learned to help you make sure you're getting the most possible value from this solution."

Maybe the seller shares a graphical implementation minefield at that point, or runs through an implementation-readiness checklist. Regardless of what they might share, Framemaking sellers are seeking to frame the implementation process—simplify it and make it feel more manageable. So the point of framing isn't to simply inventory all of the many ways implementation might go wrong, but rather to understand the key drivers of outcome variability and work with customers to ensure they have a plan in place to mitigate downside risk of underperformance and amplify the drivers most closely associated with achievement exceeding expectations.

Either way, like so many similar lessons across preceding chapters, when it comes to outcome uncertainty, Framemaking sellers run right at purchase difficulty rather than away. They've determined that the difficulty represents the single biggest hurdle preventing purchase progress as it undermines customer decision confidence.

Rather than trying to either ignore or squelch outcome uncertainty, Framemaking sellers acknowledge up front that a single purchase can lead to multiple outcomes, depending on a wide range of variables. And they proactively assume the responsibility of helping customers manage those variables: "We've come to understand the primary drivers that lead to missed value realization targets. It tends to come down to one of three things. It's probably good we talk about those and put a plan in place to ensure that doesn't happen to you."

For anyone thinking, "Our team has that conversation with customers every single day . . . on our customer success team," that's great news! The real question is, "How do we pull that conversation forward in time, making it part of the sale itself?" In an ideal world, customer success isn't initiating that conversation but sustaining it.

EXECUTING A FRAMEMAKING STRATEGY
TO REDUCE OUTCOME UNCERTAINTY

As we consider the specific tactics a Framemaking seller might employ to reduce customers' outcome uncertainty, many will feel familiar by now. In most ways, the toolkit for framing customer outcomes largely resembles the greatest hits from the Framemaking toolkit for decision complexity and objective misalignment.

That said, the application of these tactics works a little differently here as there's an important time displacement element to framing outcome uncertainty absent from any other challenge undermining customers' decision confidence. Specifically, Framemaking sellers are seeking today to boost customers' confidence in their ability to realize value sometime in the *future*. In fact, for especially long purchase cycles of highly complex solutions, customers may not realize the full value of that purchase until *years* later. To be sure, the distance in time between a seller's Framemaking efforts and customers choosing to make a purchase might, in fact, be quite small. So, sellers can determine relatively quickly whether their framing efforts around outcome uncertainty actually worked. But from the customers' perspective, they're more or less placing an often sizable bet on a future outcome. The payoff is deferred, and therefore less certain.

In many ways, that distinction may not feel particularly material to the specific tactics of framing. But it does speak in some ways to the higher burden on Framemaking sellers to build customer confidence around outcomes sufficiently high to overcome concerns from potential intervening variables that might negatively impact those outcomes over time. Bottom line, sufficiently addressing customers' outcome uncertainty is no easy feat. And as we saw earlier, many of the tools we currently rely on to do so today are just as likely to undermine customers' decision confidence as increase it. Clearly, this will take some practice.

With that in mind, let's review some of the available tools in our Framemaking toolkit through the lens of reducing customers' outcome uncertainty.

Conducting Implementation Alignment Workshops

We reviewed stakeholder alignment workshops in significant detail in Chapter 5 as an effective means for aligning customer stakeholders around a common set of objectives, tactics, and results. In some ways, a workshop designed to establish a clear path to value realization will look similar logistically, but there are some important operational differences:

1. STARTING POINT

One might assume the starting point of any value realization workshop might be a discussion of how to define value in the first place. Seems logical. But remember, that was the expressed purpose of the stakeholder objective alignment workshop. The concrete output of that meeting should be a clear articulation of the specific objectives, tactics, metrics, targets, and timelines the buying group will use to ultimately determine whether the purchase was justified. To that end, "value" is already defined.

An implementation workshop takes that OTR_{MTT} as a given and starts instead with five very practical, tactical questions:

a. How are we going to get there?

b. What resources will we need?

c. Are those resources currently available?

d. What's standing in our way?

e. How will we address/avoid those obstacles?

2. ATTENDEES

Just like the stakeholder alignment workshop, the Framemaking seller assumes the role of facilitator at the meeting (perhaps supported by one or two colleagues to capture notes and run meeting logistics). If the customer success representative likely to be assigned to the account should the customer choose to make a purchase has already been identified, it likely makes sense to have that person attend as well, as they will ultimately be responsible for shepherding the account toward value realization once they're on board. Finally, if the supplier supports new customers with some sort of implementation specialist or implementation engineer, it's a good idea to have that person there as well. (Note, these workshops can often be run quite effectively as either virtual or hybrid meetings if cost is a concern.) In both cases, the customer success rep and implementation expert should be active participants in the meeting, prompting (and bounding) consideration of important dimensions of implementation that customers might otherwise overlook. After all, they're the experts who work with existing customers every single day on executing implementation and value realization plans.

On the customer side, it's possible the same stakeholders who attended the OTR workshop may also attend the implementation alignment workshop. However, that may not always be the case, or even completely necessary. Essentially, setting objectives, tactics, and results is a strategic question, requiring input from senior executives. An implementation alignment workshop, on the other hand, is designed to answer an operational question: How shall we proceed in order to ensure we meet our agreed-upon targets on the agreed-upon timeline? The group of individuals responsible for crafting and then executing that plan may include professionals one or more levels deeper in the organization or attendees from functions directly connected to operational implementation but not involved in the strategy setting.

3. ROLE OF PROMPTING AND BOUNDING

Just as we saw in the OTR stakeholder workshop, the primary role of the Framemaking seller here is to prompt customers to consider implementation challenges (and opportunities) they might have otherwise overlooked on their own. This is where the homework laid out in "establish" above really pays off. That said, it's important for facilitators to guide participants to a short, bounded list of action items as a result of the workshop. Remember, the central goal of all Framemaking is to help customers feel more confident, not more overwhelmed.

As one facilitates an examination of obstacles potentially standing in the way of successful value realization, it's easy to let a meeting like this slip into a general airing of grievances and lamentations. Rather than allowing the meeting to devolve into a venting session, the Framemaking seller should direct participants to analyze root causes of obstacles and brainstorm potential solutions rather than simply catalog them. Ultimately, the meeting should feel optimistic and future oriented.

4. MEETING OUTPUT

Ideally, the concrete output of the meeting is a kind of roadmap to value realization. Whether it simply takes the form of a bulleted list or is eventually converted into something more graphical, the objective is to create a framework for value realization—an actual artifact depicting the journey to outcome certainty that both participants and members of the buying group can look at and feel sufficiently confident to make the purchase as a result.

Mapping the Minefield of Solution Implementation— Sequence of Events Revisited

Picking up on the output from the implementation alignment workshop, one might imagine either depicting or converting that artifact as a sequence of events similar to the document we encountered in Chapter 3. Here, the design principles—including its use as a customer verifier—and use case are largely identical, with the one critical difference being this sequence of events is designed to map the step-by-step journey to value realization rather than to purchase decision. In other words, the two operate in sequence—a roadmap to purchase, and a roadmap to value—each providing step-by-step verification of customers' progress along that journey.

In the case of a value realization sequence of events, however, we encounter the time-displacement phenomenon we encountered earlier. The *creation* of the document is a powerful means to boost customer confidence prior to purchase by decreasing outcome uncertainty. The *execution* of the document, on the other hand, serves as a valuable means for customers and customer success to collaboratively make good on that value promise, once the purchase is made.

Providing Social Proof Through Community Participation

Throughout this book we have examined many ways in which social proof can play a powerful role in boosting customers' decision confidence. When it comes to reducing customers' outcome uncertainty, the potential power of social proof in alleviating customers' fears of implementation missteps and unrealized value is no different. As we saw in the data, one way to make that happen is through a customer community.

The operational nuts and bolts of establishing a customer community lie well beyond the scope of this book, but for Framemaking sellers with access to a customer community already, there is a wide variety of powerful ways one might use that community to boost customer decision confidence.

Sellers might tap community members to establish a frame for managing potential buyers' outcome uncertainty—by asking existing community members to reflect on lessons learned post purchase that would have helped them feel more confident when they made their purchase, for example.

Sellers can create any number of ad hoc or recurring events inside the community to specifically address prospective customers' implementation concerns. Webinars, brown bags, panel discussions. Really, the sky's the limit.

Sellers can set up moderated topic boards inside online communities, inviting existing customers to share their experiences on effective value realization.

Or, of course (and especially if your organization doesn't already have a dedicated customer community), sellers can simply broker connections between prospective customers and existing customers, suggesting they connect and discuss the topics causing the prospective customer the most agita.

We've come to the end of our deep dive into the four challenges dramatically undermining customers' decision confidence today.

Across the following three chapters, we'll broaden our scope a bit and set Framemaking into the broader organizational context of sales training and methodology, organizational capabilities, and marketing. After all, there's no doubt that individual sales professionals adopting a Framemaking posture can dramatically impact the likelihood that customers will complete a high-quality, low-regret purchase. But the real opportunity lies in an entire commercial team working together as a Framemaking organization.

CHAPTER 7

The Framemaking Mindset

A few years back, we were in Florida at Expedient's annual sales kickoff meeting. We'd just presented the idea of boosting customers' decision confidence through sensemaking when chief sales officer Bryan Smith stood up, looked around, and summarized the message in a single powerful sentence for his sales team: "Our team has one mission: to help our customers make the best decision they can, in as little time as possible. That's it," he said. "If we do that first, we'll win at everything else."

Today, Expedient is thriving, Bryan is CEO, and those sixteen words have stuck with us ever since as the single best summary of a Framemaking mindset. As sellers, we have one job above all others: to help our customers make great decisions. Decisions that they feel good about, that they're confident in, and that make sense for their company. Decisions customers can look back on, even years later, without regret.

We've since heard Bryan repeat those words on multiple occasions, and nearly every time, almost inevitably someone asks the obvious question: "But, Bryan, what happens if we help customers make the best decision they can, but the 'best' decision turns out to be buy from the competition?"

Bryan has always been the first to admit, it's a completely fair question. To which he offers an utterly defensible two-part answer:

"First, that's why we must strive to be the best. To offer our customers better solutions, greater value, and a world-class experience. That's why we need to help them understand why our unique strengths are also the capabilities they need most.

But, second, that's why 'in as little time as possible' matters. If we're gonna lose, let's lose early."

For Bryan, "in as little time as possible" isn't just a mandate to help customers move efficiently through their purchase process. It's also a reminder that, if customers are going to choose someone else, then let's figure that out sooner rather than later, and then go find a customer we actually can help. In that sense, Bryan has turned a Framemaking mindset into a powerful qualification tool.

But even in these cases, Bryan leans into the bigger, long-term picture:

"At the end of the day, if customers see our people as the one team truly dedicated to helping them make good choices on behalf of their company, then even if we lose that deal today, you can bet, we'll be the first ones they call when it's time to do the next deal. And over time, *that's* where we want to be: the first people customers call when they're looking to solve their toughest cloud computing challenges."

It's such a powerful perspective. As much as Expedient competes every single day with competitors boasting household brands, in Bryan's mind, Expedient isn't competing against the competition nearly so much as customer indecision, confusion, the status quo, and skepticism. If Expedient can conquer *those* competitors, then over time, they'll win disproportionately in a crowded, competitive market.

Strategically, Bryan isn't solving for Expedient selling more nearly so much as he is solving for helping customers with buying more. And buying better. Effectively, it's a supplier agnostic sales approach geared to generating more sales without directly solving for selling more.

MINDSET OVER SKILLSET

We started this book with a simple but powerful question: In a world where nearly three-quarters of B2B buyers of complex solutions report they'd prefer to make that purchase without ever speaking to a sales professional *at all*, how do we become the one sales professional—or sales team—that customers actually *do* want to talk to? Taking Bryan's lead, the answer doesn't start with a skillset, but a mindset:

How do we help customers make the best decision they can, in as little time as possible?

In Bryan's case, many of his sellers were already highly skilled, with years of tenure and sales experience. What he was ultimately trying to do was encourage his sellers to apply those skills in a dramatically different manner, inspired by a completely different view of how to conduct customer interactions altogether.

Undoubtedly, Framemaking requires strong ability across a range of sales skills considered by some, perhaps, to be more advanced—things like empathy, teaching, and trust building. But at a high level, all these skills have long been recognized as differentiating the very best sellers from everyone else. So, while they're critically important for sales success, they're neither particularly new nor sufficiently effective in the abstract to win back customers increasingly turned off from traditional sales interactions. What's critical for sales success today is the *application* of those skills in a specific manner to create deeper customer connection and drive real commercial impact. That application is Framemaking. It's the mindset that resets the skillset. To be sure, there are certain things sellers need to do differently for effective Framemaking, and we've laid those out in detail across preceding chapters using the lens of establish, engage, and execute. But at the highest level, Framemaking is first and foremost about *thinking* differently about our role as sales professionals, and then applying sales skills we've long recognized as important in new and powerful ways to build human connections and drive commercial results in today's radically different world of B2B buying.

So, let's dive into these two dimensions of connections and commerce and examine exactly how we might apply these sales skills specifically to support a Framemaking mindset.

CREATING A HUMAN CONNECTION

Shifting the prevailing B2B sales mindset toward a stronger customer orientation has been a common theme for years. Indeed, many sales leaders have enthusiastically embraced increased customer centricity in an effort to help their sellers stand out as trusted advisors in the eyes of customers, hoping that customers return the favor by putting the supplier first when it comes time to buy.

The Framemaking mindset, however, works in the exact opposite direction. Framemaking is far less about changing the way customers feel about *our* ability to impact their business, and far more about changing the way customers feel about *their* ability to impact their business, specifically through effective purchase decisions. To be sure, the ultimate goal is to increase sales, retention, and expansion, but for all the reasons we've laid out thus far, everything in the data tells us the best way by far to influence those results resides in our ability to ensure customers feel confident in their decision prior to feeling confident in our value. In many respects, it's not unlike how we might seek to interact with other individuals beyond a sales setting—in a manner that leaves them feeling better about themselves as a result of that interaction—more positive, more confident, more capable. Indeed, Framemaking arguably represents more of a human mindset than a sales mindset. It's about boosting sales by making a human connection over a business connection.

And lest you might think that sounds too touchy-feely for the traditionally rough-and-tumble world of B2B sales, where the only goal that matters is winning, hopefully we've laid out a sufficiently compelling case by now as to why this kind of human connection represents what we believe to be the shortest path possible to the kind of winning we all want to achieve: more high-quality, low-regret deals.

Building Human Acumen

We've seen "better business acumen" atop the list of desired sales skills in annual sales leader surveys for years. In interviews, we find the reasons are always the same: "We need our sellers to understand our customers' business, their strategic priorities, how they operate, and where they're struggling." Typically, the solutions were similar too: training on company financials, coaching on improved discovery, roleplays with internal executives, organizing into industry verticals, sourcing sellers from the target market. All in an effort to ensure sellers conduct better, deeper, more relevant customer conversations about their business.

Yet, if our primary opportunity to drive more high-quality, low-regret deals means making a *human* connection, then we'll need to think just as carefully and systematically about building human acumen as we currently do about business acumen. For some, that statement might sound like a horribly misguided idea, while to others it will carry a strong whiff of "no duh."

For the more skeptical, rest assured, we're emphatically *not* saying that business acumen doesn't matter, simply that human acumen equally does. To be sure, sellers still need to understand how customers' businesses operate, how they make money, the top challenges they face. But what's often missing from those efforts is an equally deep understanding of how customer stakeholders currently *feel* about their business. Are they confident? Worried? Frustrated? Excited? What about their colleagues? Their frontline employees? What kinds of hopes, aspirations, concerns, and conflicts currently impact those business decisions? How confident are individual stakeholders in their ability to drive change, win over colleagues, or even remain at their current employer? Are they excited about the future? Or exasperated by the current state of play? None of these things—at least on a personal level—show up in a company's annual report. Nor do many stakeholders openly discuss these feelings unprompted with a salesperson. Yet, these kinds of human forces dramatically shape business decisions every single day, even large, complex, strategic ones. It's funny, we're all taught to believe that companies operate in a predictable, rational manner, when in fact the only thing that's truly predictable is that they're run by humans (for now) and, as Dan Ariely puts it, humans aren't anything if they're not "predictably irrational."[1] And, in many ways, tapping into this behavioral and emotional side of business decisions is often the secret to sales success. Indeed, today's star performing sellers often fail to appreciate that they've already mastered this skill because, from their perspective, they're just being themselves when it comes to human interactions.

In fact, this is likely the single biggest objection on the "no duh" side when it comes to flagging the importance of human acumen. It all feels sort of patently obvious. After all, sellers are human beings (for now), so the human-interaction operating system comes pre-installed. No training necessary.

But that couldn't be further from the truth. If we're going to tap into the world of emotion and feeling, then we're going to need a robust toolkit that equips sellers not only to understand that world but to influence it productively. Fortunately, the skills best suited to helping customers feel more confident about themselves can absolutely be learned, practiced, and improved over time in very practical ways—skills like empathy, teaching, and trust building. No doubt, these are skills we've always recognized as valuable as they're all fundamental to every kind of human interaction. But let's face it, most of us have not mastered them by any stretch (including us), and for most companies these skills typically take a distant back seat in formal sales training programs to a more traditional focus on product knowledge and business acumen, simply because they feel less urgent. Even when training does touch on something like empathy or curiosity, it generally falls far short of highly tactical advice carefully tailored to the specific context of today's B2B buying and selling, as it's often designed to be more inspirational than practically applicable. So, let's take a brief, practical tour of what that kind of skill building might look like within a Framemaking mindset, starting with making an emotional connection in the first place.

What to Know vs. What to Feel

When we first unpacked the attributes of customers' decision confidence associated with an HQLR deal in Chapter 1, you may remember, none of those dimensions had an objective finish line. For example, whether customers feel confident that they've asked the right questions or conducted sufficient research can be determined only within the context of an agreed-upon definition of "right" or "sufficient." There is no absolute truth for "right" or "sufficient" when it comes to questions or research in the context of B2B buying. Rather, "right" and "sufficient" are based largely on what customers believe to be the case. The same is equally true for all other dimensions comprising decision confidence. The upshot is, the single biggest driver of a high-quality, low-regret deal in B2B buying is a direct result not of what customers *know*, but of what customers *feel*. Meaning, the ability to connect with customers on an emotional or feeling level proves critically important if we are going to help them feel something more or feel something different, relative to their current level of decision confidence.

So how exactly do we connect with customers on an emotional level? By using the language of feeling. Now, if that sounds either strange—especially in a business context—or unhelpfully vague, let's make it very concrete and extremely practical.

Over the years, we have worked with hundreds of speakers and sellers, honing their communication and presentation skills when speaking with senior business executives—everything from one-on-one conversations to main-stage keynote presentations. Over time, what has become crystal clear across all those sessions is that the single most consequential tactic for effectively engaging and then moving an audience to action is a technique we've come to call "what-to-know vs. what-to-feel."

Usually when we teach this, we gather a group of five to eight client-facing colleagues in a room and ask them to present three to four slides that they might typically share as part of a customer conversation—maybe data-driven research, a best practice profile from another company, or the demonstration of a new solution or product use case. One person presents as if they were in a live conversation—on stage, as it were—and the rest of us observe. Upon finishing we gather feedback from the group, offer suggestions, reflect on what worked and what didn't, and then run it again. Usually three to four times per person.

After running this exercise countless times, we started to notice a pattern. Generally, the first time through, the delivery was accurate, polished, and professional (especially considering the often nerve-wracking nature of presenting to one's colleagues). But virtually every first attempt seemed to fall flat somehow. It was fine, but it lacked that certain spark that made someone really lean in and engage. It always felt like something was missing, but none of our participants could put their finger on what exactly. The missing ingredient is emotion. Think of it this way. Every slide, every bar chart, every product capability, every idea or concept you share with a customer has two dimensions: a teaching point and an emotional point. For every idea you share with a customer, you need to be able to answer the two questions, "What do I want my audience to *know* as a result of sharing this information?" and "What do I want them to *feel*?" So, in our group exercise, after a participant had presented and gathered feedback, we'd ask them these two questions.

Typically, the knowing part was relatively straightforward. We'd clean up any misunderstandings or misrepresentations and then move to the emotional side, where participants would often draw a blank. They'd never been asked the question before. It's such a critical point, and yet many of us walk right past it as we're completely focused on getting the messaging right. After all, we've been trained to a fare-thee-well on product features, content details, value propositions, ROI documents, and cost calculators, such that we're laser focused on getting all that right. Honestly, the whole idea that there's an emotional component to every customer conversation simply gets lost in all that focus on repeatedly rehearsing what we've been trained to say.

So, after some back-and-forth discussion on the intended emotional point of the message, we'd settle on a single word—say, for example, "frustrating," ask the room for three to four other words that signaled the same emotion, and then write that list on the white board—perhaps "exasperating," "maddening," "disheartening." Finally, we'd ask our colleague to present the same information one more time, but as part of the presentation use any three of those words as part of the presentation.

> "You know, one of the things that's so frustrating about this challenge is simply how widespread it is. We feel like we've got it under control in one place, and it pops up in another. It's maddening. So, we spend our time putting out fire after fire, but can never get sufficiently ahead of things to really address the underlying problem. It's kind of disheartening, isn't it?"

Every single time, after they'd finish, virtually everyone in the room would look at the speaker, look back at us with surprise, and ask, "What did you just do?" They were blown away by how completely different it felt. To which we'd always reply, "We didn't do anything. We just put the emotion back in that we inadvertently took out thinking it doesn't belong in this kind of conversation." In business settings, we forget, we're talking to human beings. And human beings engage on an emotional level as much as on a rational level.

And that's really what we're solving for with Framemaking. Beyond all the guidance, advice, tools, workshops, verifiers, and frameworks, we're seeking to create a visceral feeling of decision confidence. Do facts, data, and evidence matter for customer confidence? One hundred percent. But all that evidence absent an emotional context can easily wash over someone with little impact, as it fails to connect to the way customers either currently feel or aspire to feel.

So, what might this technique sound like inside a Framemaking conversation? The opportunity to experiment is limitless, but here are a couple of examples to get you started.

Example 1:

You know, it's funny, in working with other customers like you, we've often found that the excitement of finally getting after this challenge can evaporate overnight when it comes to getting frontline staff excited about making the change. It's sort of soul crushing watching your excitement for improvement land with a thud when you ask for team input.

One thing we've found more and more customers doing to avoid that kind of heartbreak is to involve end users from the very early planning stages. Often, they can add a whole new perspective on what they need that makes the project motivating for everyone.

Example 2:

I'm guessing you've seen the same endless stream of white papers, research, and analyst advice we have on this approach. It's a lot, isn't it? I think we're all kind of overwhelmed sorting through everything and struggling to figure out what's best for our organization.

For a lot of companies we work with, we've found that it really helped for them to boil things down to three key questions. They told us that when they started there, things felt a lot less daunting.

Once you've practiced this technique it becomes almost second nature. Why? Because most of us do it every single day in other human conversations. Framemaking sellers will naturally make an emotional connection in virtually every kind of sales interaction, whether it's a discovery call, product demo, alignment workshop, or a conversation with procurement.

A Key Role for Empathy

If we're going to materially influence the way B2B buyers feel about a purchase process, it's extremely valuable to know how they feel about that potential purchase. Exactly how far from decision confidence are they now, and in what direction? Is it frustration? Fear? Exhaustion? Resignation? Uncertainty? Overwhelmedness? The journey to customer confidence can begin in many different places, depending partly on the specific challenges standing in customers' way. Decision complexity, for example, likely causes a great deal of frustration, even resignation, while outcome uncertainty probably engenders something closer to fear, concern, or doubt. Information overload, on the other hand, arguably leads to confusion and a feeling of cognitive overload.

At the same time, many of those emotions also have very different positive counterparts, indicating different antidotes best suited to boost customer confidence along that dimension. If customers are afraid (e.g., afraid of poor results, or afraid of messing up), then promoting feelings of certainty and assurance makes sense. If, however, customers are overwhelmed or frustrated, then prompting feelings of control and clarity arguably represents a better approach.

It's not enough, in other words, to make an emotional connection with customers. We need to identify with a relatively high degree of accuracy which emotions matter most for any given conversation, such that our efforts to build closer customer connections don't inadvertently exacerbate distance rather than bridge it.

Hypothesis-Based Empathy

Empathy is one of those skills largely omitted from traditional sales curricula—often reduced to a single slide followed by an inspirational video. Indeed, some argue that empathy is innate and therefore can't really be taught. After all, it's not especially easy to see the world through someone else's eyes or to *feel* the world through someone else's lived experience.

For our purposes, let us sidestep the debate of nature versus nurture and offer instead a practical means to at least approximate empathy, if not master it altogether, specifically suited to Framemaking objectives. This technique is especially helpful and effective for sellers who have less experience either selling to executives or working in leadership roles themselves. With this technique, one need not have served in those roles to feel their pain.

We call this approach hypothesis-led empathy. The technique unfolds across three steps.

STEP 1: LEAD WITH A HYPOTHESIS.

In speaking with a customer about their current challenges or opportunities—perhaps as part of an early discovery call—make it a point to identify how they *feel* about that challenge. However, rather than simply asking, lead with a hypothesis, or an educated guess.

"I'm guessing that's gotta feel pretty stressful! Is that right?"

If you're unsure where to start, this is where a certain amount of emotional curiosity can prove especially valuable. By wondering how customers feel about various aspects of a purchase process, Framemaking sellers can generate any number of emotional hypotheses worthy of testing with customers. Think of this as a kind of tactically targeted curiosity rather than broadly aspirational curiosity, using questions like these:

- I wonder whether that kind of meeting is as frustrating as I think it is.
- I wonder if they're as confused about what to do in this situation as the last three customers I talked to.
- I wonder whether they feel sufficiently aligned on their strategy to see the value of making a purchase.

The emotion almost doesn't matter—maddening, surprising, confusing—pick one based on your best guess, or how you imagine you'd feel in a similar situation.

More often than not, if you get it right, the customer will agree with you: "Yeah, it's incredibly stressful. I know I look sixty-five, but I'm actually only thirty-two!"

And if you get it wrong, they'll likely correct you, telling you how it really feels. "No, we're fine. It's not too bad. We're actually pretty excited about some of the changes we can now make as a result."

To be sure, you have to be confident enough in yourself to remain comfortable if corrected, because you're nearly guaranteed not to get it right every time. One, because you're guessing, but two, because not everyone feels the same way in similar situations. But notice, either way you win. You have now confirmed an accurate articulation for how that kind of challenge actually feels to that particular customer. Even better, after you've done this two or three times with customers in similar situations and heard the same—or similar—answers each time, now you're ready to generalize.

STEP 2: LEAD WITH SOCIAL PROOF.

In step 2, we aggregate what we've heard and share it proactively with the next customer.

"You know, we talk to similar customers all the time who tell us this is really stressful. One even joked he has gray hair at thirty-two! Is that what you're finding too?"

What's especially nice about this approach is, you're still testing the accuracy of your hypothesis, but you're now simultaneously establishing both credibility and value as a connector. You're on the inside now, because you know how it feels. And you're connected to other executives who feel the same way. But perhaps most powerful is the third step.

STEP 3: LEAD WITH EMPATHY.

Once you've tested your hypothesis enough times and heard the same answer over and over, now you're ready to assume full-on empathy.

"We all know how that feels—it's really stressful, isn't it?"

Notice, social proof is still subtly baked into the question ("we all know"), but now you're assuming the status of a peer. You have the confidence to assert a specific emotion because you've very purposefully tested it again and again. That said, you're still leaving room for the customer to disagree or add their own personal perspective to the mix. You're not telling them how to feel; rather, you're offering a likely feeling as a means of finding a common bond. Essentially, this kind of empathy enables you to provide validation to a customer that they're not alone, that it's safe to speak of how hard things are, not just practically but personally. Instead of thinking, "Ugh, another sales call," your customer is far more likely thinking, "This person really gets it." Not because you've presented a detailed ROI calculation or explained technical product features in a compelling manner, but because you've established a human connection. You've won access to a side of the customer many sellers never see, their humanity. As a result, you're now in a far better position to go on an emotional journey with that customer, guiding them closer and closer to decision confidence.

Now, all that said, what matters above all else with this kind of technique is that it's meant, and delivered, in an authentic manner with sincere intentions. The challenge with laying out this process in a series of tactical steps is that it's easy to turn empathy into a rote skill rather than an authentic interaction. In a word, it becomes performative. As we seek to make a human connection, the thing we must remember is, it needs to be a genuine connection, not simply the result of a scripted set of prompts. It's a mindset as much as it is a skillset. Without the former, the latter is little more than a mechanical activity.

The Framemaking mindset is steeped in empathy. Almost instinctively, Framemaking sellers are looking to continuously improve the precision with which they connect to customers about how they feel about the challenges they're facing and the outcomes they're achieving. If, on the other hand, making that kind of connection with customers doesn't motivate you or get you excited, then it's very possible that sales may prove to be an increasingly tough place to thrive over time, especially given how modern B2B buying has evolved. After all, if a seller is unwilling—or unable—to make this kind of connection, then why do customers really need to connect with them at all? If customers simply need to gather information and make a straightforward decision, they can do that on their own—probably on your website. The reason they want to talk to you rather than consulting your website is because of the thing you offer that your website can't: humanity.

Teaching with a Twist

Finally, shifting to a Framemaking mindset means thinking differently about how we teach customers what we need them to know.

Sales skills have traditionally leaned heavily on a seller's ability to present information, whether it's product specs, features and benefits, speeds and feeds, or solution attributes, bookended by discovery skills up front to determine the size and relevance of the teaching opportunity in the first place, and negotiation and closing skills on the back end to ensure customers buy in (literally) to whatever was taught along the way. In between, the bulk of sales activity comprises sharing information, demonstrating capabilities, and explaining differentiators. That's a lot of teaching. And, of course, it all still really matters.

Yet, insofar as "teaching" simply means "imparting information," we now live in a world where much of that activity can be done online, leaving customers struggling to see the need to speak with a seller who is only able to teach them things they already know through their own independent learning. Essentially, sales' traditional role as teacher has been outsourced to the Internet.

Which returns us to the core question at the heart of Framemaking selling: How can we be the one seller—or sales team—that customers actually *do* want to talk to?

When it comes to teaching, the answer is a purposeful shift away from *presenting* information, and a principled move toward helping customers make the best decision they can (in as little time as possible). For some, that may not even sound like teaching at all. It might be better described as guiding or coaching. For all the reasons we've laid out here, we call it Framemaking. But it's still teaching. It's just teaching with a twist.

The teaching objective in Framemaking is less about giving information and more about creating a context for productive learning. What's the difference? And why does it matter? It may sound like semantics to some, but it's absolutely a distinction with a difference. Remember, our primary objective with Framemaking is to build customers' confidence in *their* ability to make complex purchase decisions on behalf of their company. Their sense of agency is critical. As a result, we aren't seeking to convince them of our expertise but to instill in them the conviction of their conclusions. To that end, our job isn't so much to provide teaching, but to facilitate learning. To help customers feel confident they're asking the right questions, conducting sufficient research, and thoroughly considering alternatives.

For many sellers, it's a very different posture—seller as facilitator. But it's completely consistent with our high-level objectives in Framemaking. Effectively we're still teaching, but we're teaching by helping customers discover answers that make the most sense to them rather than simply providing them answers that cynically suit our needs. We've seen examples of this approach in everything from our phrase that pays—*In working with customers like you, one of the things we've found other companies struggling with this is*—to customer alignment workshops where our role isn't so much to connect individual stakeholders to us, but to create a structured interaction whereby individual stakeholders are more likely to productively connect with *each other* across objectives, tactics, and results. The Framemaking approach to teaching proves profoundly important as it allows customers to retain a sense of control across a complex sale where so many things feel completely out of their control. They're the ones making decisions; we're simply setting them up for success by providing clear, easy framing to promote that process.

The fields of adult education, cognitive psychology, and even behavioral economics have a great deal to say on the topic of teaching, which falls well outside the scope of this book, but a brief look at some of the key attributes of a more Socratic teaching style will hopefully provide at least a sense of why this kind of customer engagement strategy foots so well to a sales approach designed to guide customers to their own conclusions:

Dialogue-driven: Engage customers in a conversation rather than a presentation. Learning is the result of exploring perspectives rather than receiving them.

Question-based: Use open-ended questions to explore concepts and ideas. Open-ended questions allow customers to construct an answer for themselves. (Again, Framemaking has a certain therapy feel to it as it's designed to accomplish much the same outcome—more positive, productive self-perceptions.)

Critical thinking: Encourage customers to analyze and evaluate their own thoughts, priorities, objectives, motivations, capabilities, and resources. We see this especially clearly in a formal setting like a customer alignment workshop, but it can be baked into any conversation.

Reflective: Promote self-examination and deeper understanding. Prompting can play a powerful role here: "In talking to other customers like you, we find a lot of concern about necessary support from the IT team. Is that something you're concerned about as well?"

Explorative: Seek to uncover underlying assumptions and beliefs. This is where exercises like the five whys of root causing and the five hows inside of an OTR exercise can be especially valuable.

No question, sales has always been about effective teaching. That hasn't changed. But what *has* changed, and changed dramatically, is customer *learning*. Today's information and technology landscape no longer requires customers to lean on sellers for *access* to information. They know that on their own. However, that very access has proved a double-edged sword as customers empowered to learn now find themselves overwhelmed. Meanwhile, increased organizational complexity and outcome uncertainty leave customers struggling to find answers online or off.

By adopting a Framemaking mindset, sellers reveal a completely different teaching opportunity inside this current buying environment. While customers may not need more teaching as we've come to understand it, they could absolutely use more *guidance*.

Rewriting the Trust Equation

Sometimes when sales leaders first encounter Framemaking, their immediate reaction is, "This is great, but you can't engage customers in that way unless they trust you first. So, first we need to build trust!"

However, when we respond with, "Fair enough. So, how do we build trust?" we typically find leaders falling back on something like, "Have something valuable to say about their business."

Honestly, it's not a bad answer. But it nonetheless raises the exact same question: "How do we win the right to share something valuable if customers don't trust us enough to engage in the first place?"

And around and around we go.

Sometimes, it's easy to feel like we've solved a problem simply by diagnosing it. But that's almost never the case. So let's see if we can break this circular conundrum of customer trust. If we return to Bryan's perspective at Expedient, you'll remember his simple but powerful point of view. We help customers make the best decision they can in as little time as possible for two reasons. First, it's simply the right thing to do—for all the reasons we've laid out here. And second, it's how we win in the long run—if not on this deal, then on the next one, and the one after that. Implicit in Bryan's thinking, we believe, is a productive way to think about building customer trust: this is where you start. You don't establish customer trust in order to earn the right to engage in Framemaking. You engage in Framemaking in order to establish customer trust.

Or put another way, trust isn't the gateway to human connection; human connection is the gateway to establishing trust. Does it eventually evolve into a virtuous circle, where connections build trust and deeper trust builds closer connections? Almost certainly. But you have to start somewhere.

CREATING COMMERCIAL OPPORTUNITY

Not to be crass, but let's be very clear: Framemaking is absolutely an effective approach for building closer, deeper human connections, but ultimately, it's about making more money.

If customer decision confidence wasn't the number one driver of the likelihood of a high-quality, low-regret deal—by far—then we'd be writing this book about something else. But in all our experience, the best possible route to commercial success that we can find lies along the path paved with customer confidence. So here we are.

If the human side of the Framemaking mindset is all about creating closer, deeper human connections, the commercial side of the Framemaking mindset is all about "How do we get our customers to make bigger decisions that they feel better about in less time?" No doubt, Framemaking sellers want to hit quota and go on incentive trips to all-inclusive oceanside resorts just like everyone else (and many do). But the data tell us the single biggest lever at sellers' disposal for making that happen is by helping customers get more buying decisions done in less time.

To that end, just as the Framemaking mindset leads to a rethink of specific customer engagement skills, it will equally lead to a rethink of certain commercial execution skills—in particular, opportunity qualification. We've already seen the application of a very different set of qualification criteria across several preceding chapters. If customer stakeholders are unwilling to commit to a sequence of events, for instance, their ability to successfully navigate that purchase decision should be suspect at best. Meanwhile, customers unwilling to commit to at least some kind of stakeholder alignment workshop should undoubtedly be downgraded in terms of likelihood to close. That said, adopting a Framemaking mindset does not require wholesale rewiring of the entire organizational machine. Think of it as a powerful supplement rather than a full-blown substitute.

Mindset vs. Methodology

Framemaking isn't meant to represent a formal, end-to-end sales methodology or sales process. Instead, a Framemaking mindset can easily sit on top of virtually any popular sales methodology or qualification framework (Challenger, MEDDPICC, Richardson, Sandler, gap selling, Miller Heiman, SPIN, TAS, value selling, etc.). That said, regardless of existing methodology, a Framemaking mindset reorients virtually every sales activity around *purchase*-process execution rather than sales-process compliance. Framemaking sellers approach their day, prioritize their time, and allocate their attention very purposefully through a lens of "What do I need to do today to help customers in my pipeline advance along their purchase journey with increased confidence?" If any, or all, of these methodologies can help bring structure to that kind of activity, that's a complete win. As long as it's mindset over methodology, a Framemaking approach can likely be integrated into any existing methodology.

To demonstrate, here's a story from our friend Kevin, the chief sales officer from Chapter 2. A few years ago, Kevin was on stage at his annual sales kickoff meeting presenting "the year in review" to his team of five hundred mostly tenured, highly trained sales professionals. Kevin's company was—and still is—known globally for its huge investments in sales training and performance, having built a virtual sales machine on top of a leading-edge sales methodology. Compliance was great, and engagement was strong. So, it was a bit of a surprise when Kevin took the stage to review another banner year of sales performance and told his team the following story.

After walking through a long list of new-logo wins from the previous year, Kevin came to the final logo on the slide and with a flourish of excitement announced the single biggest deal to date in the history of the company—a multimillion-dollar deal with a world-class brand. As the raucous applause died down, Kevin looked out across the room thoughtfully and said in a reflective tone, "You know, it's funny. Let me tell you something about this deal." He paused as the room fell still. "Yes, it is the single biggest deal in the history of our company." Pause again. "But it had been in our pipeline for over *five* years." Pause. "And we had forecast it every single month for the last three." Not knowing exactly how to react at that point, a certain nervous laughter coursed through the room. But everyone knew. That's not good. If nothing else, there was a real question as to the opportunity cost of a five-year deal to overall margins. To be sure, no one likes to lose slowly, but few in the room had ever really considered the all-in cost of *winning* slowly.

But more importantly, Kevin wasn't making a point about selling. He was making a point about buying. The reason it took so long wasn't because Kevin's team failed to "execute with precision," "comply with sales process," or "follow the methodology." Instead, the reason why Kevin's team was selling so long was because the customer's team was "buying so slow." They were wandering aimlessly through their spaghetti bowl of B2B buying for *years*. Literally.

This is why Framemaking is so important. Irrespective of sales methodology, applying a Framemaking mindset helps customers move with far greater intentionality through an otherwise sometimes nearly endless purchase process. It's about moving customers through a purchase far more than moving sellers through a sale. And it makes you wonder, what's it worth to win a multimillion-dollar deal in three years instead of five? Or even faster still? For most of us, it's a lot.

Getting Paid for Framemaking

For those still concerned about getting paid for Framemaking, there are a couple important points worth mentioning to possibly allay those concerns.

It's only fair to openly acknowledge that Framemaking is by no means some kind of commercial panacea. Of course it is unrealistic to think that adopting a Framemaking mindset and applying the three E's of establish, engage, and execute will automatically convert a deal to a win every single time. That's not only unrealistic, it's completely unimaginable. The reality of B2B buying is simply far too complex to provide any kind of guaranteed outcome from *any* sales approach. Indeed, holding a sales tactic, process, method, or idea to that kind of unmeetable standard before taking it for a test drive leads to little more than a "never mind, let's try nothing" mentality that leaves sellers falling ever further behind.

Instead, Framemaking is built on a set of probabilities. Strong probabilities, mind you, but probabilities nonetheless. That's why the data behind this book matter so much. If we could find anything else even in the same ballpark as increasing decision confidence on the probability for HQLR deals, we would mention it here. But nothing else is even close.

That said, Framemaking is subject to the exact same free consulting trap as *The Challenger Sale* before it. The free consulting trap refers to the exact same objection raised against Bryan's mandate to his team. What happens if we help customers make the best decision they possibly can, and they ultimately decide that the best decision is to buy from the competition? We've essentially sold them right into the arms of a top competitor. We'd all agree, that doesn't feel particularly good.

So, beyond losing "in as little time as possible," let's briefly address three ways to mitigate the risk of free consulting.

LEAD TO YOUR UNIQUE STRENGTHS.

While Framemaking is supplier agnostic, that doesn't necessarily mean that we can't prompt customers to consider a question or include a metric that leads back to something our company does better than anyone else. After all, you wouldn't be doing this if you didn't think your solution would solve their business problem.

However, it's by no means easy; in order to lead to your unique strengths, you must actually have a clear understanding of what those unique strengths are. It sounds sort of obvious, doesn't it? But years of experience have taught us that identifying your unique strengths is quite difficult. At the end of the day, the question isn't "What is your company good at?" but "What is your company *uniquely* good at?" And in the world of complex B2B solutions, it turns out that's an extremely hard question to answer for many. But it's a question well worth the effort.

Ultimately the question isn't so much a sales question as it is an organizational strategy question, requiring input from across senior leadership. For example, in Chapter 3 of *The Challenger Customer*, we tell the story of a chief sales officer (since retired) at a global food-ingredients company who shared this about one of their business units: "We sell salt. Not fancy salt, kosher salt, or sea salt. Just plain old salt. It's not different than the salt you get anywhere else. It comes in a mountain, on a barge." He then asked, "Where's the 'unique strength' in that?"[2]

It was a totally fair question, to which we offered a completely honest answer: "No idea." We went on to suggest, however, that if they were seeking to charge a premium for what is definitionally a commodity, then they'd have to find some other source of differentiation. Perhaps it was in their mining operations—because their highly distributed shorter supply lines allowed for just-in-time delivery. Or maybe it was some sort of unique financial hedging instruments the company offered, allowing customers to avoid unpredictable variations in salt prices. Ultimately, that's the key to identifying unique strengths: brainstorming with a diverse group of colleagues either the subset or unique combination of company capabilities that no one else can offer. Almost inevitably, the companies we've conducted this exercise with in the past have had to travel through a valley of despair where it appeared there was literally nothing they did sufficiently better/differently to merit the label "unique strength." But after enough iterations many landed on surprising articulations of their capabilities that they themselves hadn't fully appreciated up to that point.

Either way, it's critically important to remember, the fundamental premise of Framemaking is to boost customers' confidence in their ability to make the right decision for their company. If at any time along a purchase journey, therefore, they become either suspicious or skeptical of your Framemaking help as a self-serving attempt, you can pack up your Framemaking toolkit and head for the door. Once customers have lost faith in your intentions it becomes virtually impossible to see you as an effective agent of building faith in their decision-making ability.

So, proceed with caution. You should remain a supplier agnostic guide through the spaghetti bowl of B2B buying. There are times, of course, when customers are going to want specific information about your capabilities and how they might address their priorities, but at a natural point, Framemaking conversations will return to helping customers figure out which questions to answer for themselves in order to determine whether that capability represents a priority for them. And if it doesn't, hopefully you've helped them realize this early enough in the process for you to move along to a new customer who might be a better fit.

CREATE A VALUE EXCHANGE.

What's especially powerful about Framemaking, however, is that framing customers' thinking in a way that leads to your unique strengths isn't the only way—and may not even be the best way—to ensure that customers buy from you over anyone else as a result of your Framemaking efforts.

A few years ago, we had the honor of interviewing Dr. Robert Cialdini, a pioneer in human motivation and persuasion. Among other things, we discussed the power of something called a "value exchange."[3] In essence, a value exchange captures the simple but powerful idea that humans feel obliged to reciprocate to others something of value in return for a gift received. If a friend invites you to dinner, you feel the need to return the gesture. If a colleague provides a favor, you feel you owe them one in return.

Now, this idea certainly isn't new in sales. Promotional giveaways have been common for years ranging from inexpensive tchotchkes to VIP trips to major golf tournaments. However, what's especially interesting is that the value one might provide isn't limited to items with clear monetary value. Value can be derived, for example, from an uplifting feeling or positive impact on self-perception. Which, of course, is exactly the goal of Framemaking with respect to customer confidence.

Even though this dynamic works largely at an almost subconscious level, the way it plays out in a typical Framemaking interaction is easy to see. A customer who feels better and more confident about themselves, their company, and the decisions they're making is strongly inclined to do business with the person who helped them feel that way. Again, no guarantees, but more often than not—and certainly over time in the aggregate—Framemaking pays simply due to human wiring.

TAKE YOUR SHARE OF A BIGGER PIE.

Finally, it's important to remember, Framemaking isn't nearly as much about winning against the competition as it's about winning against the status quo.

No doubt, most every company has two or three tough competitors against whom they compete on a regular basis for their fair share of the market (or their outsized share, if they're especially successful). And it's easy for sellers and leaders alike to get caught up in these tough, competitive battles, pouring disproportionate time and energy into beating the competition at all costs. After all, there are only so many deals to go around, and survival depends on winning what we can.

But if we think all the way back to Chapter 1, we started this story in a very different place. By far, customers' greater challenge isn't choosing one supplier over another; it's managing to make it all the way through the spaghetti bowl of B2B buying. Truly, sometimes it seems a bit of a wonder that B2B commerce happens at all. But when it comes to getting paid, that's the key insight to the Framemaking story. Watching B2B buyers struggle to buy—or simply struggle to decide—really makes you wonder how much *more* commerce could happen if customers simply felt more confident in the decisions they're making on behalf of their company. Ultimately, that's the true commercial opportunity of Framemaking selling—boosting the size of the pie altogether by helping more customers navigate to a successful purchase decision. If 40–60 percent of B2B deals end in status quo, imagine how much opportunity one might generate simply from shaking just a few more deals lose from the depths of indecision.

Of course, with a nod to Dr. Cialdini, if we're the ones actually providing customers the guidance they need to feel sufficiently confident to make that purchase decision, then we're well positioned to win that incremental business as we generate it, potentially taking far more of the pie as it expands.

Bottom line, it's hard not to see the potential commercial goodness from adopting a Framemaking mindset across the entire organization. Indeed, that's where we'll turn next, to the broader organization. To ensure everyone is working from the same page when it comes to enabling Framemaking, we'll look at key Framemaking design principles and the tools we can use to support them.

CHAPTER 8

Framing Framemaking for Framemakers

Throughout the book, we've seen many examples of how Framemaking can help customers navigate complex decisions, analyze and prioritize information, align with colleagues on objectives, and reduce uncertainty around outcomes. In each example, the foundation of sellers' Framemaking efforts was some form of tactical guidance—sometimes quite informal, other times highly structured—designed to help customers address the challenges most likely to undermine their ability to reach a confident purchase decision.

In this chapter, we provide some suggestions on designing and deploying that guidance that both individual sellers and the broader commercial organization—sales enablement, marketing, customer experience—can use to determine what kind of guidance, and in what form, will prove most valuable in framing customers' buying journeys. Essentially, think of this chapter as an introduction to guidance on guidance.

To get there, let's dig a bit deeper into a few important nuances of Framemaking.

FRAMEMAKING 101

At its most basic, Framemaking is an action: it is the act of making a complex task or decision feel more manageable. It's something sellers **do** as part of customer engagement to boost customers' decision confidence. As part of that engagement, sellers will need a set of tools in order to offer useful guidance to buyers along the way. In the case of Framemaking, sellers engaged in the act of guiding are naturally going to need some actual guidance to serve as the basis of that action. We call this guidance *framing*.

Framing can take numerous forms, spanning a spectrum from conversational/informal at one end to well-documented/highly structured at the other. Sometimes, Framemaking simply entails sharing a piece of helpful advice. Other times, it means working with customers collaboratively through an assessment of some aspect of their current organizational context (e.g., priorities, expectations, budget, current level of consensus).

As we move along this spectrum toward higher levels of formality, we shift into the world of *frameworks*. Frameworks are simply the formal rubrics we use to help customers structure their thinking and organize their thoughts. Not surprisingly, frameworks can take many forms—from the very simple to the highly complex—each designed to help customers address different obstacles they face as they move through a complex purchase.

Naturally, then, we'll want to determine a number of things as we seek to support sellers' Framemaking efforts. At the highest level, we'll need some criteria to determine where our guidance should land along that spectrum. In other words, when is simple framing sufficient, and when would a more formal framework prove especially helpful in guiding customers? Second, we'll need to understand the range of form factors of frameworks at our disposal. Of course, the sky is the limit as there are untold different forms, flavors, and functions of frameworks depending on what help a customer needs. We'll focus here on the design principles for creating the framing that will help customers make the best decision they can, as quickly as possible, while making sure we are supporting both the customer's ease as well as their agency. And finally, we'll want to make sure that whoever is using that framing—sellers, account executives, customer success representatives, subject matter experts—is able to deploy the framing as designed to ensure maximum positive impact on customers' decision confidence.

Framing with a Framework

Arguably, "framework" might be the single most overused word in business speak today, which is why it is important to clarify what it means in the context of Framemaking. In short, a framework is a concrete tool that helps structure a person's thinking.

Some more common frameworks include checklists, 2x2 matrices, and process diagrams. The idea here is that a buyer might have only a general sense of the problem, and a framework gives a buyer a concrete way to think about it that makes the problem feel more manageable.

We can see a concrete example of how a framework can make a customer's struggle more manageable by looking at how sellers help customers shop for diamond engagement rings. For someone planning to get engaged, shopping for an engagement ring can produce a jumble of emotions ranging from excitement about their relationship and the big step they are about to take to fear of what that big step means on many levels. However, the purchase of the ring might be especially daunting as there is a good chance the customer has never purchased something so small and so expensive ever before. There is a lot of pressure to get it right. But where to start? What ring is right? How much should it cost? Why is this ring so much more valuable than that ring?

Fortunately, an experienced seller will likely be ready to help the customer with the framework of the 4Cs:

"Over the years, I've worked with a lot of young people like you looking for an engagement ring. It can be really overwhelming. There are so many questions to consider, and it is so hard to figure out what you want most based on your budget.

What most people find helpful are the 4Cs: color, clarity, carat weight, and cut. The 4Cs are the framework for how diamonds are valued so you can decide what is most important to you. Some customers really want a large stone and are less concerned about other factors. They might choose a stone with lower clarity to get more carats. Others want a specific color and cut but are OK with a diamond that has fewer carats. Once you have figured out what matters most, it tends to be easier to figure out what tradeoffs you want to make to fit your budget."

Without the 4Cs, the customer would have found it really hard to compare two diamonds and understand why one that seemed more sparkly was less expensive than another diamond that seemed to be the same size. Is it something about the number of facets? Or maybe the craft of how the facets were cut? Or is there a defect in the less sparkly diamond? But then why would it be more expensive? Deciding which diamond to pick would feel so arbitrary and out of control.

By using the 4Cs framework, the customer now has a structure to understand the small number of factors that matter, but more importantly, the customer now feels in control. They feel in control over the tradeoffs that they can make and most importantly of all, in control to pick the diamond that is right for them.

The 4Cs is just a list with four items. But that short list makes all the difference. It's a concrete tool that helps structure a person's thinking. This framework has been adopted globally—even if it's not called the 4Cs in every language. The tradeoffs between color, clarity, carat weight, and cut are a helpful tool to structure a buyer's thinking and help them make a purchase with confidence.

Many of the examples of framing in the book use one form of framework or another. However, when designing framing to help guide your customers, don't assume that you need to create a framework. In many cases, framing without a framework is a much better option.

Framing Without a Framework

One of the simplest examples of Framemaking we have discussed is the story of procurement from Chapter 2. In that example, the seller Tara helped her customer appreciate the benefit of involving procurement early. In this case, there is no framework involved. Tara's guidance was basically a quick tip, a suggestion, a fairly simple idea the customer would likely have missed on their own.

But notice that this very simple example still qualifies as a great example of Framemaking. The seller is providing guidance and making the complex task of navigating the purchase process in the customer's company a bit easier. Now the seller doesn't attempt to make the overall buying process more manageable—that would almost certainly require a framework to understand all of the people and processes involved. But one of the tasks in the overall buying process is to get signoff from procurement. To make that one task just a bit easier, the seller prompts the customer with the guidance that it is beneficial to involve procurement early and helps make one part of the buying process a bit more manageable.

It is important to note that the biggest advantage of framing without a framework is its inherent simplicity. Imagine if instead of guiding the customer with the simple idea to include procurement early, the seller instead suggested the customer fill out a multi-question self-assessment tool as part of a framework to help the customer recognize the benefits of including procurement early. Sounds ridiculous, doesn't it? That would be way too much club to determine whether to bring procurement in early in the process.

In this case, a framework would actually make things harder, not easier. And this is why using framing without frameworks is a critical tool for sellers.

DESIGN PRINCIPLES FOR FRAMING

Now that we understand the two types of framing (with and without a framework), we can dive into design principles for effective framing starting with the first, and maybe most important: simplicity.

Design Principle #1—Simplicity: Less Is More

When designing framing that a seller will use to help a customer make a complex task more manageable, the first thing to consider is how to make the framing as simple as possible for the customer. Simpler framing should use less customer time, less mental energy, and less effort and generally make it easier for the customer to benefit from the framing's guidance.

If an idea is enough to help the customer, no need for a framework. After all, the goal of Framemaking is to make things easier for the customer. But if the complexity of the customer's decision or task can't be addressed with a tip or simple idea and instead requires structuring, a framework will likely be needed.

The following list of commonly used framework forms is roughly in order of simplicity, starting with the simplest:

1. Checklists
2. Categorizations

3. 2x2 matrices (or larger AxB matrices)
4. Process diagrams
5. Assessments (e.g., performance diagnostics, maturity models)

Selecting the best form for a framework will depend on the nature of the complexity of the specific customer decision or task that it is being designed to address. For example, when helping a customer assess the maturity of existing operational processes, it will be hard to avoid using a maturity-model assessment.

However, a good rule of thumb is to start by testing if a checklist will be effective, as that tends to be the simplest form of framework. If a checklist won't work because the list is too long to be practically usable, test if using a category-based framework like the 4Cs will work instead. Progress to more complex forms of frameworks only after you have ruled out the simpler ones.

When designing a framework for simplicity, it is also important to figure out what matters most. The 4Cs are a great example of this because the 4Cs actually aren't the only factors that affect a diamond's value. They are just the most important factors. Things like polish and shape also influence the value, but they have a much smaller effect. By simplifying the framework to the four most important factors, the customer's decision is made easier.

Now of course this raises the important question of how to balance the tradeoff between simplicity and precision. Imagine instead of the 4Cs, diamond sellers used the 4Cs&P&S? That doesn't exactly roll off the tongue, but it would be a bit more precise. But does the added precision from including the P for polish and S for shape actually help customers? Or does it just make things harder? Adding factors means more tradeoffs to consider and more complexity to manage. It is always important to remember that the primary goal of framing is to make a complex task or decision feel more manageable.

If you have a checklist that includes six items, it is worth testing if the customer really needs all six to make their decision more manageable or if any can be removed without impacting the benefit of the guidance for the customer.

Note one other factor that will affect the simplicity of a framework is the amount of input needed from the customer to use it. The 4Cs are an excellent example of input simplicity, as there is no input required from the customer at all. The 4Cs are always the same for every customer. It doesn't matter if the customer is getting married for the first time or is shopping together with their partner or any other factor that might be unique to that customer. The 4Cs are stable in the sense that the framework doesn't change based on the customer's context.

Although frameworks that never require input based on customer context are less common, the success of the 4Cs highlights the fact that the more stable a framework is, the more broadly it can be applied, making it easier for both customer and seller.

The ultimate test of simplicity for a framework is the customer. If the customer feels the framework is simple to understand and easy to use and it helps them better manage the complexity of a decision or task, that is all that matters.

Design Principle #2—Context: Putting the Customer in Focus

In the 4Cs framework, context doesn't matter. We now shift to an example of a framework where the input of customer context is critical. Recall the example of the OTR framework for helping customers align on objectives from Chapter 5. OTR is an example of a categorization framework as it structures the complexity of objective alignment using three categories—objectives, tactics, and results. These categories establish what matters when a customer is aligning on objectives.

Key to the design of this framework is the input of the customer context. For OTR, the input will include the perspective of not just one customer champion responding on behalf of the entire customer organization, but of multiple stakeholders providing their own perspective. Only by capturing OTR from multiple stakeholders, including potential conflicting responses, can the customer use the framework to identify and resolve cases of objective misalignment. Without the ability to input customer context, OTR would be completely useless.

It is important to note that OTR extends further to break out the R of results into the three categories of MTT—metrics, targets, and timelines. This makes it possible for the customer to add precision to the framework by double-clicking on results to explore if there is potential stakeholder misalignment at that more detailed level. This ability to cascade context is an advanced design approach to keep in mind when facing a framework with more than a few categories that requires significant input of customer context potentially from multiple stakeholders.

Having established the first two principles that will help establish the form and degree of flexibility in the framing, we now shift to addressing the specific help that the customer needs. This is where we explore our two primary Framemaking active ingredients: bounding and prompting.

Design Principle #3—Bounding: Setting Limits

A quick reminder that bounding establishes clear, credible guidance on what matters and more importantly what doesn't to make complexity feel more manageable. For many customers, bounding is the biggest opportunity to help increase their decision confidence. After all, how can a customer be confident that they asked the right questions, did enough research, explored enough alternatives if they don't know when enough is enough? Mastering framing that effectively utilizes bounding is absolutely critical.

When designing framing to help a customer bound the complexity of a decision, creating a framework is often the best option, as the framework's structure inherently establishes limits. Even in a checklist, the simplest example of a framework, bounding is baked right in. After all, the things that matter are included as items on the checklist, which establishes clearly defined limits. Anything not on the list is out and should be ignored. So often, the most effective guidance for a customer struggling with the complexity of a decision is a simple list that narrows the scope down to the things that matter.

Although bounding is very helpful for most customers, it is especially helpful for maximizers. You will remember from Chapter 4, maximizers are prone to boil the ocean when seeking information and struggle to know when enough is enough. Although maximizers tend to benefit the most from a framework that establishes clear limits, unfortunately, they may be likely to resist efforts to establish boundaries using frameworks (or by any other means). This may test a seller's patience, but ultimately a framework may provide the exact help that a maximizer needs—and without the benefit of the boundaries a framework establishes, a maximizer might end up trapped in an endless cycle of analysis paralysis. Of course, we've seen all too many deals where a key stakeholder is an extreme maximizer who undermines all efforts to utilize bounding to make complexity more manageable for a buying group. In these cases, it may be necessary to disqualify or at least deprioritize that customer altogether.

When designing checklists (or other forms of frameworks) where the primary goal is to establish boundaries for customers, the key question is how many items to include on the list. As we discussed in the first design principle of simplicity, it is generally better to limit the number of items as much as possible. Each item you add to a checklist makes it a little bit less simple, a little bit less easy for the customer to use. For this reason, less common items are generally not included in most checklists.

However, if you are designing a checklist where the primary goal is to establish a clear boundary, it may be necessary to make the list a bit more comprehensive. This is to avoid the risk that a customer questions why certain items aren't included, which can undermine the credibility of the boundary. To see how this might play out, recall the stakeholder alignment workshop discussed in Chapter 5.

Imagine you are the seller helping a customer prep for the workshop. To help the customer set boundaries around who should attend, the seller engages the customer with a checklist of the typical stakeholders that are commonly invited. When designing the checklist, you might find that most of your customers don't have a capital review board so you don't include a stakeholder from the CRB on the checklist. But imagine the customer's reaction (especially if they have read this book) if they have a CRB and see a critical need to have a representative participate in the workshop. Having found a "mistake" in the checklist, the customer will not only doubt its credibility but will be likely to question your credibility as the seller as well. Ugh!

If this isn't bad enough, imagine your customer is a maximizer. Now that they've found something has been missed, they will want to boil the ocean that much harder. To avoid this, you might be tempted to add every possible stakeholder you've ever seen a customer include in the workshop, but this makes the checklist much less easy to use and also raises doubts in its credibility if the customers see a number of items that just don't apply.

Seems like we are stuck between a rock and hard place, but we can find our answer in a surprising place: a box of cake mix.

In the US after World War II, boxed cake mix sales took off as companies shifted from creating dry mixes for troops and focused on busy consumers. But by the mid-1950s, sales slowed, so market researchers held focus groups to understand how housewives felt when making boxed cakes. The troubling answer was "guilty."

The market researchers of the 1950s needed to figure out how to help housewives feel better about themselves when "cheating" and not making a cake from scratch. Essentially, they needed to figure out how to create more agency for someone making a cake from a box mix. They found a clever solution that tapped into our human psychology. The marketers simply adjusted the recipe on the box so that making the cake was just the first step. The second step was to decorate the cake and make it all your own.[1] Agency restored.

Certainly, a lot has changed since the 1950s, but the evolution of human psychology doesn't move that quickly. Customers still place significant value on getting a little bit of agency by making something their own. If you doubt that customers today will be as likely to respond to this type of technique, just take a look at the revenues for gaming companies. Gamers are spending billions of dollars a year buying in-game cosmetics that have no effect on game play. Much like 1950s housewives decorating boxed cakes, gamers today use cosmetics to make their avatar their own. Sometimes, the more things change, the more they stay the same.

Returning to the example of the checklist for the stakeholder alignment workshop, we can see it isn't actually a question of whether to add one more role to the checklist. The question is how to add a little dash of agency. The best way to do this is by simply adding a blank line for the customer to fill in for themselves. Note this does two things. First, it recognizes that each customer's situation is unique and provides the opportunity to input the context for that customer situation, creating agency for the customer. Second, it bounds that input by providing only one blank line.

Now most satisficers will likely ignore this blank line and just address the items listed. But for the maximizers, adding exactly one blank line is a critical opportunity to use bounding to help them. By signaling to the maximizer that there is only space for one addition, the maximizer receives the guidance that they should pick only the most important additional item, thus bounding their typical tendency to not know when enough is enough.

Note that this approach is needed because the checklist is a form of framework, like the 4Cs, that is very stable. There typically isn't the flexibility to input customer context. By adding the ability to add context with the extra blank line, the checklist adds a little flexibility and agency at the cost of a little simplicity and ease.

This tradeoff between flexibility and simplicity is very common when designing frameworks. To see how this plays out for a much more flexible framework, it is useful to revisit the OTR framework. It is easy to see how OTR helps create useful boundaries, as it includes just the three things that matter most when aligning objectives for a buying group: objectives, tactics, and results. This establishes a clear scope for the customer when tackling a question as complex as "What are we trying to do?" OTR is a great example of a framework that combines a simple categorization with the ability to capture customer context and focus the decision-making of a group. This type of framework is very common and especially useful when supporting customer efforts to develop consensus.

Note that OTR is especially flexible, as customers have the ability to input their context. Of course, this does an excellent job of supporting customer agency, but it comes with a cost. Unlike a simple checklist where the answers are provided, OTR provides a framework that the customer has to fill out. Far less simple and easy for the customer. I'm sure we can all imagine how maximizers might be prone to add dozens of objectives when filling out the OTR. But recall from Chapter 5 that a key element of OTR is the five hows. Customers aren't encouraged to endlessly cascade to lower and lower levels of objectives and tactics. Instead, customers are encouraged to go only five levels deep.

Having seen how to apply the design principle of bounding, we now turn to the second active ingredient of Framemaking—prompting.

Design Principle #4—Prompting: Nudging the Customer

When designing framing to help customers, the simplest way to think about prompting is how to help customers identify key considerations and prioritize next steps that they might have missed.

When prompting a customer on the steps they need to take next, sometimes they will need a framework like a process map of the steps all the way to their destination, but frequently, prompting may only require suggesting the best thing to do next. The guidance needed to prompt a customer can often be quite simple—often it's just a quick tip.

For this reason, it is important to avoid the trap of presuming a framework is needed when the primary goal is to prompt your customers. As we discussed in the first design principle of simplicity, it's best to first test if framing without a framework is sufficient before designing a framework like a full process map.

But if a framework is needed, it is important to understand the relationship between bounding and prompting, for often even a framework designed primarily to help a customer set boundaries will have an element of prompting as well. After all, even the simplest checklist will prompt customers to consider whether the items on the list have been addressed along with whether there are items on the list that customers hadn't considered before.

But it is important to be aware of when bounding and prompting can come into conflict. Recall when discussing bounding, we saw the benefits of including only common items on a checklist. However, including only the most common items risks that the checklist doesn't prompt any new ideas or next steps the customer hasn't already considered.

Now this may be fine if what the customer needs is boundaries of where to stop. But if the goal is to prompt the customer to consider possibilities that they might be missing, only including items that are already obvious to the customer is a lost opportunity. Imagine working with a customer considering a purchase of a CT scanner in a situation like the parking garage story from Chapter 5. When the seller includes marketing on a checklist of stakeholders the customer should consider including in an early discussion of objectives, the customer will be prompted to consider something they might not have thought of on their own. Now if that customer is a satisficer and prone to settle for good enough, they may well react by saying, "I don't think we need to include marketing. We've got enough people involved already. It's a pretty straightforward decision. We should be good to go." But the seller knows this might be a recipe for disaster. Thanks to the prompting from the checklist, the seller can now guide the customer to appreciate why skipping marketing might not be a good idea.

Having covered the four design principles for framing, we now turn to the question of how to make sure our framing actually provides the buyers the help they need.

Testing for Ease and Agency

When designing framing, it is important to remember why we are doing all this. Our goal is to boost our customers' confidence so they can buy better. Of course, we've seen throughout the book that the key to increasing customer confidence is supporting both buyer ease and agency, so we need to test the framing to make sure our guidance is supporting both.

For the most part, designing guidance that helps make complex decisions more manageable will produce framing that makes things easier for the customer. Especially by following the design principle of simplicity, ease should be supported. In fact, most framing tends to be designed with ease as the priority, and if the framing isn't making things easier for the customer, then you need to go back to the drawing board.

Often context can be a primary source of agency for a customer, but as we've seen, some forms of framing like the 4Cs or static checklists do not provide an opportunity to capture customer context, creating the risk that agency becomes a secondary consideration. The good news is that even engaging with a framework where agency wasn't a primary focus will typically produce at least a mildly positive boost to a customer's sense of agency. This has less to do with how we design the framework and more to do with how we all as humans process information.

Typically, a customer will attempt to apply the new perspective introduced by the framework to their own situation. As this happens, the customer is in control. They are actively imagining how this new idea plays out in their world. This process is often characterized as constructing knowledge for yourself and is a core process in how humans learn.

But maybe more important than the design of the framework is how the seller helps the customer engage with the framework. In the case of a simple checklist, if the seller just tells the customer to go do the things listed on the checklist, the customer's agency will likely be undermined. They aren't in control. They are taking orders from a seller. Let's now imagine a seller that instead engages the customer with the checklist by saying, "Here is a list of things that other customers like you have found useful. Let's go through it together and figure out which apply to your situation." Potentially this involves suggesting what to add to the checklist even if a blank line isn't provided. Now the customer is engaging with the framework. Now they are applying it to their situation and constructing knowledge for themselves. Now their agency will be supported.

Certainly, this is another reason for sellers to focus on developing sensemaking skills and avoiding the telling posture, but it also highlights the critical importance of making sure sellers are prepared to effectively engage customers with framing that increases both ease and agency.

Guiding the Guides

As we have discussed throughout the chapter, one of the simplest but still very effective forms of framing is the checklist. So we end this chapter with a checklist of questions that sellers should ask themselves before they put Framemaking into practice. The answers to these questions function almost like a teacher's manual for the seller, making sure that sellers are able to effectively use their framing to help their customers.

1. What help does this framing provide to the customer?
   This question checks to make sure the seller understands what the customer is struggling to address and how the customer will benefit from engaging with the particular framing. This will be key not only to establish the correct framing to use with a customer, but also to convince the customer to engage with the framing.

2. How does the framing work?
   The seller will need to understand the content of the framing, especially how the framing was designed to provide the help the customer needs. This will typically include the form of the framing (whether it's a framework or a simple suggestion), the input of context, as well as the way bounding and/or prompting are built into the framing.

3. Why this framing?
   The seller needs to be able to explain to the customer why this framing will make the customer's struggle more manageable. In some cases, this may include data on how the use of the framing has proven useful, but often simple anecdotes about how other customers found the framing helpful will be sufficient.

4. How do you run a conversation using the framework?
    This is the how-to guide the seller uses with all of the steps they need to follow to help the customer benefit from the framing. This will typically include any specific details related to any aspect of the three E's that the seller will need to effectively guide the customer as well as detailed guidance on how to communicate the framework and engage the customer so they can construct the knowledge for themselves.
5. What are the next steps?
    A successful framing conversation that helps a customer overcome a challenge creates positive momentum. The seller needs to be ready to build on that momentum with a clear sense of how to best prompt the customer with the next steps to make the best decision they can.

So much of what we have discussed to this point involves sellers working directly with customers. But of course, marketing plays a key role in getting customers to engage in the first place. This is where the story of Framemaking shifts to marketers and the role our digital channels and content need to play to unlock the power of Framemaking.

CHAPTER 9

Building a Framemaking Content Strategy

In a world where so many customers would prefer to learn on their own and avoid sales conversations altogether, any attempt to propose a new sales technique, like Framemaking, inevitably confronts a confounding conundrum.

If we modify our sales approach and become the sellers that customers actually *do* want to talk to, how will customers know? Sure, the ones who are already talking to us will benefit from the guidance we provide as we use Framemaking to increase their confidence and help them buy better. But what about the buyers who need our help but don't know we are the seller that they would actually want to talk to if they aren't actually talking to us already? This is the critical question. After all, Framemaking sellers can provide help and guidance to customers only if they are willing to engage in the first place. So how do we make *that* happen? How do we win access to customers who aren't already speaking to our sellers?

For most customers, the answer is to meet them where they already are and then draw them into a seller-led, person-to-person

Framemaking conversation. And if we think about where customers are already, at least in terms of buying activity, chances are they're online conducting research, assessing needs, and seeking answers from websites, white papers, videos, assessments, you name it. And hopefully some of that content is ours. So the question becomes, How might we design that content to establish a Framemaking posture with online learners, and then use that engagement to direct them, willingly, to a sales-led conversation far better suited to guide them more fully through a complex purchase?

For that, we'll need a Framemaking content strategy.

Whether led by marketing, sales enablement, or another part of the commercial organization, that strategy will need to complete the following steps:

1. We'll need to map the buyer's journey through the spaghetti bowl of B2B buying. This includes identifying where along that journey customers are most likely to go astray, get stuck, or need help. What questions are they most likely to have? Which ones present the best opportunity for Framemaking guidance?

2. We'll need to tune our content strategy for Framemaking and design content that specifically targets the questions that impact customer decision confidence.

3. We'll have to determine which questions are more suited to being addressed by digital content and which require help from a seller.

4. To make sure our content is performing, we need to implement a feedback system to make sure buyers are getting the guidance they need to buy better with confidence.

That's a lot. But really, it's no different than the steps one might follow to design any kind of content strategy. In fact, for marketers, much of this will feel comfortably familiar, but it is important to note that each step comes with a twist, as each step requires a certain departure from conventional content-creation wisdom to ensure it's purpose-built for a Framemaking strategy.

So, let's work through each step, starting first with mapping the customer's B2B buying. Once we've nailed that down, we're ready for a journey of our own, a step-by-step rethink of a conventional content strategy to ensure it not only supports but actually initiates Framemaking selling.

MAPPING THE BUYER JOURNEY

Of course, the foundation for any content strategy has to be the buyer. After all, if we don't know what steps the buyer needs to take, how can we design content that will help them take those steps? How can we know what content will even be sufficiently relevant to a buyer that they will be willing to spend time consuming it?

To answer these questions, many commercial teams have already invested in creating buyer journey maps to make content relevant enough to earn their attention and provide enough information to help buyers progress on their journey.

But before we address the ways a Framemaking buyer journey map needs to be a bit different, it is worth starting with a quick review of what may already be in place at your organization. Of the countless buyer journey maps we have reviewed over the years, there is a lot of variability, but they generally structure the steps a buyer goes through using some variation of the following four stages: awareness, consideration, preference, and purchase.

In this model, the primary goal of journey mapping is to track—and ultimately nudge—customers along their journey toward purchase of our solution. Many early versions of buyer journey maps were focused on awareness of our brand, through consideration of our company, to preference for our solution, and eventually to the purchase of our product. The goal was of course to put us in a far better position to both predict sales and drive growth. In other words, the model was designed to solve for more sales and better selling.

Contrast that with Framemaking, where our primary objective is to enable better buying by helping customers make the best decision they can.

And from the perspective of Framemaking, old-school buyer journey maps fall woefully short of the guidance necessary to provide customers material help. After all, we need only scratch the surface of this fairly outdated version of a buyer journey map to reveal its significant limitations:

"Awareness" of whom? Well, of us, the supplier, of course.

"Consideration" of whom? Again, us, the supplier.

"Preference" for whom? Yup, us again.

And "Purchase" from whom? Well, naturally, us, of course.

It's hard to miss the pattern, isn't it? In the end, this isn't the buyer's purchase journey nearly so much as the buyer's purchase-from-us journey. It's really little more than supplier centricity wrapped in a thin veneer of buyer consideration.

But Framemaking is all about making a supplier agnostic decision.

If we're going to accurately identify what a buyer needs to do to complete a purchase today with confidence, we're going to have to dramatically shift from a "buying from us" journey to instead understand what a buyer needs to do well beyond factors that influence their preference for a single supplier.

Over the years, many commercial organizations have made significant progress shifting the focus of their buyer journey map to really understand the perspective of the customer. For many, the first stage of the buyer journey map at your company may still be awareness, but it has shifted from "awareness of us as the supplier" to instead "awareness of the problem," and this is the first step in the right direction, but we would suggest using the following stages based on how buyers actually talk about their journey.

Start with What Customers Need to Do

From the seminal article "Know Your Customers' 'Jobs to Be Done'"[1] by Clayton Christensen et al., the jobs-to-be-done (JTBD) framework has proven to be a powerful way to analyze and influence both B2C consumer and B2B customer behavior. Collaborating with Christensen on much of that work was entrepreneur and innovator Bob Moesta, author of *Demand-Side Sales*.

In the years leading up to the global pandemic, the CEB team worked directly with Bob to apply the JTBD framework to complex B2B purchase decisions. With Bob's guidance, the effort comprised a range of highly structured interviews with senior leaders recently involved in a B2B purchase, aiming to identify the specific buying jobs customers have to complete to their satisfaction in order for a large-scale organizational purchase to actually happen. That work ultimately isolated four critical buying jobs:

1. Problem identification
2. Solution exploration
3. Requirements building
4. Supplier selection

You will recognize these four jobs from the spaghetti bowl discussed earlier in the book. These are the four critical jobs that serve as the foundation of what customers need to do to complete a B2B purchase. Whether you choose to use these four buying jobs as the stages of your journey map or choose alternatives, it will be important to use language that will resonate with your specific customers.

Years ago, we had the opportunity to listen in on a conversation between a seller and a buyer who seemed to be early on in their journey. The seller appropriately wanted to find out which stage the buyer was in, so they asked, "How is progress going on your awareness of the problem?" The buyer literally laughed at this and replied quite sarcastically, "Oh, we are quite aware of no shortage of problems at our company. Where we are struggling is identifying a problem we are actually going to go solve!"

On that call, the seller quickly pivoted and asked about how the buyer was trying to make progress on identifying the right problem, so ultimately no harm was done. But this story highlights that words truly do matter, and if internally we are talking about a stage as awareness, but that isn't the natural language of the buyer, we create unnecessary risks of lost-in-translation moments. To avoid these, it is important to try to use the buyer's own words wherever possible when mapping their journey.

Having established the primary buying jobs as the stages of your customer's journey, you might think that the next step is to map out the specific steps that a buyer will need to take to complete all of those jobs and ultimately make a purchase.

But it turns out that mapping a buying journey as a series of steps isn't the best approach. If the customer knows the steps they need to take, they don't actually need any help. They've got it covered on their own.

What matters are the steps that the buyer isn't sure about. The steps they don't know how to take. What matters are the points in the journey when they have a question and need help. If we are going to help a buyer make progress on their journey, the key will be to provide that help, to answer the questions that might undermine the customer's confidence and cause the journey to stall.

Answering the Customer's Questions

This is why it is useful to think of a buyer journey map not as a series of steps but as a series of questions. (We sometimes refer to this as the "Jeopardy!" strategy for buyer journey maps—everything needs to be in the form of a question.) Imagine a buyer who asks both of the following questions. The first is a typical "what" question—"What are the risks to our budget if our implementation takes longer than twelve months to complete?" The second is a typical "how" question—"How can we reduce the risk to our budget if our implementation takes longer than twelve months to complete?" Now of course it is quite common for a buyer to first ask a "what" question to understand an aspect of a step before they ask the corresponding "how" question as they work out how to actually take the step. Both are related to the same step, and this is part of the problem.

When creating a buyer journey map as a series of steps, there is a risk that the help that the customer actually needs gets lost in translation. If we mapped the questions in the above example as a step, it might be something like, "Reduce budget risk if implementation runs longer than twelve months." This would accurately capture the step the buyer might struggle to complete, but we wouldn't actually know whether the buyer needed help figuring out *what* the risks are or *how* to reduce their impact. By capturing specific questions, we can be confident we know precisely what help the customer needs.

To distinguish this kind of map from the various buyer or customer journey maps many will be familiar with, we often refer to this as a buyer question map to emphasize the importance of capturing the questions that buyers need help answering.

By mapping the journey as a series of specific questions in the buyer's own words, we can be confident that answering that specific question will provide the buyer the help they need, but now we need to figure out what questions we should capture in our map, because all questions aren't created equal.

Mapping the Misery

The good news is we don't actually need a comprehensive map of every question a buyer might need to answer to complete a purchase. A buyer will be able to complete much of their journey on their own and not have questions that need our help. We just need to discover where buyers are really struggling and figure out what questions they need help answering at those points.

Even though it might at first appear counterintuitive, more important than interviewing customers of successful buying journeys is documenting stuck, failed, and postponed ones, paying close attention to the specific stall points that customers struggle to address on their own. When we talk to these buyers who struggled, we want to focus on two key questions. First, "What were the questions that you struggled most to answer during your buying journey?" Second, "Did the struggle to answer those questions affect your confidence that you would ultimately make the best decision on behalf of your company?"

As we map these unsuccessful journeys, we want to pay especially close attention to the psychic or emotional toll that those stalls take on customers' confidence. By calibrating the relative impact of each potential stall on customer confidence, we can prioritize our Framemaking efforts around the specific points of greatest leverage for providing help.

After all, the purpose of the buyer journey map is to figure out where the customer needs help. Where they are really struggling. Where they may become frustrated. Where there is risk that it all becomes too much and the deal stalls and they just give up because it just isn't worth the effort. Having a comprehensive inventory of every step a customer needs to take will be far less useful than a buyer journey map that is focused on the biggest stall points.

So the best place to start is by mapping the misery. Identify where frustration and other negative emotions are at their highest and confidence is at its lowest, and capture that misery in the buyer journey map. Flag those questions that are at points that are especially painful and when confidence is being undermined. By noting the points where confidence is under threat, we can easily prioritize where customers need the most help and where the risk of failure is highest.

Creating the Buyer Journey Map

Buyer Journey Map

Problem Identification		Solution Exploration		Requirements Building		Supplier Selection	
Question	Misery	Question	Misery	Question	Misery	Question	Misery
Question 1	H/M/L	Question 1	H/M/L	Question 1	H/M/L	Question 1	H/M/L
Question 2	H/M/L	Question 2	H/M/L	Question 2	H/M/L	Question 2	H/M/L
Question 3	H/M/L	Question 3	H/M/L	Question 3	H/M/L	Question 3	H/M/L
Question 4	H/M/L	Question 4	H/M/L	Question 4	H/M/L	Question 4	H/M/L

Figure 5

Figure 5 strips down the buyer journey map to its simplest form to highlight what really matters. First and critically important are the buyer stages across the top. Note that every question will be attached to one of these stages, which at a high level will allow us to identify where the buyer is on their journey based on the questions they need help answering.

The only other two pieces of information captured are the questions the customer needs help answering and a subjective misery score (high, medium, low) that indicates the degree of struggle the customer is experiencing at the point they ask that question. That's it. Those are the basics that give us enough to get started.

Now just as we would try to capture the order of the steps in a more traditional buyer journey map, we will want to capture the order of the questions in a buyer question map. As we saw in the spaghetti bowl of B2B buying, there can be lots of looping in buyer journeys, so the order of the steps tends to reflect an idealized journey, but of course the actual journeys buyers take are often much messier. The same is true for a journey map based on questions, but we still should make our best effort to try and figure out the ideal order that a buyer should try to answer the critical questions that impact their confidence and capture that sequence of questions within each stage.

Now that we have the structure for our map, we need to turn to the question of how to start filling it out. If you have already created the inventory of buying obstacles based on the it-turns-out-that audit from Chapter 3, you can use that as a jumping-off point, as that will be a great way to identify customers who struggled, along with the nature of the struggle. If you haven't already created an obstacle inventory, the same techniques described in the it-turns-out-that audit can be applied to developing a buyer journey map simply by focusing primarily on the questions that customers need help answering when struggling through those obstacles on their buying journey.

If building a buyer journey map for the first time, it is best to limit the mapping to the most common, most painful points of stall, and often your sellers can quickly identify those from promising deals where it looked like there was a great fit, but suddenly the deal stalled. No need to try and map out every point where the customer is struggling and every question they need help answering before you get started designing ways to help your buyers buy better with confidence. There will be ample opportunity to expand the journey map over time. Periodically, it will be valuable to repeat this exercise to confirm both that the prior points of greatest misery are still priorities, but also to explore if new points of misery are emerging. Buyer journey maps should be treated as living documents, and their development should be thought of as iterative.

So now we have our buyer journey map and are ready to start creating our content strategy to answer the buyer's questions so they can proceed with confidence.

CREATING A FRAMEMAKING CONTENT STRATEGY

As you tune your content strategy to enable Framemaking, two components will deserve particular attention to unlock its potential for your commercial organization.

The first component to revisit is the business goals your content strategy seeks to support. As discussed at length throughout the book, customer decision confidence is the critical goal to drive growth and should be a primary goal of your content strategy. If we hope to sell more by helping customers buy better, we need to guide customers to overcome decision complexity, information overload, objective misalignment, and outcome uncertainty. Only by helping address these challenges to customer confidence can we help more customers successfully navigate their buying journeys and ultimately close more deals.

Just as we saw the benefits of adopting the Framemaking mindset for sales in Chapter 7, our content strategy should adopt the goal of helping customers make the best decision they can in as little time as possible. By doing this throughout our content strategy, we will soon see how it helps us better nurture customers to be ready for sales conversations and ultimately better qualify leads and drive more sales.

The second components of your content strategy that will need attention are the content pillars. The content of our content, if you will. This is where the investment in developing your buyer journey map really pays off. If we have clarity on the guidance our customers most need and can prioritize our content based on the relative level of misery, it is quite straightforward to select key topics that best address the specific questions customers struggle with the most.

Capturing the buyer journey map as a collection of questions pays dividends here as well, as it provides clear guidance for our content strategy. When creating an individual piece of content, it becomes very easy to test if that content is likely to actually help the customer answer one of the priority questions on the buyer journey map. If not, it may be time to go back to the drawing board.

Creating Verifier Content

Designing content to answer specific customer questions has an additional benefit that can significantly improve customer qualification as well.

When a supplier creates a buyer journey map based on questions, then the opportunity to develop content that specifically answers one and only one question proves to be incredibly useful in determining where that customer is on their buying journey. It is easy to see how this works by returning to the example of a customer asking the question, "What are the risks to our budget if our implementation takes longer than twelve months to complete?" If a buyer consumes a piece of content addressing this question, we can be quite confident that this customer is likely trying to answer a question related to outcome uncertainty and is far along in the buying process.

Recall from Chapter 3 that a customer verifier is simply a specific, clear, predictable customer action that objectively demonstrates their progression through a purchase journey. If a customer engages with content that helps them answer a specific question they have on their buying journey, then that act of engagement can be thought of as a verifier. If the consumption of a piece of content identifies where a buyer is on their journey based on the question the content answers, we refer to it as verifier content, and it can be an incredibly effective tool for qualifying potential buyers.

Now of course, verifier content won't be as accurate as the customer verifiers that can be observed by sellers. Verifier content will be limited by the typical challenges of digital content, for even if the buyer views or downloads the content, it can be difficult to know if they actually fully engaged with it or if it actually maps to where they are in the process.

Even with these limitations, the advantages are quite obvious when compared to more traditional content, especially anything long form like white papers and customer buying guides. Those types of longer-form content will typically attempt to answer many customer questions. We can't begin to count how many definitive buying guides we have evaluated as part of our research over the years. That type of content often tends to not be very helpful in verifying where a customer is on their journey, especially if the content answers questions ranging from very early questions related to problem identification all the way through questions related to implementation.

It can be challenging to determine if a customer is ready to talk to sales or especially if a customer is close to buying based on engagement with this kind of long-form content. Now of course putting a white paper or buying guide behind a gate may be a very useful tactic for capturing a buyer's contact information, but it often doesn't tell us much about where they are on their buying journey.

But remember why we created our journey map. We need to identify where customers need the most help to feel confident, where they feel fear, feel uncertain, or simply feel overwhelmed. The goal for our content creation is the same: to provide help to customers by answering the questions they face at those points where things are most likely to go wrong. By creating verifier content that targets those points by answering those specific questions, we can help our customers while also gaining a much better sense of how close they are to buying.

With our strategy for the content of our content established, we turn to optimizing our channel strategy for distributing that content.

How can we most effectively engage customers with the guidance that will help them make the best possible decision and buy better?

To answer this question, we first need to pull up and take a big-picture look at the nature of the questions customers ask.

FRAMEMAKING CHANNEL STRATEGY—HORSES FOR COURSES

With the customer journey mapped as a set of questions and our strategy for our content designed around those questions, the next step is to determine how best to design our channel strategy to deliver content to customers to answer those questions. This may feel like a complex challenge, but as we've seen throughout this book, a simple framing can make the complexity of designing a channel strategy much more manageable. In this case, the variety of questions customers may need help answering can be framed with a simple continuum.

On one end are what we typically think of as the simpler, quicker-to-answer questions (what we call "just the facts" questions). These include questions about things like feeds and speeds and other product specifications.

On the other end are what we typically think of as the more complex, harder-to-answer questions (what we call "it depends" questions). These questions require more context, as there isn't a single simple answer that applies to every situation. These are questions like "How long should implementation take for a customer like us with twelve plants spread across three countries?"

Simply flagging each question in the buyer journey map as either "just the facts" or "it depends" helps us optimize our channel strategy for helping customers through both digital channels and human sellers.

Digital Channels Are Suited for "Just the Facts"

For "just the facts" questions, customers expect to be able to find answers quickly. Because customers see these questions as inherently easy, the critical element that can impact customer confidence is agency. Customers expect to be able to answer these questions on their own without needing help from anyone. If they can't, or it takes longer than they expect, then feelings of frustration will be a threat to confidence.

Companies simply need to make sure their websites and other digital channels are optimized to answer customers' "just the facts" questions as easily as possible. While ease may not necessarily generate customer confidence, difficulty certainly can erode it. Making customers work for those answers or struggle to interpret something relatively straightforward is committing an unforced error when it comes to customer confidence. Rather than making less-confident customers more confident, we're doing the exact opposite, inadvertently making potentially confident customers feel more unsure at a moment when creating greater uncertainty is absolutely unnecessary.

Human Sellers Handle "It Depends" Questions

Many of the questions customers face aren't so simple. Answers can depend on a seemingly infinite variety of variables that may be very difficult to anticipate. Among these are the more complex questions that require the power of Framemaking. Not only are "it depends" questions hard to answer, but often the customer will feel very little agency over how to address them.

As a buyer will tend to feel a low level of confidence when facing a hard question where they feel low levels of agency, these are the types of questions that can produce stalls. It is critical for suppliers to help customers address these questions while increasing the customer's confidence.

As we think about the best channel to use to help customers in this situation, it is useful to recall from Chapter 4 the three approaches a seller can take when providing information to a customer—telling, giving, and sensemaking. We saw that sensemaking techniques are more successful than giving or telling techniques as they help structure challenging questions in a way that increases ease while simultaneously increasing the customer's feeling of agency as they are empowered to use the framing to help construct the answer for themselves. As "it depends" questions tend to both be hard and undermine buyer agency, it is especially important for our channel strategy to adopt a sensemaking approach.

Unfortunately, if we take a hard look at the approach our digital channels use to present information to buyers, it typically ends up being some combination of giving and telling.

There are good reasons why we design our digital channels this way. We are proactively putting information on our digital channels to give it to our customers. To help them find it. To help them benefit from it. Almost the definition of giving. Likewise, digital channels also tend to display telling tendencies as they typically present information along with evidence as to why the information is valid and the best answer to the question.

So it's not wrong that our digital channels primarily adopt some mix of giving and telling. In fact, this combination works very well when addressing "just the facts" questions. However, this becomes problematic when trying to answer "it depends" questions.

To help customers with these complex questions that can feel unmanageable, sensemaking is critical, as it is less about providing information and instead focuses on helping prioritize perspectives and quantifying tradeoffs. This is exactly what customers need when facing "it depends" questions. Sensemaking does this not by telling customers what to think and believe, but by suggesting a framework for deciding and then guiding the customer to construct the knowledge for themselves. Of course, in many cases it will make sense to make the relevant frameworks available to your customers through digital channels. However, when it comes time to guide the customer on how to think about the framework, how to tailor it to the situation in their own company and think through the complex dimensions upon which a decision will depend, this is where the sensemaking skills of the seller are critical.

Bottom line, human sellers utilizing sensemaking tend to be the best channel to help customers answer "it depends" questions.

But how does a buyer with an "it depends" question, who may be part of the 75 percent of buyers who would like a rep-free buying experience, go from looking up information on a website to wanting to talk to a human seller?

Designing Digital Content to Connect Customers with Sellers

Commercial organizations need to focus digital content for a buyer struggling with an "it depends" question with a single, clear call to action for the customer—get help by talking to a member of our team. At its most basic level, that is the goal.

Now of course, so much of our digital content efforts are geared toward getting customers ready and willing to talk to a seller, but here again we need to do things a little bit differently. When designing digital content to get customers to be willing to talk to sellers who can help them answer "it depends" questions, there are three key design principles to keep in mind.

1. HELP CUSTOMERS APPRECIATE THAT THEY NEED HELP.

When designing content that will encourage customers to seek help from a seller to address an "it depends" question, it is important to appreciate that not all customers will be coming from the same perspective. There tend to be two distinct groups of customers, and it will be critical to think through the needs of each group separately and design content accordingly.

Group 1 can be a bit tricky. These are the customers who incorrectly think they are dealing with a "just the facts" question that is really an "it depends" question. These customers can become frustrated as they fail to find an answer that addresses the complexity of their context and the various dimensions on which the answer might depend. Designing content for this group often includes explicitly listing some of the dimensions that the answer depends on as a prompt to help the customer appreciate what they might be missing. For example, "How can we reduce the risk that our implementation takes longer than twelve months to complete?" is a question whose answer will likely depend on the type of risk that is delaying the implementation. If the risk is primarily due to resource availability, it might require support from HR, while if it is due to regulatory risk, there might be a need for legal involvement.

Designing content that picks one of these possibilities and treats it as if it were a "just the facts" question may serve the needs of any buyers who only care about that one risk. But adding a prompt to the content that suggests consideration of a few of the other leading sources of risk along with hints at who might need to be involved to reduce that risk can help the customer appreciate that the question is more complex than they realize. In this case, it is helpful to add a call to action that includes something like "If some of these other risks apply to your situation, please contact us for help."

Group 2 are the customers who need help because they are aware of how challenging the question is. In many ways, this group is easier to support because they don't need help understanding the nature of their question, they just need to be aware that they can talk to someone who can help them. This group might ask a question more like, "What are the various risks that could cause our implementation to take longer than twelve months to complete, and how can we reduce the impact of those risks?" Notice that this question has "it depends" baked right into it as the "how" depends on the answer to the "what." Content targeted to this group should focus on the variety of risks along with the implications for how to address them. It is important to emphasize the complexity of it all and the need to talk to someone who can help make it more manageable.

2. INCLUDE A CALL TO ACTION FOCUSED ON HELPING ANSWER ONLY ONE QUESTION.

If the customer has an "it depends" question, especially one that needs framing from a seller, the call to action should exclusively focus on getting a call scheduled for that customer and avoid attempting to answer any potentially related "just the facts" questions as part of the same piece of content. Of course, there may be related questions with which the customer may need help, but once the seller has the customer on a call, there will be opportunities to help with those. When it comes to getting the customer to take the step to schedule the call, you don't want to highlight all the different questions a seller can help answer, as that risks creating distraction or, worse, overwhelming your customer.

3. PREP THE SELLER TO HELP ANSWER THE ONE QUESTION—AND QUALIFY THE BUYER.

Of course, all of this effort to get the customer to talk to the seller only works if the seller has the necessary framing or other resources and is actually able to help the buyer. When producing content to guide customers to seek help, it is critical that the corresponding sales enablement resources are made available to anyone likely to take a call from customers seeking that help.

We've primarily focused on sellers helping customers in these Framemaking situations, but in some cases, other members of the commercial team might be well suited to answer particular types of customer questions. Regardless of who ends up helping the customer, it is valuable to anticipate that even if the customer is now able to answer the question that they called about, there may be related follow-up questions they may or may not know to ask. Including these enablement resources for the person helping this customer presents an excellent opportunity to guide the customer to other critical questions they will need to answer.

After helping a customer with an "it depends" question, we will have a much better sense of where the customer is on the journey. Have they been able to answer the question that caused them to contact the supplier? If so, we can now hopefully use that connection to further guide them on their journey. If they haven't been able to answer that question, that might be a red flag about whether they are going to be able to make progress toward a purchase decision and should be disqualified.

Now that we have worked through the changes needed to our content and channel strategy, we will want to make sure our content is performing.

CHECKING YOUR WORK—BUYER JOURNEY AUDIT

To test that the overall content strategy is effectively helping the customer make the best decision they can as quickly as possible, it is important to perform an audit to test your buyer journey mapping to confirm where customers can actually find the best answers. Think of it as a reverse content audit, where instead of reviewing the content that you have produced, you analyze the content customers need.

This audit starts with the questions on your buyer journey map. It is best to start by checking that customers are quickly and easily able to answer their "just the facts" questions. For each question, have a member of the commercial team seek an answer to the question as if they were a customer. Best to use someone who is customer facing so they can try to channel their inner customer with as much empathy as possible. It can also be beneficial to pick someone fairly junior who may not be burdened with a lot of knowledge that an average customer might not possess. For these "just the facts" questions, the person playing the role of the customer will want to try and find the answer quickly using a couple of approaches.

First, use whatever method finds an answer as quickly as possible regardless of source. The goal is to replicate the customer experience and check how long it took to find an answer. Note it is not necessarily a problem if the quickest answer comes from an independent source or even the competition. These "just the facts" questions need to focus on customer ease and agency, so whether they find an answer on your website or your competitor's doesn't matter much as long as the customer can find the right answer quickly. However, if it is not quick and easy to find the right answer that you have made available through digital channels, there may be search optimization opportunities.

Next, compare the answer your company has made available through digital channels (if one exists) to the answer found most quickly from another source. For "just the facts" questions, both will likely be roughly the same, but you may find cases where there is inconsistency. This is especially problematic, for it not only creates risk for the customer's self-confidence but may raise questions about your company's reliability as a source of help. If this occurs, and your company's answer is the best one, it may be necessary to adjust your content to explain why the alternative answer(s) are inferior.

Auditing the "it depends" questions follows a similar process. You will especially want to look for any examples of frameworks available from competitors as well as third-party experts. If you find something that looks potentially useful to customers and is significantly different from the framing you are using, it may be worth checking if an existing customer had experience using the framework and what guidance they might have received on how to apply the framework to their situation. This will not only identify opportunities to improve your frameworks but may reveal new approaches sellers can use when engaging customers with your framing.

As with "just the facts" questions, when reviewing the framing that sellers will use to help customers answer "it depends" questions, it is important to find any conflicting information that might confuse the buyer. It will be critical that the seller is not only aware of these potential conflicts but is enabled with approaches to help the customer make sense of any conflicts.

One final note is that after completing this audit, commercial teams will likely discover that they have content that fails to answer any questions on the customer's journey map. It is worth considering whether this content should be retired to reduce clutter and make it easier for customers to find what they actually need.

No question, there are many layers to Framemaking selling, spanning customer challenges, seller skills and mindset, and broader organizational capabilities. We hope we've given you a strong sense for the incredible opportunity in front of all of us to employ Framemaking to better align selling with today's B2B buying. As we bring our story to a close, let's take a moment in Chapter 10 to place Framemaking into its broader historical context and wrap things up with a few powerful, higher-level themes we find weaving through this entire body of research. As we do, we hope you'll see what we see in Framemaking—a powerful opportunity to drive greater, more differentiated commercial performance by creating far closer customer connections.

CHAPTER 10

Framemaking, the Big Picture

We started this book with a simple, powerful question: How can you be the one sales professional—or the one sales team—that customers actually *do* want to talk to?

Across the last nine chapters, we've covered a lot of ground in a wide range of dimensions exploring an answer: decision confidence, customer centricity, ease and agency, decision complexity, information overload, objective misalignment, outcome uncertainty, mindset versus skillset, sales methodology, digital engagement. It's a lot.

No doubt the opportunity associated with adopting a Framemaking mindset is as vast as it is potentially powerful. But, as we draw to a close—at least for now—if we were to step back and sort of squint across the entire Framemaking landscape, three powerful higher-level themes really shine through, each delineating Framemaking from any other sales approach. As we review each theme in turn, we gain richer perspective into Framemaking's profound potential to set sellers apart in customers' eyes. But just as valuable, connecting these themes allows us to wrap a bow around the book in a way that helps synthesize what might otherwise feel like a very large, multifaceted idea.

So, let's put a frame around Framemaking.

THEME 1—CHASING DIFFERENTIATION

Sales success has always been a story of setting oneself apart, standing out in the eyes of potential customers such that they buy from you over anyone else and ideally pay a premium to do so.

Yet, across the last thirty years, we've arguably seen more change in B2B commerce than in the previous hundred, leaving suppliers struggling to adapt fast enough to stay ahead and stand apart. Massively disruptive commercial, technological, sociological, logistical, and behavioral changes brought on by the World Wide Web, the Information Age, globalizing supply chains, mobile computing, Big Data, and AI have repeatedly forced suppliers to rewrite the rulebook on how they go to market. In fact, if we step back and take in the last three decades together, three distinct shifts in commercial strategy really stand out, providing extremely helpful insight not only into how sales has evolved, but where we're likely going next (see Figure 6). This evolution, in turn, allows us to place Framemaking in its historical context, even as that history continues to evolve.

Shifting What We Sell

Historically, efforts to stand out in sales focused primarily on product attributes. Sellers were taught to direct customers' attention to the unique features and benefits of their products in order to appear not just different but materially superior in the eyes of customers. For the best sellers, those individual skills were honed to a razor's edge and celebrated in both sales offices and popular movies where would-be sellers were admonished to "Sell me this pen!" and only

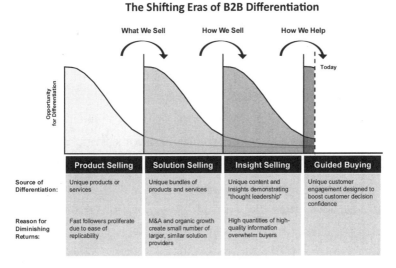

The Shifting Eras of B2B Differentiation

	Product Selling	Solution Selling	Insight Selling	Guided Buying
Source of Differentiation:	Unique products or services	Unique bundles of products and services	Unique content and insights demonstrating "thought leadership"	Unique customer engagement designed to boost customer decision confidence
Reason for Diminishing Returns:	Fast followers proliferate due to ease of replicability	M&A and organic growth create small number of larger, similar solution providers	High quantities of high-quality information overwhelm buyers	

Figure 6

the very best earned jealous admiration from their peers, along with the good leads and dibs on the coffee.

However, in the world of enterprise B2B sales, things began to shift dramatically starting in the mid-1990s (sooner in some industries). Across the 1990s, a rapid rise in fast followers and cheaper alternatives available through globalizing supply chains meant many suppliers of premium products found it increasingly difficult to stand out in the eyes of customers more than willing to settle for cheaper, look-alike products and good enough alternatives. It was a race to the bottom that many name-brand B2B enterprises simply couldn't afford.

Heading into the late 1990s, then, the immediate answer for most B2B suppliers made a ton of sense: We need to rethink what we sell. If stand-alone products are easy to replicate at far lower prices, then let's bundle those products, wrap them with services, and call them "solutions" instead. It was (and still is) a world where 1 + 1 + 1 is meant to equal 4. In other words, customers could achieve the true, incremental value of a supplier's unique solution only if that combined set of capabilities remained intact. And through both organic growth and a massive amount of merger-and-acquisition activity, B2B organizations began rolling up ever broader sets of capabilities designed in aggregate to "solve customers' broader business needs."

As a result, sales forces around the world were retrained on "selling solutions." In particular, it became critical for sellers to connect with senior leaders in customer organizations who had both the authority and the budget to sign off on bigger, broader deals meant to connect more parts of their company. At the time, CEB was writing studies with titles like "Simplifying Solutions Execution" and "Resisting the Forces of Unbundling" as we sought to support a wholescale shift in B2B commerce to larger, more complex deals.

All in an effort to maintain differentiation and protect margins.

Shifting How We Sell

Somewhere around 2006, however, we began to detect a "disturbance in the Force," as it were. What had quickly become tried-and-true solution-selling strategies were beginning to show signs of diminished impact. In a particularly memorable moment at a Chicago meeting of chief sales officers that year, an attendee who is now CEO at a Fortune 25 company joined the discussion with a question that ultimately launched a decade worth of research. Looking around the room, he asked his peers, "Is anyone else seeing deals with more and more stakeholders involved?" So much for selling solely to the corner office.

In the meantime, however, solutions roll-ups continued apace as companies raced to expand the value their solutions could deliver to address an ever-broader range of customer challenges. As an example, FedEx, a shipper of overnight envelopes, added trucking, shipping, retail, and global freight to become a world-class provider of global logistics. It was a massive (and expensive) expansion of capability that allowed them to stake out a highly differentiated position in the global shipping marketplace. Mostly. The only real challenge was that UPS, a trucking company known for moving boxes and freight, pursued almost the exact same strategy across the exact same timeframe, acquiring almost the exact same set of capabilities: planes, small-package services, retail. In the end, UPS also managed to stake out a highly differentiated market position in global logistics. Mostly. But now, at least from the outside, the two looked almost identical (right down to globally recognized, completely iconic logos). To be sure, their teams would be quick to point out the differences between the two (as they rightly should), but by and large, these are two world-class companies with world-class brands competing head-to-head across nearly every dimension of a dramatically expanded set of solutions capabilities.

Their story is in no way unique, really. Indeed, we could find similar examples across virtually every major industry. But their example is helpful nonetheless in explaining what happened across the late 2000s. Simply put, the solution-selling strategies B2B companies put in place a decade earlier to drive differentiation and escape commoditization were themselves becoming commoditized. After all, from a customer's perspective, when considering a choice between two more or less equivalent providers of a world-class solution, one doesn't really need to know who's better, as they're both great. What most customers really want to know is "Who's cheaper?" because, let's face it, both are good enough. And suddenly, here we are, right back to facing the very problem we were seeking to solve, competing on price.

It was right around this time—late 2008, to be precise—that we first conducted the research that eventually became the book *The Challenger Sale*.[1] That research is best known for showing that 53 percent of customer loyalty—over half—is a result not of *what* you sell, but *how* you sell. As we put it there, the single biggest incremental opportunity for a supplier to stand out in the eyes of their customer was less the result of the products and services they sold, and far more the result of the quality of *insight* they delivered as part of the sale itself. Eventually, insight about a customer's business that challenges their thinking while leading back to your unique strengths became the newest, biggest opportunity for thousands of B2B companies to stand out and drive growth.

All in an effort to maintain differentiation and protect margins.

Shifting How We Help

Somewhere around 2018 we began to see problems—which we've detailed here. First, the Chicago question from 2006 proved to be deeply prescient—buying groups *were* getting bigger. Broader solutions meant more stakeholders leading to increased buying complexity and exhausting, dysfunctional B2B buying journeys. More-complex buying decisions also contributed to stakeholder struggles to align on objectives and predict outcomes. But for suppliers seeking to differentiate themselves in the marketplace, perhaps the most dramatic problem was the rise of thought leadership leading to a smartness arms race where every supplier sounds smart, but no one sounds different. Over time, competition between suppliers resulted in not only commoditizing solutions but eventually commoditizing insight. And efforts to make up for that lack of differentiation through sheer volume of thought-leadership content has only exacerbated the problem.

That's where we are now. Right back where we started: struggling to stand out.

Yet, we now face the exponentially tougher challenge of solving (or at least navigating) for B2B buyers who are struggling to buy. No question, many other factors have contributed to today's deficit of decision confidence, but there's equally no doubt that suppliers themselves, in an ironic twist, have been complicit in aggravating the problem. In an effort to sell more stuff, we've landed in a place where buyers are far more likely to actually buy less.

Enter Framemaking. Framemaking isn't really about changing the way we sell nearly so much as it's about improving the way customers buy. It's the act of making a complex buying task or purchase decision feel more manageable by providing customers the guidance they need to progress with confidence. In many ways, Framemaking marks an important shift away from improving selling to improving buying. At the beginning of *The Framemaking Sale* we wondered whether today's dramatically evolving B2B buying behavior marks an end of sales as we know it, or even of sales altogether. Clearly the answer is an emphatic no, at least regarding the end of sales altogether. But it may serve us well going forward to reframe much of what we currently do in the name of sales less as solution selling, value selling, or insight selling, and more as guided buying.

How do you stand out in the marketplace and become the one supplier, the one seller, that customers actually *do* want to talk to? By *helping* rather than *selling*. Framemaking is about providing the guidance that struggling customers are going to absolutely need if suppliers hope to stand out not only from the competition but from the status quo.

"What we sell" to "how we sell" to "how we help." Thirty years of B2B selling wrapped up in three key shifts. All in an effort to maintain differentiation and protect margins.

THEME 2—PREPARATION, PREPARATION, PREPARATION

Way back in 2003, CEB published a landmark study on sales rep time spend that corroborated with data something many had suspected but no one could ever prove: Star performing sellers significantly overweight time spent on precall planning relative to core performers.[2] They are meticulous when it comes to preparation.

They understand the customer's business, hypothesize their needs, plan their engagement all before engaging in a customer-facing interaction.

Almost every sales leader would tell you, they wish sellers spent more of their time actually interacting with customers. They lament persistently low levels of customer face time and repeatedly call for a reduction in all internal, non-customer-facing activity. The thinking is almost always the same: "We could sell so much more if we just spent more time with customers." Yet, these original data—along with a mountain of evidence we've encountered since—clearly tell us a different story: Time in front of customers without proper preparation is ineffective at best and dramatically damaging at worst. If sellers simply jump into customer conversations without a relatively deep understanding of their business, their challenges, and their objectives, they're far more likely to exacerbate customers' deep-seated dislike of sellers rather than overcome it. Especially when those conversations start with open-ended questions like "What's keeping you up at night?" and "What's top of mind for your team heading into the new year?" If anything, questions like these prove what customers already feared: they're talking to someone who couldn't be bothered to learn about their company in advance. The key to sales success is preparation.

In the Framemaking world, the exact same principle applies. While we provided three E's for each Framemaking approach—establish, engage, and execute—those three E's are not created equal. Without spending the time in *advance* of customer interactions to *establish* a frame for decision-making, information, value, or expectations, sellers will struggle to engage and execute an effective Framemaking strategy. Bottom line, do the due diligence. Adopting a Framemaking posture toward any of the four customer challenges we reviewed here means you need to understand those dimensions as well as, if not better than, customers themselves. After all, those are the four areas where they're struggling and they're looking to someone—hopefully you—for help.

Establish is first among equals. It is the key activity that sets up everything else. In many ways, however, it is also the step that might feel like the most work or most like someone else's job. But rest assured, you can't execute a Framemaking strategy if you're not sure how to make things easier in the first place. And you can't make things easier if you haven't taken the time to determine what's hard. Not for you, the seller, but for the customer. Star performers will intuitively know this and prepare accordingly. The rest of us will need to repeatedly remind ourselves to sit down and do the work of establishing frames first. That said, the good news is, over time it turns into muscle memory. It gets easier and easier, almost instinctive, as patterns emerge and problems become increasingly predictable. But until then, don't let the whole "customer face time is everything" mantra lull you into a false sense that you can wing this stuff.

THEME 3—THE ULTIMATE ANSWER

Let's go all the way back to where we started. With a simple, powerful question: *How do you become the one seller—or sales team—that customers actually do want to talk do?*

Now, we have an answer.

In B2B business, we're all trained to believe that companies act rationally. The best way to close a deal is through logic, numbers, business cases, and value calculations. But companies are made up of buyers. And buyers aren't robots, they're humans (at least for now). And the most successful sellers are specifically focused on helping those customers feel more confident in themselves using a toolkit designed for emotional connection. They're appealing to customers on an emotional level, not just a logical one, as the single biggest driver of high-quality, low-regret deals isn't based on something customers know but rather on something they *feel*. While the traditional sales toolkit might be loaded with persuasion, discovery, objection handling, and closing, Framemaking sellers level up with empathy, guidance, and trust building.

Great selling isn't that much different from any other great human interaction. To demonstrate, take a moment to think about some of the people you care about most deeply in your life. The people you truly love. Maybe it's a spouse, or a child, or a friend. Maybe it's someone from your past.

If you think about that relationship—the kind of relationship that makes you sort of warm and fuzzy inside—chances are pretty good that when you really consider that relationship you might find yourself thinking, *You know, I love you not just because I love you. I love you because I love* me *when I'm around you.*

If we're lucky, we have one or two of those people in our lives—or at least we've had one in the past. The people that you want to be around simply because when you look at yourself from the outside you think, "I love that version of me." I want to be that person all the time. It's a deeply powerful question. Who is that person for you? I want to be around you, because I like *me* when I'm around *you.*

What does that have to do with Framemaking? It helps us answer the question we started with at the beginning of this book. Really, what we're trying to understand is, how can you be that kind of person for your customers? How can you interact with a customer in such a way that the result of that interaction isn't that the customer feels better about you, but better about themselves? More confident in the decisions they're making. More confident in their ability to navigate their organization. More confident in their ability to win over colleagues. That's powerful.

If you can be the person who helps customers feel better about themselves, you win. Not just at sales, but also at humanity.

It turns out, Framemaking isn't just a selling story or a buying story. It's a human story. For, never has there been a time when doing what's right for selling and doing what's right for human relationships has been more closely aligned than it is today.

And we think that's really inspiring. We hope you do too.

Cheers.

ACKNOWLEDGMENTS

In a world awash in "thought leadership," it is easy to dramatically underestimate the amount of time, resources, and talent necessary to produce the breadth and depth of work supporting a project of this magnitude. To paraphrase Isaac Newton, if we have seen farther, it is by standing on the shoulders of giants. The foundational quantitative and qualitative research supporting these findings traces its roots to the scores of talented individuals we've had the honor of calling colleagues while at CEB, both prior to and after its acquisition by Gartner—many of whom we're proud to call friends still today. The countless hours spent studying, discussing, and debating the finer points of B2B selling, marketing, and buying with those individuals served as the critical kernel of an idea that eventually evolved years later into Framemaking. There aren't enough words to express our respect, admiration, and appreciation to everyone involved in that foundational research. Your talent, curiosity, enthusiasm, discipline, and plain raw intelligence are utterly unmatched. And your friendship is deeply appreciated. Today, the CEB diaspora continues to dramatically impact B2B business for the better as so many have moved into C-suite positions all over the world. Experience tells us, any attempt to list everyone who influenced these ideas by name would inevitably, inadvertently, and undeservedly leave someone out. Rather than run that risk, we extend a collective and deeply heartfelt thank-you to all of you. We imagine, most of you look back on those days with a powerful sense of collective nostalgia and pride, just as we do, as we share the pursuit of productive disruption across the balance of our careers and beyond.

For all the executives who have contributed to this work, we can't thank you enough for your curiosity, generosity, and unbending resolve to understand and improve the world of B2B sales and marketing as it evolves dramatically. Your support, friendship, and willingness to experiment make this book worth all the effort. Your fearlessness in adopting these ideas is both humbling and inspiring.

This book literally wouldn't exist without the massive support and invaluable guidance from both our agent Jill Marsal of the Marsal Lyon Literary Agency and our editor Emily Taber. We are deeply indebted to you both and even more grateful for your boundless Framemaking capability.

Personally, Brent would like to thank Karl for coming along on this crazy ride. For those who've had the misfortune to work with me know, the way my brain is wired means I'm not particularly easy to work with at times, so thank you, Karl, for your patience, boundless curiosity, and unwavering intellectual rigor. This project wouldn't have happened without you.

For over fifteen years at CEB, and then Gartner, one of the greatest highlights of my career was the opportunity to lead a group of highly progressive commercial leaders we called the Guru Group. Many members of that group have been featured in our work over the years, including in this book. To all past Gurus, I would simply say, "Thank you. Thank you, for *everything*." It is one of the single greatest honors of both my professional and personal life to count so many of you today as incredibly dear friends. I would not be the person I am without your friendship.

Of course, a project of this size never happens in a vacuum. To my wife and two daughters, I can't thank you enough for your patience—which I try on an ongoing basis—support, and faith in me. You are why I do any of this, and I couldn't do any of it without you. Especially to my two daughters as you head out into the world, may you go forward with the kind of empathy in your hearts that enables you to be the people who lead others to love themselves just a little bit more as a result of their connection to you. There is truly no greater gift that we can either give or receive.

Finally, to my parents. *The Framemaking Sale* is undoubtedly built on research, developed from a set of skills and a level of discipline you taught me from an early age. But it is also built on a set of values—generosity, empathy, curiosity, hard work—that you've instilled in me from the very beginning. This book represents my attempt to capture those values and translate them to the world of business in a meaningful way.

Two weeks after completing this manuscript, my dad was diagnosed with an inoperable, aggressive brain cancer, which more than likely means he won't see its actual publication. I'm so incredibly proud of my dad and everything he's taught me at every stage of my life. There is no better role model for the man I have become than my dad. It's only fitting to me that this book is scheduled to release on his birthday. I love you, Dad.

Karl would like to thank Brent for being the best (and most patient) partner I could hope for. Your intelligence and commitment to the creative tension that turns half-baked theories into ideas that put a dent in the universe are truly remarkable. Maybe even more impressive is your ability to simplify even the most complex ideas in a way that makes them sing—truly Framemaking at its very best.

To my wife, Kerstin—since we first met as teenagers, I can say with confidence that any growth I've managed over the years is thanks to you and our children. I am so grateful to continue this journey with you, no matter where it takes us.

To the many teachers, especially my parents, who tried to guide whatever potential I was given to more productive pursuits—I felt your presence deeply throughout this project, which was greatly inspired by the way you lit up with joy when one of your students figured out something difficult. I only hope this book helps sellers feel a little of that same joy when guiding customers to make the complex a little easier.

NOTES

Introduction

1. Brent Adamson, "Opening Keynote: Rewriting B2B Selling for Digital Buying," presented at Gartner CSO and Sales Leader Conference (virtual), May 17, 2021, www.linkedin.com/video/live/urn:li:ugcPost:6800072650547834880, 3:40, accessed May 13, 2025.

2. 6sense, "Don't Call Us, We'll Call You: What Research Says About When B2B Buyers Reach Out to Sellers," January 8, 2024, 6sense.com/blog/dont-call-us-well-call-you-what-research-says-about-when-b2b-buyers-reach-out-to-sellers/, accessed May 26, 2025.

3. Gartner, "Gartner Says B2B Sales Organizations Need to Give Customers a Seller-Assisted Digital Buying Experience," Stamford, CT, May 17, 2021, accessed May 26, 2025.

4. Matthew Dixon and Ted McKenna, *The JOLT Effect: How High Performers Overcome Customer Indecision* (New York: Portfolio, 2022), 182.

5. Matthew Dixon and Brent Adamson, *The Challenger Sale: Taking Control of the Customer Conversation* (New York: Portfolio, 2011); Brent Adamson, Matthew Dixon, Pat Spenner, and Nick Toman, *The Challenger Customer: Selling to the Hidden Influencer Who Can Multiply Your Results* (New York: Portfolio, 2015).

Chapter 1: Solving for Customer Confidence

1. Matthew Dixon and Brent Adamson, *The Challenger Sale: Taking Control of the Customer Conversation* (New York: Portfolio, 2011), 47.

2. Brent Adamson, "Opening Keynote: Rewriting B2B Selling for Digital Buying," presented at Gartner CSO and Sales Leader Conference (virtual), May 17, 2021, www.linkedin.com/video/live/urn:li:ugcPost:6800072650547834880, 11:22, accessed May 27, 2025.

3. Sam Nathan and Karl Schmidt, "From Promotion to Emotion: Connecting B2B Customers to Brands," Think with Google, October 2013, www.thinkwithgoogle.com/consumer-insights/consumer-trends/promotion-emotion-b2b.

4. Justin Trudeau, "Trudeau: 'The Pace of Change Has Never Been This Fast,'" posted January 23, 2018, by World Economic Forum, YouTube, www.youtube.com/watch?v=fTl1YNTNb0g.

5. An early inspiration for this graphic came from: Gartner, "Gartner Says the Marketing-to-Sales Handoff Should No Longer Exist," Las Vegas, NV, October 9, 2018, gartner.com/en/newsroom/press-releases/2018-10-09-gartner-says-the-marketing-to-sales-handoff-should-no-longer-exist, accessed May 27, 2025.

6. Gartner, "Gartner Keynote: The New Imperative for B2B Sales and Marketing Leaders," October 9, 2018, gartner.com/smarterwithgartner/gartner-keynote-the-new-imperative-for-b2b-sales-and-marketing-leaders), accessed May 27, 2025.

Chapter 2: Introducing Framemaking

1. Amos Tversky and Daniel Kahneman, "The Framing of Decisions and the Psychology of Choice," *Science* 211, no. 4481 (1981): 453–458.

2. Gartner, "Buyer Enablement: Simplify Your Buyers' Purchase Process and Empower Sellers to Deliver Value," https://www.gartner.com/en/sales/insights/buyer-enablement, accessed May 27, 2025.

3. Gartner, "Gartner for Sales: The Sense Making Seller," 2021, 2.

4. Brent Adamson, "Sensemaking for Sales," *Harvard Business Review* (January–February 2022), https://hbr.org/2022/01/sensemaking-for-sales.

5. Matthew Dixon and Brent Adamson, *The Challenger Sale: Taking Control of the Customer Conversation* (New York: Portfolio, 2011); Brent Adamson, Matthew Dixon, Pat Spenner, and Nick Toman, *The Challenger Customer: Selling to the Hidden Influencer Who Can Multiply Your Results* (New York: Portfolio, 2015).

6. Adamson, "Sensemaking for Sales."

7. Adamson, "Sensemaking for Sales."

8. Adamson, "Sensemaking for Sales."

9. Adamson, "Sensemaking for Sales."

Chapter 3: Untangling Decision Complexity

1. We reported on these data in detail in Brent Adamson, Matthew Dixon, Pat Spenner, and Nick Toman, *The Challenger Customer: Selling to the Hidden Influencer Who Can Multiply Your Results* (New York: Portfolio, 2015).

2. Karl Schmidt, Brent Adamson, and Anna Bird, "Making the Consensus Sale," *Harvard Business Review* (March 2015).

3. Robert B. Cialdini, *Influence*, 5th ed. (London: Pearson, 2024).

4. Adamson et al., *The Challenger Customer.*

Chapter 4: Reducing Information Overload

1. Brent Adamson, Matthew Dixon, and Nick Toman, "The End of Solution Sales," *Harvard Business Review* (July–August 2012), https://hbr.org/2012/07/the-end-of-solution-sales.

2. Brent Adamson, "Sensemaking for Sales," *Harvard Business Review* (January–February 2022), https://hbr.org/2022/01/sensemaking-for-sales.

3. Amos Tversky and Daniel Kahneman, "Judgment Under Uncertainty: Heuristics and Biases," *Science* 185, no. 4157 (1974): 1124–1131.

4. Herbert A. Simon, "A Behavioral Model of Rational Choice," *Quarterly Journal of Economics* 69, no. 1 (1955): 99–118.

Chapter 5: Addressing Misaligned Objectives

1. Brent Adamson, Matthew Dixon, Pat Spenner, and Nick Toman, *The Challenger Customer: Selling to the Hidden Influencer Who Can Multiply Your Results* (New York: Portfolio, 2015).

Chapter 6: Mitigating Outcome Uncertainty

1. Matthew Dixon and Ted McKenna, *The JOLT Effect: How High Performers Overcome Customer Indecision* (New York: Portfolio, 2022).

2. Matthew Dixon and Brent Adamson, *The Challenger Sale: Taking Control of the Customer Conversation* (New York: Portfolio, 2011); Brent Adamson, Matthew Dixon, Pat Spenner, and Nick Toman, *The Challenger Customer: Selling to the Hidden Influencer Who Can Multiply Your Results* (New York: Portfolio, 2015).

3. Daniel Kahneman, Olivier Sibony, and Cass R. Sunstein, *Noise: A Flaw in Human Judgment* (New York: Little, Brown, 2021).

Chapter 7: The Framemaking Mindset

1. Dan Ariely, *Predictably Irrational: The Hidden Forces That Shape Our Decisions* (New York: HarperCollins, 2008).

2. Brent Adamson, Matthew Dixon, Pat Spenner, and Nick Toman, *The Challenger Customer: Selling to the Hidden Influencer Who Can Multiply Your Results* (New York: Portfolio, 2015).

3. Robert B. Cialdini, *Influence, New and Expanded: The Psychology of Persuasion* (New York: HarperCollins, 2021).

Chapter 8: Framing Framemaking for Framemakers

1. Laura Shapiro, *Something from the Oven: Reinventing Dinner in 1950s America* (New York: Viking, 2004).

Chapter 9: Building a Framemaking Content Strategy

1. The jobs-to-be-done framework has proved a powerful way to analyze both consumer and business buying behavior. Clayton Christensen, Taddy Hall, Karen Dillon, and David S. Duncan, "Know Your Customers' 'Jobs to Be Done,'" *Harvard Business Review* (September 2016).

Chapter 10: Framemaking, the Big Picture

1. Matthew Dixon and Brent Adamson, *The Challenger Sale: Taking Control of the Customer Conversation* (New York: Portfolio, 2011).

2. Corporate Executive Board, *Shifting the Performance Curve: Exporting High-Performance Sales Disciplines to the Core* (2003), https://anyflip.com/gper/ybie/basic, accessed May 27, 2025.

INDEX

Brent Adamson is a world-renowned researcher, author, presenter, trainer, and advisor to B2B commercial executives. The former "chief storyteller" of the sales, marketing, and customer service practices at CEB, now Gartner, he is the coauthor of the bestsellers *The Challenger Sale* and *The Challenger Customer.* He lives outside of Washington, DC.

Karl Schmidt is an award-winning research leader, author, strategy consultant, and corporate executive focused on driving growth for organizations from the Fortune 500 to start-ups. While practice vice president at CEB, now Gartner, he led over fifty researchers solving the most challenging problems faced by heads of sales, marketing, and communications. Those insights have appeared in the *Harvard Business Review, Forbes,* and *The Challenger Customer.* He lives in Bethesda, Maryland.

RAISING READERS
Books Build Bright Futures

Thank you for reading this book and for being a reader of books in general. As author, I am so grateful to share being part of a community of readers with yo and I hope you will join me in passing our love of books on to the next generatic of readers.

Did you know that reading for enjoyment is the single biggest predictor of child's future happiness and success?

More than family circumstances, parents' educational background, or incom reading impacts a child's future academic performance, emotional well-bein communication skills, economic security, ambition, and happiness.

Studies show that kids reading for enjoyment in the US is in rapid decline:

- In 2012, 53% of 9-year-olds read almost every day. Just 10 years later, in 2022, the number had fallen to 39%.
- In 2012, 27% of 13-year-olds read for fun daily. By 2023, that number was just 14%.

Together, we can commit to **Raising Readers** and change this trend. How?

- Read to children in your life daily.
- Model reading as a fun activity.
- Reduce screen time.
- Start a family, school, or community book club.
- Visit bookstores and libraries regularly.
- Listen to audiobooks.
- Read the book before you see the movie.
- Encourage your child to read aloud to a pet or stuffed animal.
- Give books as gifts.
- Donate books to families and communities in need.

BOB1217

Books build bright futures, and **Raising Readers** is our shared responsibility.

For more information, visit **JoinRaisingReaders.com**

Sources: National Endowment for the Arts, National Assessment of Educational Progress, WorldBookDay.org, Nielsen BookData's 2023 "Understanding the Children's Book Consumer"